Not in God's Image

WOMEN IN HISTORY FROM THE GREEKS TO THE VICTORIANS

the text of this book is printed on 100% recycled paper

Other books by the Authors

JULIA O'FAOLAIN
We Might See Sights and Other Stories
Three Lovers

LAURO MARTINES
The Social World of the Florentine Humanists
Lawyers and Statecraft in Renaissance Florence
(Editor) *Violence and Civil Disorder in*
Italian Cities: 1200-1500

NOT IN GOD'S IMAGE

edited by Julia O'Faolain
and Lauro Martines

HARPER COLOPHON BOOKS
Harper & Row, Publishers
New York, Hagerstown, San Francisco, London

A hardcover edition of this book is available
from Harper & Row, Publishers, Inc.

Contents

Illustrations

The illustrations numbered 15 and 17 are reproduced by courtesy of the Warburg Institute, London; those numbered 11 and 19 by courtesy of Alinari, Florence; 25 by courtesy of Mr Brian Reade; all others, including the title-page illustration, by courtesy of the British Museum.

Note to the Reader

Throughout the book our commentary appears in one type, the readings in another. The texts are thus made to stand out. The only exception to this involves the bracketed material—explanatory notes —inserted into the texts. Readings conclude with a reference to author and source, and the Notes supply additional credit. We have been careful to indicate the names of translators; where such an indication does not appear, the translation is ours.

J O'F
L M

. . . but separately, as helpmate, the woman herself alone is not the image of God; whereas the man alone is the image of God as fully and completely as when the woman is joined with him.

ST AUGUSTINE

. . . woman taught once and ruined all.

ST JOHN CHRYSOSTOM

Foreword

If her bowels and flesh were cut open, you would see what filth is covered by her white skin. If a fine crimson cloth covered a pile of foul dung, would anyone be foolish enough to love the dung because of it? ... There is no plague which monks should dread more than woman: the soul's death. [From the *Carmen de Mundi contemptu*, ascribed to Roger de Caen, a French monk, died 1095.]

'Do you know the latest definition of a wife?'
'No.'
'A handy little gadget to screw on the bed that does all the work.' (American joke doing the rounds in the late 1960s.)

These two items are vibrant with tension. To appreciate the tone and thrust of either, one must know a little about its historical context. The mediaeval monk, for instance—supposing he were to come back to life—would probably miss the indignation in the modern joke. Its irony would escape him and so would the fact that it is pro-woman and *against* exploitation, dehumanization and a number of other twentieth century sins not mentioned in his canon. A twentieth-century reader, on the other hand, might sift the monk's misogyny for some parachronistic motive instead of relating it to the religious climate of the time.

So much for the dangers of presenting history through documents. The reader has been warned. The advantage is obvious: direct contact with the past.

This book focusses on women in European societies from early Greece down to the middle of the nineteenth century. By collating testimonies left by men and—when possible—women who lived in those societies, it aims at presenting a close-up picture of the lives of ordinary women from different social classes: of their status, social roles, degrees of freedom or tutelage, and of the mental conditioning which has survived to leave its residue in the attitudes of our own time. The book differs from others recently published in that its aim is not polemical. Its usefulness as a book of readings must centre on the fidelity with which it picks up and transmits voices from the past, allowing them to explain behaviour which might at first sight strike a modern reader as cruel, arbitrary or perhaps abject. The editorial comment is designed to put the readings into their historical context and bridge unavoidable gaps.

We move in time from prehistoric Greece to the political and industrial revolutions of the nineteenth century. Geographically, we have limited ourselves to Greece, Rome, Byzantium and, from the Middle Ages on, to Europe. In view of the impact of Islamic culture on mediaeval Europe, it seemed appropriate to include a chapter on Islam. Though clearly of immense importance, the Americas have been excluded partly, though not solely, because of space. The major themes in the history of Western women are traceable in Europe and more successfully represented if confined there, provided the story goes no further than the middle of the nineteenth century which is where we stop. Thereafter, the position of ordinary European women changed: they began to contend on increasingly equal terms with men. New problems arose; the progress of organized feminism accelerated; documentation becomes more and more abundant and women's history moves into a dramatic period which is being treated in a large number of studies.

With minor exceptions, the readings chosen have little to do with those few unrepresentative women — queens, female regents, courtesans—who happened, through exceptional circumstances, to emerge into the foreground of history. Only a tiny minority actually wielded power, thereby becoming about as typical of the rest of their sex as a wolf-boy on the roll-call of a nursery-school.

It would be foolish to pretend that a book of readings can avoid bias completely or tell the whole story. Such a book is limited by the availability of material, and the most readily available material is the propaganda put out by groups in power. Individual women, as has just been indicated, rarely held power; collectively, they never did.

The resultant situation is acidly pinpointed by the New York joke of some years ago, about an astronaut who had seen

God and was asked on his return to describe Him. 'Well fellas,' he warned, 'this'll be a shock but, first off, SHE'S BLACK !'

It is a protest-joke. Images, it implies, promote the values of the powerful. And if the Western image of God has not even now grown noticeably dark or androgynous, then that goes to show whose grip is still on the reins in our society. Weaker elements do, to be sure, try to promote counter-images, but rarely with success. In the words of a South African poet:

> In human history, and rightly so,
> The Final Word is with the knockout blow.

He or she who is knocked out is not in the best position to give his or her version of events. This was even truer in the centuries before television teams tended to be on hand to record the words of the defeated. The weak may now get a microphone long before they get a share in government—and this has given rise to a whole rhetoric of protest of which the astronaut joke is itself an example. But it was not always so. Most opinions coming down to us from the past are those of victors.

When we try, across some centuries, to pick up the voice not of a subject race or class but of a subject sex, we may hear nothing but interference. No underground protest documents survive from the centuries of female subjection in Europe. Probably none ever existed. Women then did not think of their interests as distinct from those of their male protectors. A history of the West told in terms of women would not therefore be a counter history; it would not be, as is sometimes claimed for histories of the working-class, a reversal of the coin. Rather more would it be in the nature of a supplement: a groping back into the shadowy areas behind the dominant male figures to where sustaining, attendant females submissively and more or less contentedly keep their place. Bred to be loyal and obedient, women accepted this status and the rules governing it.

Very rarely, before the sixteenth century, do we pick up the faint, uncertain whimpers of complaint. What we pick up instead is the voice of the male, a voice often tremulous with anxieties that go back at least to the makers of the Eve myth and probably beyond, to memories of matriarchies and female aspirations after power. These memories seem to have persisted less in female rebellion than in male suspicion of it. The wife who was financially and legally dependent on her husband — for long periods he had the right to kill her if she proved adulterous — had everything to gain by reassuring him of her submission. Unsurprisingly then, when we do catch an echo of the female voice, it is nearly always soothingly pitched.

The reasons for keeping women in subjection were cogent and once widely recognized, being tied to the interests of the family. A family's wealth, social leverage and connections, endowed each member with status and could be called on by him in time of need. In return, the individual was expected to contribute his or her utmost toward strengthening the family's position. Woman's role was to provide heirs who might continue the collective endeavour — and who must be incontestably legitimate. To ensure this, women must be pure and be seen to be pure. The double standard had no other basis and neither had the practice of keeping women in relative seclusion and subjection. Individual women might try to infringe this double standard, but the code remained triumphant well into the eighteenth century. During the mediaeval and early-modern periods, even sex-war jokes turned less on a challenge to male authority than on amusement at the feminine guile which could on occasion outwit it. Servants and peasants were also credited with guile: a slavish attribute whose display — like mettlesome temperament in a horse — only proved the need for keeping them well in hand.

Such jokes, it might be objected, come down to us through the writings of men. True, but there is no evidence that women would have challenged their premise. When women did accede to an education and learned to write, they enthusiastically parroted the opinions of their male teachers, supported the double sexual standard and were, if anything, more stringent than men in demanding submission and nun-like propriety from their own sex. Their one request was that the privilege granted themselves — that of receiving an education — might be extended to other deserving women. If any of their male contemporaries had had prophetic vision, he might have seen here another example of feminine guile — for surely this mini-reform, first lobbied for in the late fourteenth century, was the root of all the later trouble? By the time the Reformation had success-fully challenged the established hierarchies and habits of thought, a number of women were capable of inferring that changes in their own condition were now no longer inconceiv-able. The growth and spread of this awareness was slow and fluctuating. The relation of woman to her lord is like no other. In the acceptance-world prior to the sixteenth century, she more easily sank her interests in his; in the seventeenth and eighteenth centuries, she might be more prone to question the double sexual standard and resent his authority; in the nine-teenth to demand professional and economic parity, and in the twentieth to grapple with the psycho-sexual conditioning which survives all her earlier disabilities. But there were reversions and mutations in every period. Timidity, emotional confusion and backtracking are essential components of women's groping progress towards a perception of their needs. To leave this out would be to falsify the story, since it would be to deny the difference between their case and that of other social groups struggling for equality.

Not every aspect of women's history can be given play in a collection of documents. It took place on very different levels and ours here will be largely that of discernible event. We have tried to show what women did and were allowed to do and how and why they were prevented from doing anything else. Where myths had a demonstrable impact, we represent them too: for example, the flattering-threatening propaganda whereby soci-eties beguile women into accepting ancillary status or the fantasies which women themselves summon in order to enlarge the narrow scope of their lives. This traffic with fancy and pro-paganda had long-term effects on women's psychology, but such effects cannot emerge from short, encapsulated illustration. Collections of readings are uniquely limiting: they must depend heavily on the quotable document or self-contained text. These more easily illustrate external circumstances: scales of wages paid for female labor, conditions of employment, laws govern-ing behaviour, presuppositions of biologists, taboos imposed on women and the ideals proposed by the writers of manuals and sermons, the rules of etiquette designed to condition the female conscience to the point where their infringement must set up alarms and guilts. More difficult to illustrate in brief readings—and so we shall discuss them here—are the side-effects such mystification sometimes had: a tendency to succumb to fantasy, to mysticism, to exaggerated preoccupations and attitudes. Since women led distinctly narrower lives than men, these mental evasions could become surrogates for the realities denied them. Dreaminess and its corollary, timidity—an unreadiness to face dangerous actuality—have been traditionally regarded as female characteristics. Extreme acts of violence or courage can have their source in the same estrangement from a physically and emotionally restrictive life. The woman who believed she was a witch, the bride of Christ who keenly imagined his embraces and smelled his presence, the nun subject to ecstatic seizures, the barbarian queen (Radegonde) who burned Christ's initials into her flesh, the ladies who spent years discussing the refined and over-refined subtleties of Platonic love—each of these, in her way, is a female Don Quixote. For better or worse, they have lost touch with the actualities around them and live in a formally-organized fantasy-world. The warnings of writers against allowing women to read novels are very frequent. They intuited a propensity among them to be carried away by dreams and imagined perfections. Diderot said women were 'Pythian'. Flaubert, bearing out the warnings of earlier moralists, has left us the sardonic word '*bovarysme*' defined by the Petit Larousse dictionary as 'a Romantic dissatisfaction which consists in trying to escape one's own reality by inventing an idealized persona for oneself, as the heroine did in Flaubert's novel, *Madame Bovary*'. James Thurber's Walter Mitty indulged in the same escapism, and in recent fiction male characters are presented more and more frequently by male writers—who, presumably, should know—being driven to fantasy by the arid routines of contemporary life. This is considered a fairly new (and so a remarkable) phenomenon for men. But women's lives were *always* dominated by routine, narrower than men's, often confined physically and hemmed in by strictures of 'do and don't'. An Athenian male might be attended by three different women: courtesan, mistress and wife. Each had her separate functions. His world was the world, hers was a third of it. Even down to our own century, women of 'the better classes' have been more or less restricted to the confines of home and family. The exceptions, interestingly, were most likely to be seen at the top and bottom of the social hierarchy—in the princely courts and fashionable drawing rooms, among petty tradeswomen and perhaps the peasantry, where women were associated through their labour with nearly all aspects of the life of rural working men.

Another unavoidable gap in our coverage of European women concerns the female slave in the ancient world and the serf in mediaeval Europe — large percentages of the population. We find no incisive or detachable texts to offer snapshots of the lives of female slaves in Greece and Rome, which by no means signifies that nothing is known about them. Passing references, archaeological remains, and a multitude of inscriptions add up cumulatively to a picture which cannot be rendered by a few pages of readings.

Again, to illustrate the absence of something very nearly defies doing. The fact that women were not ordinarily educated in classical Greece rarely drew any serious attention. Texts do not say 'women are not being educated'. A few philosophers aside, it occurred to no one that they might be.

The part played by men in the birth and growth of feminism is given no prominence in the concluding chapters of this book. We chose, instead, to listen to the emerging voice of women. But the reader should keep in mind that the new voice was often an echo—personal, strongly felt, but an echo. This is no disparagement of women. Men were given a superior preparation; they were more advantageously placed to grasp the significance of the new social trends. They pointed these out to women, just as bourgeois thinkers, in the middle decades of the nineteenth century, were to take the lead in the perception of working-class interests. So women, in a quite different but analogous situation, could not have waged tellingly the nineteenth-century struggles for emancipation without the help of men. From the father of Christine de Pisan, who insisted that his daughter should be educated like a boy, to Talfourd and John Stuart Mill, who sponsored feminist legislation in a parliament which admitted no women, men mediated between women and power, women and the state, women and freedom. This is no longer true, but it remained largely so down to the middle of the nineteenth century.

We come to a final point: women's resistance to their own emancipation. This was based on fear and the fear was well grounded. Submission, not competition had been for millennia the woman's way to her meal-ticket. The transition had to be tricky. To betray competitiveness before one can compete is self-destructive. Agrippa d'Aubigné (1552–1630) was a realist when he warned his daughters to conceal any learning they might acquire—particularly from their husbands. The image of the mindless, delicate female was reassuring to husbands: it signified docility and the man of property needed reassuring. He was beset with terror lest his name and possessions pass to the issue of his wife's adulterous loves. So, pliantly, women conformed to the desired role, internalized it and made it their reality. It had another, more pleasing significance: it was upper-class. The female laborer, servant, tradeswoman, or fishwife could not afford to be weak or feather-brained. Delicacy and idleness became a caste-code. One thinks of the lady in a Wilde play who answers someone's invitation to call a spade a spade by denying that she has ever seen one. It was when poor women worked hardest—in the factories and workshops of the nineteenth century—that rich women were idlest. Landed women who ran estates, and merchants' wives in the seventeenth century had been far more active. The consumptive weakling of the Romantic era — floral imagery was ransacked to describe her — got a nasty jar when Mary Wollstonecraft summoned her to get up off her *chaise longue* and be independent. Traditionally, independence had been possible only for unmarried women and they were failures: old maids, spinsters. The charged words still arouse a shudder.

If we think of the confrontations outside Miss World contests, we see at once that the female preference for the dependent life and its rewards is still with us. Inherited conditioning? Not entirely. There are still rewards for the ultrafeminine woman and these are no longer reserved for the upper classes. A 'disadvantaged' girl may hope to grow up to be a model or star, if she is lucky enough to have the sort of appearance that fashion demands at the time. There are not, however, enough of these rewards to go round. The more available ones— marriage and a meal-ticket—are acknowledged to be like leprechauns' gold: disappointing in the long run. The survival of the feminine woman is therefore like that of a folk-tale whose meaning has been lost. The courtship and dating rituals, habits, language and old images printed on the racial retina preserve her artificially. But the vital need which created her type— men's need to be assured that the heirs to their property were truly the heirs of their own bodies—has all but evaporated from the modern world.

I Greece

1 The Pre-classical Period

Despite the pots, the paintings, and the excavated palaces, the great period of Minoan civilization at Crete belongs to prehistory: there are no decipherable texts. So our view of women in that society, pieced together from legend and iconography, may be presented only as surmise: a surmise that they enjoyed a far superior status to that of their successors in historic Greece. The Minoan Ariadne, originally a goddess, appears in later legend as a princess whose freedom of movement would have been unthinkable in classical times. She went, for instance, to the games:

And as it was a custom in Crete that the women also should be admitted to the sight of these games, Ariadne, being present, was struck with admiration of the manly beauty of Theseus. [Plutarch, 'Theseus,' *Lives*][1]

Frescoes at Knossos bear this out. They show women watching the bull-leaping from balconies, and some frescoes actually have white-skinned figures—women—in male attire, engaging in bull-leaping themselves. The palace at Knossos did not contain the closed-off women's quarters or gynaeceum found in classical Greek dwellings. In Minoan religious art, mother-goddesses and priestesses take precedence over male figures. According to Herodotus, the Lycians, who were descendants of Cretan immigrants, traced their descent matrilineally. Such evidence concurs in suggesting that a matriarchy may once have flourished in some form on Crete. It has been argued too that Alcinous and Arete, king and queen of the Phaeacians, described by Homer in The Odyssey, *were inspired by the rulers of Minoan Crete, and his account of their palace by legendary memories of Knossos.*

Alcinous made her [Arete] his wife and gave her such homage as no other woman receives who keeps house for her husband in the world today. Such is the extraordinary and heartfelt devotion which she has enjoyed in the past and still enjoys, both from her children and Alcinous himself, and from the people, who worship her, and greet her when she walks through the town. For she is not only the Queen but a wise woman too, and when her sympathies are enlisted she settles even men's disputes. [Homer, *The Odyssey*]²

Homer, writing in a time when such reverence for a woman is astonishing, gives mythic dimension to what may be a folk memory of earlier mores.

The Lycians came originally from Crete, which in ancient times was occupied entirely by non-Greek peoples . . . . In their manners they resemble in some ways the Cretans, in others the Carians, but in one of their customs, that of taking the mother's name instead of the father's, they are unique. Ask a Lycian who he is, and he will tell you his own name and his mother's, then his grandmother's and great-grandmother's and so on. And if a free woman has a child by a slave, the child is considered legitimate, whereas the children of a free man, however distinguished he may be, and a foreign wi͝   ͝ mistress, have no citizen rights at all. [Herodotus, *The Histories*]

HOMER

From roughly 1600 to 1100 B.C. flourished Mycenae, 'the rag and bone shop' of all Greek myth and imagery. The Homeric poems are assumed to reflect its warrior splendors. So is Greek mythology, which took shape then and whose vigorous female figures, if not supreme like the goddess-mothers of Crete, are not subject either. Homeric queens do not themselves hold power, but men obtain it by marrying them. Aegisthus became king by his marriage to Clytemnestra, and any suitor who won Penelope's hand would have got the crown with it. Telemachus says of Eurymachus that he 'is most eager to wed my mother and to have the sovereignty of Odysseus' (Bk XV). Homer's world is a hybrid one, part memory, part contemporary (ninth century B.C.), and women's position in it is hard to sum up. Queens enjoy status and freedom of speech but share their husbands' favors with concubines. The Achaean warriors had sexual companions throughout their ten years' absence from home but expected all their womenfolk to await them in chastity. Even the female slaves of Odysseus' household owed him fidelity. His first inquiry, after killing his wife's suitors, was:

'But what of the women-servants in the house? Tell me which have been disloyal to me and which are honest.'

'My child,' his fond old nurse replied, 'I'll tell you exactly. You have fifty women serving in your palace, whom we have trained in household work and to card wool and make the best of slavery. Of these there are twelve all told who have taken to vicious ways. . . .'

. . . said the wise Odysseus, ' . . . tell the women who have disgraced themselves to come here.'

The old dame left the hall to inform the women . . . while Odysseus called Telemachus. . . . 'Take the women out of the hall . . . and use your long swords on them, till none are left alive to remember their loves and the hours they stole in these young gallants' arms.'

(Telemachus herds the women into a courtyard:) 'I swear I will not give a decent death,' he said, 'to women who have heaped dishonor on my head and on my mother's. . . . '(Whereupon he hangs them.) [Homer, *The Odyssey*] [4]

Honor was a collective, not an individual matter. A woman's sexual lapse reflected on the house as a whole, the more so as these women were property, with no right to dispose of themselves.

PANDORA'S BOX

Hesiod lived in the Greek Dark Ages, the eighth century B.C., a transitional time when clan-administered justice was breaking down and the state was not yet strong enough to impose its own. He was a resentful, pessimistic, rural misogynist who liked the Pandora story—the Greek version of Eve—and used it in two poems. In the Works and Days *he tells how Prometheus stole fire and gave it to men to make their life easier and how Zeus, to make them pay for this, presented them with something evil : woman.*

'As the cost of fire, I shall send them a plague. Their hearts shall delight in it and they shall cherish their own scourge.' So spoke Zeus, the father of gods and men, then burst into laughter. . . .

The lame smith (Hephaestus) then molded from clay a body like that of a shy virgin. . . .

Hermes . . . slipped lies, wheedling words and a bent for treachery into her heart. He . . . gave her speech and called the woman 'Pandora' because she was the gift offered for the sorrow of men, the bread-eaters, by the dwellers on Olympus. . . .

Up to this time the races of men had lived on earth free from harm, from toilsome labor and from the painful diseases which bring death to humankind. But the woman's hands raised the lid of the great jar, scattered the evils within it and laid up harsh troubles for men. Only hope stayed where it was. . . .

Don't let any woman dazzle you with her decked-out rump; behind the twaddle, she's after your barn; anyone who trusts a woman is trusting thieves . . . .

First get a house, a woman and a plow ox—not a married but a purchased woman who can, if necessary, follow the oxen.

Bring home a wife when you are ripe for marriage. You should be neither far past nor short of thirty. The woman should be in her fifth year after puberty. Marry a virgin so you may teach her good habits and, above all, marry someone from your own neighborhood after first looking into everything to make sure you are not giving your neighbors something to laugh at. A man can acquire nothing better than a wife if she's a good one and nothing more disastrous than a bad one whose only thought is eating well. Such a one consumes him without fire and makes even a strong man old before his time. [Hesiod, *Works and Days*][5]

2 Sparta

The two states of classical Greece about which most is known are Sparta and Athens. Sparta, originally no different from other Greek cities, became an anomaly in the sixth century, when its aristocracy froze the institutions, making change impossible and attributing their legislation to a mythic lawgiver, Lycurgus, whom they projected back into a vague past. In this militaristic, hierarchized society, the role of free women is clearly defined. Of Helot or Perioeci women we know nothing. One of the main sources of information about Sparta is the Constitution of the Lacedaemonians written by Xenophon (c. 430–c. 355 B.C.) while in exile from Athens. The Spartan blueprint has fluttered in the minds of eugenists and elitists from Plato to our own day.

Here then, to start at the beginning, is their approach to procreation. Elsewhere, young girls who are destined to become mothers and considered well brought up are stinted in their basic diet [cereals, wheat, barley, etc.] and eat as little as possible of other foods. As for wine, they are either deprived of it completely or allowed it only when diluted with water. Then other Greeks want young girls to lead the sedentary life of artisans and spend their time quietly working wool. . . .

But Lycurgus considered that garment-making could be left to slaves and that the essential role of free women was to have children; accordingly, he prescribed bodily exercises for the female as well as the male sex. He also decided that, just as boys do, girls should compete with each other in speed and strength, for it was his belief that if both parents are sturdy, then their children will be too.

Seeing that elsewhere, at the beginning of their marriages, husbands had excessive intercourse with their wives, Lycurgus opposed such intemperance. He made it a disgrace to be seen going to or leaving one's wife. Thus hampered in their relations with each other, married people desire each other more and the children they may beget will be sturdier than if the parents had been mutually sated. Moreover, Lycurgus. . . laid it down that each man should marry when at the height of his physical powers, for this, he believed, would also favor successful procreation. It might, however, happen that an old man had a young wife. Lycurgus, having observed that such men guard their wives more jealously than any others, strove to change their ways by establishing the following custom: an old man who admires the physical and moral qualities of a young one may introduce him into his house in order to have children by him. If, moreover, a man did not want to sleep with his own wife but did want to have children whom people would admire, Lycurgus allowed him to have them by some other woman whose fine offspring and noble soul he had observed, once he had obtained her husband's permission. [Xenophon, *La République des Lacédémoniens*] [6]

Spartan men of the warrior class slept in barracks until they were thirty— whether married or not—and dined at mess halls until they were sixty. The aim was not, of course, to liberate women, but this, according to critics of the system, was what happened.

In fact, my friends, your public table for men is an admirable institution . . . but it is a grave error in your law that the position of women has been left unregulated and that no vestige of this same institution of the common table is to be seen in their case; no, the very half of the race which is generally predisposed by its weakness to undue secrecy and craft—the female sex—has been left to its disorders by the mistaken concession of the legislator. . . it would be better from the point of view of the good of the state, to submit this matter to revision and correction and devise a set of institutions for both sexes alike. . . . [Plato, *The Laws*] [7]

Odysseus had wielded total power over his household. That was the patriarchal way. Plato (c. 427–347 B.C.) imagined a state which would draw all family matters into its purview, where life would be in common and 'secrecy and craft' impossible. Aristotle (384–322 B.C.) too would have extended the Spartan state's vigilance.

. . . the license of the Lacedaemonian women defeats the intention of the Spartan constitution, and is adverse to the happiness of the state. For, a husband and a wife being each part of every family, the state may be considered as equally divided into men and women...the legislator...has neglected the women, who live in every sort of intemperance and luxury. The consequence is that in such a state wealth is too highly valued, especially if the citizens fall under the dominion of their wives.... This license of the Lacedaemonian women existed from the earliest times and was only what might be expected. For during the wars of the Lacedaemonians ... the men were long away from home, and, on the return of peace, they gave themselves into the legislator's hand, already prepared by the discipline of a soldier's life ... to receive his enactments. But when Lycurgus, as tradition says, wanted to bring the women under his laws, they resisted, and he gave up the attempt. [Aristotle, *Politics*][8]

3 Athens

Mistresses we keep for pleasure, concubines for daily attendance upon our person, wives to bear us legitimate children and be our faithful housekeepers. [Demosthenes, 'Against Neaera,' *The Orations*][9]

These categories are recognizable: even if the barriers between them are down, they have survived. A woman today may slip from one to another, combine all three, or throw all up for something else. Not so in Greece. Categories there were segregated, and you did not choose your own. Athens, though less rigid than Sparta, also had a caste system: slaves, noncitizens, and citizens. A woman was never a citizen. She had neither political rights nor legal capacity and, being subject to a guardian, was unable to dispose of her own person. Guardians must once have had the life-and-death powers enjoyed by Odysseus, for a law of Solon (c. 640– c. 553 B.C.) restrains them:

He made it unlawful to sell a daughter or a sister, unless, being yet unmarried, she was found wanton. [Plutarch, *Lives*][10]

Demosthenes (c. 383–322 B.C.) mentions a case of sister-selling as something shameful and likely to discredit the seller with a jury:

He sold his sister—not a sister by the same father, but his mother's daughter and his own sister, at all events, whoever the father was (for that I pass by)—he sold her, I say, to be taken into a foreign country, as is stated by the plaint in the action which was brought against him on that very account by his worthy brother here, who will presently assist in his defense. [Demosthenes, 'Against Aristogiton'][11]

But who was a girl's guardian likely to be? Normally her father; after his death, her nearest agnate. Rarely did her husband become her guardian. For example, if an adopted son married his adoptive father's daughter, he became her nearest agnate after the father's death and therefore her guardian too. Aristotle's will (below) envisages such an arrangement. In such a case nobody could break up the marriage against the husband's wish. In other cases, however, the woman's guardian could do so. He could also remarry his ward off when she became widowed and dispose of her in his will. Guardianship, when vested in someone other than the husband, restricted marital power, providing the woman with someone to whom she might appeal. Demosthenes' father, being guardian of both his wife and his daughter, disposed of both in his will:

My father died, possessed of property to the amount of nearly fourteen talents. He left two children, myself aged seven years, my sister aged five, and a widow, my mother, who had brought him a fortune of fifty minas. Being anxious to make the best provision for us, when he was on the point of death, he left the whole of the property to the care of the defendant Aphobus and Demophon the son of Demon, who were his nephews.... To Demophon he gave my sister with a portion of two talents to be paid immediately; and to the defendant he gave my mother with a portion of eighty minas and the use of my house and furniture. [Demosthenes, 'Against Aphobus I']¹²

The following extract is from Demosthenes' speech to the jury on behalf of Phormio, an ex-slave, now married to the mother of the plaintiff, Apollodorus.

It is no secret that Socrates the banker, having got his freedom from his master, did what the plaintiff's father did, gave his wife to Satyrus, who formerly belonged to him. Socles, another banker, gave his wife to Timodemus, who . . . formerly belonged to him. And it is not only here, men of Athens, that people in this line of business so act; but in Aegina, Strymodorus gave his wife to Hermaeus, his own slave, and again, upon her death, he gave him his daughter. And many such examples could be quoted, and no wonder. For although to you, men of Athens, who are citizens by birth, it would be disgraceful to prefer wealth, however great, to honorable descent, yet those persons who have obtained citizenship as a gift either from you or from others, and who owe that honor . . . to their having prospered in business and made more money than their neighbors, are obliged to preserve these advantages. Therefore it was that your father

1   Greek dancing girl
From a Greek vase dated about 520 BC

2   Leading the bride home
Greek vase dated about 460 BC

Pasion [Demosthenes here addresses Apollodorus directly] did
what he has done : he was not the first or the only person that
ever did such a thing: he did it not to disgrace himself or you
his sons; but seeing that the only way to keep up his business was
to attach this man to you by a binding connection, for that
reason he gave his own wife, your mother, to him in marriage. . . .
That the thing took place by your father's desire and
direction ... appears from the will.... [Demosthenes, 'For
Phormio']¹³

Aristotle's will is given by Diogenes Laërtius (c. A.D. *200–250):*

I appoint Antipater to be my executor. Until my adopted son,
Nicanor, comes of age, let Aristomanes, Timarchus, Diocles and
Theophrastus, if they are willing to shoulder this burden, be the
guardians of my children, of my estate and of Herphyllis. When
my daughter is old enough to be married, let her marry Nicanor.
If she should happen to die—which may the gods forbid—before
her marriage or before having children, then let Nicanor take
charge of my natural son, Nicomachus, and of my estate in a way
worthy of himself and of me. He shall provide for my daughter
and for Nicomachus so that they lack nothing, and behave
toward them as a brother and father.... If he prefers to let
Theophrastus take my daughter, then the same conditions shall
obtain for him.... I want the guardians and Nicanor to remember what my relations were with Herphyllis and her fidelity to
myself. If she wishes to take a husband, they should not give her
to a man unworthy of me. Apart from what she has already received from me, let her have a talent from my estate and three
slave girls if she wants them, the girl she already has and the
boy slave, Pyrraios. If she chooses to live at Chalcis, she is to have
the house by the garden, and if she prefers Stagyra, then let her
have my parents' house. The guardians shall have her house
furnished fittingly and to her satisfaction. [Diogenes Laërtius,
*The Lives, Opinions and Remarkable Sayings of the Most Famous
Ancient Philosophers*]¹⁴

*In the Athenian system neither women nor minors could be left to their
own devices:*

A minor is not allowed to make a will; for the law expressly forbids any child—or woman—to contract for more than a bushel of barley. [Isaeus, 'Against the Estate of Aristarchus']¹⁵

INHERITANCE AND PROPERTY

One thing is admitted, that males and the issue of males have the first title to inheritances: for the law positively declares that inheritances shall go to the nearest relations in the male line, when there are no children.   [Demosthenes, 'Against Leochares']¹⁶

It was important to every Greek to leave a male heir who could save his family and its religious cult from extinction. A daughter could not continue this cult, but a man without male issue had two remedies: (a) he could adopt a son or (b) resort to a device whereby his daughter married her nearest agnate. The male offspring of such a marriage, being descended on both sides from the dead man, was an acceptable heir for religious as well as financial purposes. A girl without legitimate brothers was an 'heiress.' It was the nearest agnate's duty to marry her and, having done so, to sleep with her at least three times a month. She enjoyed the usufruct of her father's fortune—if he had one—until her son came of age. Then the fortune became his. The heiress was truly no more than the channel of life, an appendage to her father's fortune. The agnate who wanted the money could not get it unless he took her too. If she was poor, the agnate had to take charge of her anyway from regard for family honor. If a man left several daughters and no son, they were all 'heiresses' and divided the fortune's usufruct. The institution was not peculiar to Athens; it existed in Thurium, Mytilene, Sparta, Crete, and, according to Isocrates, all over the Archipelago.

With respect to those heiresses who are in the class of Thetes [small peasants, laborers], if the next of kin does not choose to marry one, let him give her in marriage with a portion, if he be of the class of Pentacosiomedimni [owners of land yielding 500 measures of corn or oil], with a portion of five hundred drachmas, if of the class of Knights [whose land yields 300 measures], with a portion of three hundred, if of the class of Zeugitae [whose land yields 200], with a hundred and fifty in addition to what she has of her own. If there be several in the same degree of consanguinity, each of them shall give a marriage gift to the heiress ratably.... And if the nearest of kin will not marry her, or give her in marriage, let the archon compel him either to marry her himself, or give her in marriage. [Demosthenes, 'Against Macartatus'][17]

Eagerness to marry an heiress was likely to be proportionate to the fortune going with her. As the nearest agnate was automatically her guardian, he could, if she was already married, break up that marriage and claim her—and her money—himself.

The law ordains that daughters who have been given in marriage by their father and are living with their husbands... in spite of the fact that they are thus married, shall, if their father dies without leaving them legitimate brothers, pass into the legal power of their next of kin; and indeed it has frequently happened that husbands have thus been deprived of their wives. [Isaeus, 'On the Estate of Pyrrhus'][18]

Until their sons grew up and could defend them, female wards could easily be cheated by their guardians.

If a son is born to an heiress, two years after he has attained puberty he shall enter into possession of the estate, and he shall pay alimony to his mother. [Demosthenes, 'Against Stephanos II'][19]

If such a boy's estate had been misappropriated, he could sue the guardian. It is from the speeches made by litigants in such cases that we get our information about Athenian law and usage.

CRETE

In another part of Greece, in Crete, the Gortyna law tables, dating from sometime between 350 and 450 B.C., show the same institution developing differently. The heiress here had the option of refusing to marry her next of kin.

The heiress shall marry her father's brother, the eldest if there are several.... If there are no brothers but there are sons of such brothers, then the heiress shall marry the son of her father's eldest brother....

If an heiress, old enough to marry, refuses to marry the one who has a right to her, she shall have the house, if there is one in the town, with all it contains, and half the remaining property and shall marry whomever she chooses of the other members of the clan who ask for her hand. She shall divide the property with the one who had a right to marry her.

If a man dies leaving a widowed heiress with children, she may marry any member of the clan, but shall not be forced to do so. If the deceased left no children, then she shall marry her next of kin as it is written.

While she is below the age of puberty, her paternal uncles shall administer her property and she shall have half the income.

If the heiress is below the age of puberty and there is no next of kin with a right to claim her, then she shall have possession of the property and its income and, as long as she is below the age of puberty, shall be brought up at her mother's; if she has no mother, she shall be brought up in the house of her maternal uncles. [*Gortyna Law Tables*][20]

The Gortyna laws allow no power of willing. Children, and eventually kinsmen, have a prospective claim on their parents' property. Girls here have a claim to a share in their own right: half that due to a son.

If a man dies, his town houses and all they contain ... shall belong to his sons.

The rest of the property shall be fairly divided: sons, no matter how many of them there are, shall each receive two shares: daughters, no matter how many, shall each have one share.

The mother's property, if she dies, shall be divided in the same way.

If there is no property apart from the house, then the daughters shall have a share in that proportionately to what is written above.

If a father wishes to give a daughter her marriage portion

during his own lifetime, he may give her the amount due to her
but no more.

Any woman who has received no property, either outright or
pledged by her father or brother as dowry, or in a partition . . .
shall share in [her parents'] estate. Daughters previously provided for shall have no further claim, nor shall any claim be
entertained against them.

Husbands may no longer sell or pledge their wives' property,
nor sons their mothers' property. [*Gortyna Law Tables*][21]

MARRIAGE

Surely, of all creatures that have life and will, we women
Are the most wretched. When for an extravagant sum,
We have bought a husband, we must then accept him as
Possessor of our body. This is to aggravate
Wrong with worse wrong. Then the great question:
    will the man
We get be bad or good? For women, divorce is not
Respectable; to repel the man, not possible.
. . . And if in this exacting toil
We are successful and our husband does not struggle
Under the marriage yoke, our life is enviable.
Otherwise death is better. If a man grows tired
Of the company at home, he can go out, and find
A cure for tediousness. We wives are forced to look
To one man only.

[Euripides, *Medea*][22]

*Respectable Greek women were bred for marriage — there was no
alternative. A guardian's duty to his ward was to dower and marry her
off suitably when she came of age and as many times thereafter as might
be necessary. Her consent was not required.*

That improvement has occurred is shown by the fact that the old
customs are exceedingly simple and barbarous. For the ancient
Hellenes went about armed and bought their brides of each
other. [Aristotle, *Politics*][23]

For this is matrimony, when a man begets children, and

introduces the sons to the members of his clan and township, and affiances the daughters to their husbands as his own. [Demosthenes, 'Against Neaera'][24]

In a transaction of such importance [marriage] no man would have taken steps without a witness.... It is for this reason we hold marriage feasts, and invite our intimate friends; because the affair is one of moment; we are giving to the charge of others the happiness of our sisters and daughters, for whom we are anxious to make safe provision. [Demosthenes, 'Against Onetor'][25]

Marriage contracts did not exist in classical Greece; thus the need for the banquet offered by the bridegroom to his phratry shortly after the marriage. Testimony that such a banquet had been given would, should need arise, prove that the woman had entered the man's house as a wife and not as a concubine. The bride did not attend this banquet — or many others: women's place was at home, in the women's quarters or gynaeceum.

THE GYNAECEUM [WOMEN'S QUARTERS]

Many things which we consider proper are thought shocking in Greece. What Roman, for instance, has any scruples about taking his wife to a dinner party? What Roman matron does not appear in the reception rooms of her own house and take part in its social life? But it is quite different in Greece, for there a wife may not be present at dinner, unless it is a family party, and spends her time in a remote part of the house called 'the gynaeceum' which is never entered by a man unless he is a close relative. [Cornelius Nepos *Vitae*][26]

It is better for a woman to stay inside the house instead of showing herself at the door; for a man, on the other hand, it is a disgrace to be concerned with household matters instead of outside ones. [Xenophon, *The Economist*][27]

A decent woman must stay at home; the streets are for low women. [Menander, c. 342–292 B.C.]

Rich women whose men or slaves did the marketing hardly emerged

except for funerals or festivals. Poorer women were out much more often,
might even be obliged to sell things in the market, and probably did not
have separate apartments because their houses were small. Even the
houses of rich Greeks were not large. A picture of their domestic arrange-
ments emerges in the following extract from a speech made before a jury
by Euphiletus, an Athenian citizen who has murdered his wife's
adulterer.

When I, Athenians, decided to marry, and brought a wife into
my house . . . I kept a watch on her as far as possible. . . . But
when a child was born to me, I began to trust her . . . presuming
that we were now in perfect intimacy. . . . But as soon as I lost
my mother, her death became the cause of all my troubles. For
it was in attending her funeral that my wife was seen by this
man, who in time corrupted her. He looked out for the servant
girl who went to market, and so paid addresses to her mistress. . . . Now in the first place I must tell you . . . my dwelling
is on two floors, the upper being equal in space to the lower,
with the women's quarters above and the men's below. When
the child was born to us, its mother suckled it; and in order
that, each time that it had to be washed, she might avoid the
risk of descending by the stairs, I used to lie above and the
women below . . . it became such a habitual thing that my wife
would often leave me and go down to sleep with the child.
[Lysias, 'The Murder of Eratosthanes']²⁸

She slept not only with the child but also with her lover, Eratosthanes,
who used to enter the house with the connivance of the servant girl.
Eventually Euphiletus discovered them and killed the lover on the spot:
a justifiable homicide if the jury accepted his version of the facts. Any
invasion of the gynaeceum by outsiders was in itself shocking. Lysias,
the orator, speaks for another client whose rival for the affections of a
boy was driven by jealousy to burst into the client's house and even the
gynaeceum:

We felt desire, gentlemen, for Theodatus, a Plataean boy; and
while I looked to win his affection by kindness, this man thought
by outrage and defiance of the law to compel him to accede to
his wishes. . . . Hearing that the boy was at my house, he came

there at night in a drunken state, broke down the doors, and entered the women's room: within were my sister and my nieces, whose lives have been so well ordered that they are ashamed to be seen even by their kinsmen. [Lysias, 'Against Simon'][29]

A client of Demosthenes was presumably wrongly accused of a similar offense, since no prosecution was made in the proper quarter.

The plaintiff ... alleged that Eurgus came to his house in the country and intruded into the apartments of his daughters (who were heiresses) and his mother; and he brought the law concerning heiresses to the court. Not to this day has he ever appeared before the archon, whom the laws appoint to attend to such matters, and before whom the offender is in peril either of corporal punishment or pecuniary fine. [Demosthenes, 'Against Pantaenetus'][30]

Husbands did not stay home with their wives. The center of life for them was the market, a sociable, clubby, male world described quickly here by Demosthenes in attacking an opponent:

He walks through the market place like a viper or a scorpion with his sting uplifted, hastening here and there, and looking out for someone whom he may bring into a scrape, or fasten some calumny or mischief upon, and put in alarm, in order to extort money. He does not frequent any of the barber shops in the city, or the perfumers; or any such establishment; he is implacable, undomiciled, unsociable, having no feeling of kindness or friendship, nor any other which a right-minded man has. [Demosthenes, 'Against Aristogiton I'][31]

BIRTH CONTROL AND EXPOSURE

Wives, then, stayed at home, getting only a fraction of their husbands' attentions (though in some cases this must have been a deliverance). In restrictive societies neglected wives devote themselves to their children, and no doubt Greek women did. The aim of marriage was, after all, to produce an heir. Not too many heirs though. Greek families were not normally copious.

May you have no more than a single son to keep the patrimony together. That is the way to preserve wealth. [Hesiod][32]

Even a poor man will bring up a son, but even a rich man will expose a daughter. [Posidippus][33]

Abortion, contraception, and exposure of newborn infants were means used to limit the family. Since the law left such matters to the head of the family, it had no power to interfere if he himself decided to suppress the children. If someone else — the mother — did so without his permission, then he could dole out punishment. Only with regard to exceptional cases does the law discuss the right to expose.

If a divorced woman has a child, it shall be presented to her former husband in his house and in the presence of three witnesses. If he refuses to take it, the woman may choose whether to bring it up or expose it.

A divorced woman who exposes her child before presenting it in accordance with the law, shall, if she is convicted, pay fifty staters if the child was free and twenty-five if it was a slave.

If the man has no house in which the presentation may be made, or if he cannot be found, the woman shall not be penalized for exposing the child. [*Gortyna Law Tables*][34]

Since, according to Solon's law quoted earlier, an unmarried mother could be sold by her father for wantonness, the pregnant girl who tried to conceal her pregnancy and expose her child is a common figure in the Greek theater. The children of slave women belonged to the slave owner, and freed slaves might or might not have the ownership of their children. A document granting a slave, Diocléa, her freedom contains the following clause:

Should a child be born to Diocléa while she is still working for her mistress, Diocléa will have the right to smother it if she wants to; if she wants to raise it, it will be free; but she will not, in any circumstances, have the right to sell it. [Cited in G. Glotz, *L'Exposition des Enfants*][35]

Now the midwife, having received the newborn, should first put it upon the earth, having examined beforehand whether the infant is male or female, and should make an announcement by signs as is the custom of women. She should also consider whether it is worth rearing or not. And the infant which is suited by nature for rearing will be distinguished by the fact that its mother has spent the period of pregnancy in good health, for conditions which require medical care, especially those of the body, also harm the fetus and enfeeble the foundations of its life. Second, by the fact that it has been born at the due time, best at the end of nine months, and if it so happens, later; but also after only seven months. Furthermore by the fact that when put on the earth it immediately cries with proper vigor; for one that lives for some length of time without crying, or cries but weakly, is suspected of behaving so on account of some unfavourable condition. Also by the fact that it is perfect in all its parts, members and senses; that its ducts, namely of the ears, nose, pharynx, urethra, anus are free from obstruction; that the natural functions of every [member] are neither sluggish nor weak; that the joints bend and stretch; that it has due size and shape and is properly sensitive in every respect. This we may recognize from pressing the fingers against the surface of the body, for it is natural to suffer pain from everything that pricks or squeezes. And by conditions contrary to those mentioned, the infant not worth rearing is recognized. [Soranus of Ephesus, *Gynecology*] [36]

THE EDUCATION OF A HOUSEWIFE

'Here's another thing I'd like to ask you,' said I. 'Did you train your wife yourself or did she already know how to run a house when you got her from her father and mother?'

'What could she have known, Socrates,' said he, 'when I took her from her family? She wasn't yet fifteen. Until then she had been under careful supervision and meant to see, hear, and ask as little as possible. Don't you think it was already a lot that she should have known how to make a cloak of the wool she was given and how to dole out spinning to the servants? She had been taught to moderate her appetites, which, to my mind, is basic for both men's and women's education.'

'So, apart from that', I asked, 'it was you, Ischomachus, who had to train and teach her her household duties?'

'Yes,' said Ischomachus, 'but not before sacrificing to the gods.... And she solemnly swore before heaven that she would behave as I wanted, and it was clear that she would neglect none of my lessons.'

'Tell me what you taught her first....'

'Well, Socrates, as soon as I had tamed her and she was relaxed enough to talk, I asked her the following question: "Tell me, my dear," said I, "do you understand why I married you and why your parents gave you to me? You know as well as I do that neither of us would have had trouble finding someone else to share our beds. But, after thinking about it carefully, it was you I chose and me your parents chose as the best partners we could find for our home and our children. Now, if God sends us children, we shall think about how best to raise them, for we share an interest in securing the best allies and support for our old age. For the moment we only share our home...."'

'My wife answered, "But how can I help? What am I capable of doing? It is on you that everything depends. My duty, my mother said, is to be well behaved."'

' "Oh, by Zeus," said I, "my father said the same to me. But the best behavior in a man and woman is that which will keep up their property and increase it as far as may be done by honest and legal means."'

' "And do you see some way," asked my wife, "in which I can help in this?"'

Ischomachus next lectures his wife on the complementary relationship of male and female, describing marriage in terms of a business association.

' " ... it seems to me that God adapted women's nature to indoor and man's to outdoor work.... As Nature has entrusted woman with guarding the household supplies, and a timid nature is no disadvantage in such a job, it has endowed woman with more fear than man.... It is more proper for a woman to stay in the house than out of doors and less so for a man to be indoors instead of out. If anyone goes against the nature given him by God and leaves his appointed post ... he will be punished.... You must stay indoors and send out the servants whose work is outside and supervise those who work indoors, receive what is brought in, give out what is to be spent, plan ahead what should be stored and ensure that provisions for a year are not used up in a month. When the wool is brought in, you must see to it that clothes are made from it for whoever needs them and see to it that the corn is still edible.... Many of your duties will give you pleasure: for instance, if you teach spinning and weaving to a slave who did not know how to do this when you got her, you double her usefulness to yourself, or if you make a good housekeeper of one who didn't know how to do anything...." Then I took her around the family living rooms, which are pleasantly decorated, cool in summer and warm in winter. I pointed out how the whole house faces south so as to enjoy the winter sun.... I showed her the women's quarters which are separated from the men's by a bolted door to prevent anything being improperly removed and also to ensure that the slaves should not have children without our permission. For good slaves are usually even more devoted once they have a family; but good-for-nothings, once they begin to cohabit, have extra chances to get up to mischief. After our tour, we began sorting things according to their function. We began with the vessels used for sacrifices. Then we collected together all the women's holiday wear, the men's holiday and battle clothes, the blankets in the women's quarters and in the men's, women's footwear and men's. We stacked weapons in one pile; implements for spinning in another; those for making bread in another; in another all the kitchen tools, in another the washing things, in another things for kneading, and in another those for table use. Then we divided things used every day from those reserved for holidays. We separated supplies used by the month from those expected to last a year....' [Socrates expresses his admiration for the industry shown by Ischomachus' wife and the enthusiasm with which she accepts her husband's training:] 'From what you tell me, Ischomachus, your wife has a truly masculine mind!'

'Well,' said Ischomachus, 'let me tell you of some of her other traits which reveal a lofty soul and of how a word from me was enough to ensure her immediate obedience.'

He then recounts how his wife had taken to wearing cosmetics but how he gently and wisely showed her the folly of this conduct and persuaded her of the uselessness and dishonesty of trying to pass herself off as other than she was. The above extracts are from a treatise on husbandry written in the form of a dialogue within a dialogue. Socrates, speaking to Critobulus, tells him of a conversation he had with Ischomachus, a skillful householder. [Xenophon, *The Economist*][37]

ADULTERY AND DIVORCE

Solon, the famous lawgiver, has written in ancient and solemn manner concerning orderly conduct on the part of women. For the woman who is taken in the act of adultery he does not allow to adorn herself, nor even to attend the public sacrifices lest by mingling with innocent women she corrupt them. But if she does attend, or does adorn herself, he commands that any man who meets her shall tear off her garments, strip her of her ornaments and beat her (only he may not kill or maim her); for the lawgiver seeks to disgrace such a woman and make her life not worth living. [Aeschines, 'Against Timarchus'][38]

And when he has caught the adulterer, it shall not be lawful for the person who has so caught him to cohabit with his wife; and if he does cohabit with her, he shall be disfranchised. And it shall not be lawful for the woman, who has been caught in adultery, to attend the public sacrifices; and if she does attend them, she may suffer any maltreatment short of death . . . [Demosthenes, 'Against Neaera'.][39]

Only one restraint was imposed on the Greek husband who wished arbitrarily to repudiate his wife: he must return her dowry. If she was adulterous, he was legally bound to repudiate her but must still restore her dowry. There seems to have been little ceremony involved in dismissing a wife.

Hipponicus assembled a number of witnesses and put away his wife, stating that this man [Alcibiades] had been entering his house, not as her brother, but as her husband. (Lysias, 'Against Alcibiades I'][40]

The following is an example of divorce by mutual consent:

Two or three months later, Menecles, with many expressions of praise for our sister, approached us and said that he viewed with apprehension his increasing age and childlessness: she ought not, he said, to be rewarded for her virtues by having to grow old with him without bearing children; it was enough that he himself was unfortunate.... He therefore begged us to do him the favor of marrying her to someone else with his consent. We told him that it was for him to persuade her in the matter, for we would do whatever she agreed. At first she would not even listen to his suggestion, but in course of time she with difficulty consented. So we gave her in marriage to Elias of Sphettus, and Menecles handed over her dowry to him ... and he gave her the garments which she had brought with her to his house and the jewelry which there was.... [Isaeus 'On the Estate of Menecles']⁴¹

A wife who had strong grounds for divorce had to bring a written account of them to the archon or get her guardian to do so. The archon could then ratify the divorce if he thought fit. Wives who initiated divorces seem to have been rare, and the provocation had to be extreme. Simple adultery by the husband was probably considered sufficient grounds only in the case of an heiress. In the following case, the husband had brought his mistresses into the conjugal house.

I am astonished, furthermore, at those who are persuaded that Alcibiades is a lover of democracy, that form of government which more than any other would seem to make equality its end. They are not using his private life as evidence of his character, in spite of the fact that his greed and his arrogance are plain to them. On his marriage with the sister of Callias he received a dowry of ten talents; yet after Hipponicus had lost his life as one of the generals at Delium, he exacted another ten, on the ground that Hipponicus had agreed to add this further sum as soon as Alcibiades should have a child by his daughter. Then, after obtaining a dowry such as no Greek had ever obtained before, he behaved in so profligate a fashion, bringing mistresses, slave and free, into the bridal house, that he drove

his wife, who was a decent woman, to present herself before the
archon, as she was legally entitled to do, and divorce him. At
that he gave conspicuous proof of his power. He called in his
friends, and carried off his wife from the Agora by force,
showing the whole world his contempt for the magistrates, the
laws, and his fellow Athenians in general. [Andocides, 'Against
Alcibiades'][42]

*In Crete the following laws regulated the division of property after a
divorce:*

If a man and a woman divorce, the woman will take back whatever property she brought her husband and half the profits, if
there are any, deriving from her property, half the things she has
woven, whatever they may be and, over and above this, if the
husband was responsible for dissolving the marriage, five staters.

If the husband denies responsibility for dissolving the marriage, the judge shall settle the matter on taking an oath.

If the wife goes off with something belonging to the husband,
she shall pay five staters and return whatever it was she took.
[*Gortyna Law Tables*][43]

TRADESWOMEN AND PROSTITUTES

*Respectable women stayed indoors. In the law courts, a woman's having
been seen at a banquet was frequently used to put her married status in
doubt. Not surprisingly, a stigma seems to have attached to working
in the markets. The following is from a speech by a client of
Demosthenes whose citizenship has been queried:*

I shall now proceed to speak of my mother (for they have calum-
niated her also), and I shall call witnesses in support of my statements. And, men of Athens, the calumnies with which Euboïides
has assailed us are ... contrary to the laws which declare that
whoever reproaches either a male or a female citizen with
trafficking in the market shall be amenable to the penalties for
evil speaking. We confess that we sell ribbons and live not in the
way we could desire....

It seems to me that our trafficking in the market is the strongest proof of this man's charges against us being false. For when he says that my mother was a seller of ribbons and notorious to all, there ought surely to have been witnesses speaking to this of their knowledge, not repeating hearsay only. If she was an alien, they should have inspected the tolls in the market, and shown whether she paid the aliens' toll, and to what country she belonged: if a slave, the person who bought her, or the person who sold her, should have come to give evidence of it; or, in default of them, some one else might have proved that she had lived in servitude, or that she had been set free. . . .

He has said of my mother that she was a nurse. We do not deny this. . . . And don't let it prejudice you against us, men of Athens: for you will find many women of civic origin taking children to nurse. . . . Poverty compels freemen to do many mean and servile acts . . . many women of civic origin have become nurses and wool-dressers and vintagers, owing to the misfortunes of the commonwealth at that period. [Demosthenes, 'Against Eubolides']⁴⁴

A society which demands chastity from one section of its female population is likely to demand the opposite from another. There were many varieties of sexually available women in Greece. Sacred prostitution took its origin in early fertility cults and could be temporary or, as in the case of the slave girls attached to Aphrodite's sanctuaries, permanent. Corinth was the most famous of these:

It was so rich that it acquired more than a thousand sacred prostitutes, many of whom had been offered to the goddess by individual men or women. Thus the city drew crowds of visitors and grew rich; sailors were especially prone to ruin themselves there. [Strabo, *The Geography*]⁴⁵

Athens did not have such a sanctuary but was famous for its prostitutes.

According to Philemon . . . it was Solon who, because of young men's unbridled passions, first made a law whereby women might be prostituted in brothels. Nicander of Colophon . . . adds

3   Playing knucklebones
South Italian Greek terracotta dated about 300 BC

Celtic woman warrior
Gallic coin

that he built a temple to the Public Venus with the earnings of these brothel prostitutes.

This is what the poet Philemon has to say on the matter:

You, Solon . . . seeing that the state was full of randy young men whose natural appetites were leading them where they had no right to be, bought some women and put them in certain places where they were to be public and available to everyone. They stand there uncovered. Take a good look at them, boy. Don't be deceived. Are you satisfied? Ready? So are they. The door is open; the price one obol. In with you. There is no nonsense, no chitchat or trickery here. You do just what you like and the way you like. You're off: wish her goodbye. She has no further claim on you. [Athenaeus, *The Deipnosophists, or Banquet of the Learned*][46]

These brothel inmates were the property of the brothel owner. They might be the children of slaves, exposed children, or pirates' captives.

Kept women and courtesans were several rungs up the ladder. Plays show young men ruining themselves for them. Athenaeus claims they were educated and witty, and Xenophon, in his Memoirs of Socrates, *shows Socrates engaged in bright badinage with the courtesan Theodate. In the following sketch, a widow explains to her daughter that their only hope of survival is for the girl to learn to use her resources.*

CROBYLE: All you've got to do is go around with young men, drink with them, and sleep with them for money.

CORINNA: The way Daphnis' daughter, Lyra, does!

CROBYLE: Exactly.

CORINNA: But she's a prostitute!

CROBYLE: Well, is that such a terrible thing? It means you'll get to be as rich as she is and have lots of lovers. What are you crying for, Corinna? Don't you see how people chase after prostitutes even though there are so many of them? And how rich they get! Look, I can remember myself when Daphnis was in rags. That was before Lyra grew up. Now look at the style of her! She has heaps of gold, marvelous clothes, and four servants.

CORINNA: But how did Lyra earn all that?

CROBYLE: Well, to start with she's always smartly dressed; she is good-humored with everyone, not getting the giggles for the least thing, the way you do, but smiling attractively and with charm. She knows how to handle men. She's warm and attentive with men who visit or send for her, but she doesn't overdo it. If a customer takes her to a dinner party, she doesn't get drunk, which is a degrading thing to do and turns men against us; she doesn't stuff herself with food as though she wasn't used to eating well but takes small mouthfuls, picking it up with the tips of her fingers and eating without puffing out her cheeks. She drinks slowly, in small sips, instead of gulping everything down at once.

CORINNA: Really, Mother? Even if she's thirsty?

CROBYLE: Yes, Corinna. She doesn't talk too much either or poke fun at people, and she keeps her eyes on the man who brought her. When it's time for bed, she's neither too cold nor too sexy but keeps her mind on pleasing and holding on to her new lover; so they all like her. Now if you can only learn to do as she does, you'll make both our fortunes, for in other ways you have a lot more going for you—but I'll say no more. One has to live. [Lucian, *Le Manuel des Boudoirs*]⁴⁷

4 Hellenistic Greece

*In Hellenistic Greece (third to first centuries B.C.) a change takes place in
women's status. The influence of Egypt and Rome contributes to this. In
Egypt, women exercise professions, pay taxes, have some legal capacity.
Marriage contracts of Greeks resident in Egypt, like the one quoted below,
mention the mother as well as the father of the girl and—a departure from
classical Attic law—consider the husband's infidelities to be as grave as
the wife's. The spread of the Egyptian cult of the goddess Isis is credited
with having helped to raise women's status. Evidence from inscriptions
shows that girls are being educated in this period.*

[Year 311 B.C.] Contract of marriage between Heracleides and
Demetria.

Heracleides takes Demetria of Cos as his lawful wife. He
receives her from her father, Leptines of Cos, and from her
mother, Philotis. He is a free man and she a free woman. She
brings with her clothes and jewels worth 1,000 drachmas. Heracleides will provide Demetria with all the requirements of a free
woman. They shall live in whatever place seems best to Leptine
and Heracleides.

If Demetria is found to have done something which disgraces
her husband, she shall lose everything she brought with her.
And Heracleides shall accuse her before three men chosen by
the pair of them. Heracleides shall not be permitted to wrong
Demetria by keeping another woman or having children by
another woman, nor to harm Demetria in any way under any
pretext. If Heracleides is found to have done such a thing,
Demetria shall accuse him before three men whom they shall
have selected together. Heracleides shall then pay Demetria
back the 1,000 drachmas she brought as a dowry and a
further 1,000 drachmas in Alexandrian silver as recompense.
[Claire Préaux, *Le Statut de la femme à l'époque hellénistique,
principalement en Egypte*][48]

ROMANTIC HETEROSEXUAL LOVE

In the second and third centuries A.D. a great vogue was enjoyed by romantic novels dealing with the separation, trials, hair's-breadth escapes, and final happy reunions of lovers. They are chivalrous and extravagant and break completely with the classic Greek attitude to women. The old way of thinking is confronted with the new in Plutarch's Dialogue on Love, *which precedes the novels and is a plea for heterosexual love. Plutarch claims for it that nobility which Plato had reserved for love between men. He gives his adversaries' arguments and concludes with an apologia for conjugal love in which he blends Plato's idealist, even mystic concept of Eros with a more realistic moralist's conception of marriage. He advances the idea that women may participate in heroic love and allows their virtue a wider scope than was afforded by the old domestic Greek ideal. The dialogue is occasioned by the news that a young widow, Ismenodora, has fallen so deeply in love with Bacchonis that she has had him kidnapped. This astonishing reversal of roles infuriates Bacchonis' homosexual friends. Plutarch gives their arguments first.*

'By the "most shameful act," ' interrupted Daphnaeus, 'don't you mean marriage, the union of a man and a woman, the most sacred of all bonds?'

'Oh,' said Protogenes, 'as this union is necessary for the propagation of mankind, legislators must obviously promote and praise it to the people. But not one whit of true love enters the gynaeceum. I certainly do not give the name "love" to the feeling one has for women and girls any more than we would say that flies are in love with milk, bees with honey, or breeders with the calves and fowl which they fatten in the dark.... Love inspired by a noble and gifted soul leads to virtue through friendship, but desire felt for a woman leads at best to nothing more than the fleeting enjoyments and pleasures of the body.... There is only one genuine love, that which boys inspire...it is simple and without luxury; you will see it haunting the gatherings of philosophers or the gymnasiums and wrestling schools, in search of the most worthy young men with a view to vigorously and generously exhorting them to cultivate goodness.

'But that other kind of love which is enervating and stay-at-home, which clings to the dresses and beds of women, craves sensual pleasures unworthy of a man, and is ignorant of enthusiasm or friendship, that love should be outlawed. Solon did this: he denied gymnastics and the love of boys to slaves, while allowing them to go with women; for just as friendship is fine and noble, so sensual pleasure is common and base; now the love a slave would feel for boys could not be noble or generous, all he could feel would be carnal love, the sort one feels for women....'

[Daphnaeus (a man) defends heterosexual love:] 'If love of boys disowns sensual delight, it does so from shame and fear of punishment; needing a decent pretext to approach young men, it puts forward friendship and goodness. It covers itself with dust in the ring, takes cold baths, frowns, puts on all the airs of a sage and philosopher because of the law; but then at night, when all are asleep, "The picking is sweet in the guardian's absence".'

[When news comes that Ismenodora has had Bacchonis carried off, a speaker exclaims:] 'There's the sort of love which may not be withstood! .... What it wants it buys even at the price of life. Who in this town leads a life as blameless as Ismenodora? What gossip has she ever provoked? What breath of scandal has touched her house? Clearly the woman has been seized by a divine impulse more powerful than human reason....' [Plutarch's father, one of the interlocutors, then sums up:] 'It is true that sex without love is like hunger or thirst; it is mere satisfaction of a need and leads nowhere.... As I have just demonstrated, the two sexes have the same nature. So, Daphnaeus, in defense of them both, we shall refute Zeuxippus' argument. He identifies love with those immoderate desires which lead the soul to debauchery, not because he believes this himself but because he has heard it said by bitter men who know nothing of love. Some of these ensnare women with the lure of a little money, then deliver them with the money over to the drudgery of housework, sordid account-keeping, and day-long bickering, and generally treat them like servants. Others, more interested in having children than in a wife, do as the male cicada does which lays its seed on an onion or some other vegetable: they get the first female to hand with child, gather the fruit, and say goodbye to the marriage; or else, if they do let it drag on, pay no attention to it, having no interest in loving or being loved.

'On the contrary, physical union with a wife is a source of friendship, a sharing together in a great mystery. Sensual delight is brief, but it is like a seed from which day by day there grow between husband and wife consideration for each other, kindness, tenderness, and confidence.' [Plutarch, *Dialogue on Love*][49]

II   Rome

I Patriarchal Rome

In the earliest period—to the end of the Punic wars in the second century
B.C.—*Roman society had been patriarchal. The head of each clan was
magistrate, priest, and owner of all the things and persons within it.
Guided by custom and after consultation—if he so chose—with a council
of kinsmen, he laid down the law and wielded powers of life and death.
These were justified by his religious function. With its erosion, his power,
once regarded as a divine gift, came to be seen as a concession from the
civil authority. Gradually, the rights and claims of his dependents grew
and his diminished: he had to ransom them if captured, he had to dower
his daughter, he could not break up her marriage against her will, he could
not exclude a child from the family, or sell his wife, or force a son to marry.
Wives obtained the power to repudiate their husbands. Men lost the power
to kill their wives and daughters-in-law. The father of an adulterous
daughter preserved his power to kill until the third century* A.D., *but such
survivals had diminished force in a context of altered values and habits.*

*Our information about this early period of Roman history comes from
historians who lived long after and who tended to idealize the simpler
mores of their city's past. The following texts speak for themselves, but it
should be noted that they refer exclusively to women of free birth and citizen
origin. Up to 445* B.C.—*when patricians were first permitted to marry
plebeians—this probably meant patrician women only. Slaves were beneath
the law, which neither bound nor protected them. Freedwomen were in
an ambiguous position, since they owed gratitude to their former owners
and such gratitude could be interpreted more or less narrowly. A wife was
received into her husband's family 'as a daughter', so that her status was
that of sister to her own children, and her dowry became her husband's absolute property. The legendary Romulus, credited with having founded
Rome in the year 753* B.C. *is also credited with having proclaimed the first
law of marriage.*

The law was to this effect, that a woman joined to her husband
by a holy marriage should share in all his possessions and sacred
rites.... This law obliged both the married women, as having
no other refuge, to conform themselves entirely to the temper of
their husbands and the husbands to rule their wives as necessary

and inseparable possessions. Accordingly, if a wife was virtuous and in all things obedient to her husband, she was mistress of the house to the same degree as her husband was master of it, and after the death of her husband she was heir to his property in the same manner as a daughter was to that of her father; that is, if he died without children and intestate, she was mistress of all he left, and if he had children, she shared equally with them. But if she did any wrong, the injured party was her judge, and determined the degree of her punishment. Other offenses, however, were judged by her relatives together with her husband; among them was adultery, or where it was found she had drunk wine— a thing which the Greeks look upon as the least of faults. For Romulus permitted them to punish both these acts with death, as being the gravest offenses women could be guilty of, since he looked upon adultery as the source of reckless folly, and drunkenness as the source of adultery. And both these offenses continued for a long time to be punished by the Romans with merciless severity. The wisdom of this law concerning wives is attested by the length of time it was in force; for it is agreed that during the space of five hundred and twenty years no marriage was ever dissolved at Rome. [Dionysius of Halicarnassus][1]

It is on record that for nearly five hundred years after the founding of Rome there were no lawsuits and no warranties in connection with a wife's dowry in the city of Rome or in Latium, since of course nothing of that kind was called for, inasmuch as no marriages were annulled during that period. Servius Sulpicius too, in the book which he compiled *On Dowries*, wrote that security for a wife's dower seemed to have become necessary for the first time when Spurius Carvilius, who was surnamed Ruga, a man of rank, put away his wife because, owing to some physical defect, no children were born from her; and that this happened in the five hundred and twenty-third year after the founding of the city [231 B.C.] And it is reported that this Carvilius dearly loved the wife whom he divorced, and held her in strong affection because of her character, but that above his devotion and love he set his regard for the oath which the censors had compelled him to take that he would marry a wife for the purpose of begetting children. [Aulus Gellius, *The Attic Nights*][2]

This story of Spurius Carvilius, repeated and variously dated by different authors, should not be taken literally. Divorce is mentioned as early as the Twelves Tables of 451 B.C.

Those who have written about the life or civilization of the Roman people say that the women of Rome and Latium 'lived an abstemious life'; that they abstained altogether from wine ... [and] that it was an established custom for them to kiss their kinsfolk for the purpose of detection, so that, if they had been drinking, the odor might betray them. But they say that the women were accustomed to drink the second brewing, raisin wine, spiced wine, and other sweet-tasting drinks of that kind. And these things are indeed made known in those books which I have mentioned, but Marcus Cato [232–147 B.C.] declares that women were not only censured but also punished by a judge no less severely if they had drunk wine than if they had disgraced themselves by adultery.

I have copied Marcus Cato's words from the oration entitled *On the Dowry*, in which it is also stated that husbands had the right to kill wives taken in adultery: 'When a husband puts away his wife,' says he,—'he judges the women as a censor would, and has full powers if she has been guilty of any wrong or shameful act; she is severely punished if she has drunk wine; if she has done wrong with another man she is condemned to death.' Further, as to the right to put her to death it was thus written: 'If you should take your wife in adultery, you may with impunity put her to death without a trial; but if you should commit adultery or indecency, she must not presume to lay a finger on you, nor does the law allow it.' [Aulus Gellius, *Attic Nights*][3]

Romulus also instituted certain laws, one of which is somewhat severe, which suffers not a wife to leave her husband, but grants a husband power to turn off his wife, either upon poisoning her children, or counterfeiting his keys, or for adultery; but if the husband upon any other occasion put her away, he ordered one half of his estate to be given to the wife, the other to fall to the goddess Ceres; and whoever cast off his wife, to make an atonement by sacrifice to the gods of the dead.   [Plutarch, 'Romulus,' *Lives*][4]

The poisoning meant is probably abortion, or the killing of unborn children by drinking some abortifacient. The keys referred to are probably those of the wine cellar, since women were forbidden to drink wine.

Valerius Maximus, a contemporary of the Emperor Tiberius (42 B.C. –A.D. 37), left an account of some of the more notorious penalties inflicted by early Roman husbands:

A far less weighty motive roused the anger of Egnatius Metellus, who beat his wife to death because she had drunk some wine; and this murder, far from leading to his being denounced, was not even blamed. People considered that her exemplary punishment had properly expiated her offense against the laws of sobriety: for any woman who drinks wine immoderately closes her heart to every virtue and opens it to every vice.

C. Sulpicius Gallus was another stern and pitiless husband: he repudiated his wife because she had been seen out of doors with her face uncovered. The sentence was harsh but based on reason. 'The law,' he could have said to her, 'bids you seek to please no one but me. It is for me that you must be attractive. For me that you must adorn yourself. To me you must confide the secrets of your beauty. In sum, I am to be the judge of your charms. Any other glance which you attract to yourself, even innocently, can only render you suspect of entertaining some criminal design.' [Valerius Maximus, *Facta et Dicta Memorabilia*] [5]

2 An Early Protest Movement

At a time [195 B.C.] of considerable concern over major wars which either had just ended or were impending, an incident occurred which, although it may sound trivial, aroused strong feeling and turned into a violent controversy. The tribunes of the people proposed that the Oppian Law should be repealed. By this law, which had been brought in during the heat of the Punic wars, 'no woman might own more than half an ounce of gold, or wear clothes of various colors, or ride in a horse-drawn carriage in any town or city or within a mile of its confines, except on the occasion of some public religious ceremony.' Crowds filled the Capitol demonstrating for and against the repeal, and neither modesty, nor dissuasion, nor the commands of their husbands, could keep the matrons at home. They stood in every street of the city, waylaying men on their way to the forum and urging that, during the present public and private prosperity, women should be allowed to adorn themselves as they had formerly done. Crowds of women came in from country towns and even villages and were bold enough to go up to consuls, praetors, and magistrates to solicit their support. One consul, however, they found particularly inexorable. This was Marcus Porcius Cato, who spoke as follows against repealing the law :

'Romans, if every married man had made sure that his own wife looked up to him and respected his marital authority, we should not have half this trouble with women in general. But now, having let female insubordination triumph first in our homes, we find our privileges trodden and trampled on in the public forum. We have failed to control each woman individually, and we find ourselves quailing before a body of them. As to the outrageous behavior of these women . . . I do not know whether it reflects greater disgrace on you, tribunes, or on us the consuls: on you, if you have brought them here to incite to sedition; on us, if we allow laws to be imposed on us by demonstrating women as was done formerly by a secession of the common people. It was not without strong feelings of shame that I pushed my way through an army of women on my way here. My respect for the modesty and dignity of some individuals among them—which I do not feel for them as a mob—prevented my doing anything as a consul which might seem like a use of force. Otherwise I should have asked them, "What do you mean by coming out in public in this unheard of fashion and calling out to other women's husbands? Could you not have raised all these matters at home and with your own husbands?"... Woman is a violent and uncontrolled animal, and it is useless to let go the reins and then expect her not to kick over the traces. You must keep her on a tight rein.... Women want total freedom or rather—to call things by their names—total license. If you allow them to achieve complete equality with men, do you think they will be easier to live with? Not at all. Once they have achieved equality, they will be your masters....'

The tribune Lucius Valerius answered Cato's last point as follows.

'I next turn to Cato's argument that if you repeal the Oppian Law ... your daughters, wives, and even sisters will be harder to control. My answer to this is that women escape dependence only by the death of their menfolk, and that the independence they achieve by becoming widows or orphans is one from which they pray to be spared. What they want is that you and not the law should regulate their dress. You, for your part, should prefer to hold them in guardianship rather than in bondage and prefer the title of father or husband to that of master. The consul just now made use of some invidious terms, talking of a female sedition and secession. Does he think they will seize the Sacred Hill or the Aventine, as the plebeians once did? Their weakness must submit to whatever ruling you make, and the greater your power, the more moderate you should be in its exercise.'

In spite of all the arguments which had been raised for and against the repeal of the law, the women poured out the following day in even greater numbers, blockaded the houses of those tribunes who had protested against their colleagues' measure, and withdrew only when the protests had been withdrawn. After that there was no doubt but that every one of the tribes would vote for the repeal. And so the law was annulled twenty years after it had first been passed. [Livy, *The History of Rome*][6]

3 Guardianship

Roman law provides one of the most coherent codifications of family law that we shall encounter. This and the following sections will draw heavily on it. The main corpus of Roman law was codified (A.D. *528–534*) *by order of the Emperor Justinian and has four principal parts: the* Institutes, *the* Digest, *the* Code, *and the* Novels. *Most of this material—chiefly laws, commentaries, and rescripts—dates from the first three centuries of the empire, but there is also much from the fourth, fifth, and sixth centuries. The* Novels *are all late.*

A Roman woman's competence to take legal action—e.g., testamentary capacity or the right to alienate property—was at first severely restricted. Normally, a guardian or tutor mediated all her legal relations with the outside world. In early Rome a girl passed, on marriage, from under the guardianship of the head of her own family to that of the head of her husband's family by virtue of an institution known as manus. *She was thus always more or less in subjection. Manus, or holding someone in one's hand* (in manu), *was the power exercised by the head of the family over his wife and children. It took its origin in patriarchal Rome, survived in later law, and is described by Gaius* (2nd century A.D.), *although by his time it had already fallen into disuse. There were marriages without* manus: *a girl thereby remained in the power of her father and did not become part of her husband's 'gens.' This was 'free marriage,' first achieved by a device which Gaius dates back to the time of the Twelve Tables* (450 B.C.). *It was probably devised to prevent patrician property, or that portion of it intended for the daughter, from falling into plebeian hands through mixed marriage, legalized by the Lex Canuleia in 445* B.C. *Since patrician wealth was in land—patricians were barred by law from taking up commerce—alienation of their traditional estates would have led to the ruin of the class. When a girl contracted free marriage, her property continued to be administered by the head of her own family and she enjoyed its usufruct only. By the third century* B.C., *free marriage was the general practice, with the result—though such had not been the aim—that a degree of feminine emancipation was realized. A woman thus married did not pass under her husband's absolute power and could free herself from the marriage by divorce. She was, it is true, under her father's control. If freed from this, for instance by his death, she became 'sui juris'— her own mistress. She still needed a guardian to administer her property, and her father probably had appointed one in his will. These guardians, however, took their duties lightly. If one was overbearing, the woman could apply to the praetor and have him replaced.*

A woman who married by any of the three following forms, all dating back to early Rome, passed into her husband's power. Confarreation was unpopular with women because it kept them in subjection and deprived them of the right to initiate divorce.

Both males and females are under the authority of another, but females alone are placed in the hands.

Formerly this ceremony was performed in three different ways, namely, by use, by confarreation, and by coemption.

A woman came into the hand of her husband by use when she had lived with him continuously for a year after marriage; for the reason that she was obtained by usucaption, as it were, through possession for the term of a year, and passed into the family of her husband where she occupied the position of a daughter. Hence it is provided by the Law of the Twelve Tables that if a woman was unwilling to be placed in the hand of her husband in this way, she should every year absent herself for three nights, and in this manner interrupt the use during the said year; but all of this law has been partly repealed by legal enactments, and partly abolished by disuse.

Women are placed in the hand of their husbands by confarreation, through a kind of sacrifice made to Jupiter Farreus, in which a cake is employed, from whence the ceremony obtains its name; and in addition to this, for the purpose of performing the ceremony, many other things are done and take place, accompanied with certain solemn words, in the presence of ten witnesses. This law is still in force in our time, for the principal flamens [priests], that is to say, those of Jupiter, Mars, and Quirinus, as well as the chief of the sacred rites, are exclusively selected from persons born of marriages celebrated by confarreation.

In marriage by coemption, women become subject to their husbands by mancipation, that is to say by a kind of fictitious sale; for the man purchases the woman who comes into his hand in the presence of not less than five witnesses, who must be Roman citizens over the age of puberty, and also of a balance-holder.

By this act of sale a woman can not only make a coemption to her husband but also to a stranger, that is to say, the sale takes place either on account of marriage or by way of trust; for a woman who disposes of herself in this way to her husband for the purpose of occupying the place of his daughter is said to have done so on account of matrimony; but where she does this for some other purpose, either to a husband or to a stranger, as for instance in order to avoid a guardianship, she is said to have made a coemption by way of trust.

The method by which this is done is as follows: If a woman wishes to get rid of her present guardians and obtain another in their stead, she makes this disposal of herself with their consent; and then the other party to the sale sells her again to him whom she wishes to be her guardian, and he manumits her by the ceremony of the wand of the Praetor, and by this means becomes her guardian, and is designated a fiduciary guardian, as will hereafter appear.

Parents are permitted to appoint testamentary guardians for their children who are subject to their authority, who are under the age of puberty, and of the male sex; and for those of the female sex, no matter what their age may be, and even if they are married; for the ancients required women, even if they were of full age, to remain under guardianship on account of the levity of their disposition.

Therefore, if anyone appoints a guardian for his son and daughter by will, and both should arrive at the age of puberty, the son will cease to have a guardian, but the daughter will nevertheless remain subject to guardianship; for it is only under the Lex Julia et Papia that women are released from guardianship by the birth of children. Those whom we speak of do not include Vestal Virgins, whom the ancients desired to be free on account of the honor of the priesthood; hence this was provided by the Law of the Twelve Tables.

A testamentary guardian can be appointed for a wife who is in the hand of the testator; just as if she were a daughter; and, likewise, one may be appointed for a daughter-in-law who is in the hand of a son, just as if she were a granddaughter.

The choice of a guardian may be left to a wife who is in the hand of the testator.... In this instance, the wife is permitted to appoint a guardian either for the administration of all the property or only for one or two things.

Moreover, the choice may be granted absolutely or with restrictions.

... according to the Law of the Twelve Tables, females had agnates as legal guardians, but afterwards the Lex Claudia ... abolished the guardianship of agnates, so far as females were concerned....

... by a Decree of the Senate, women are permitted to demand another guardian to take the place of one who is absent; and this having been granted, the first guardian ceases to hold his office, nor does it make any difference how far he may be from home.

An exception, however, is made in the case of an absent patron [i.e., former owner], as a freedwoman is not permitted in this instance to demand another guardian.

There does not seem to be any good reason, however, why women of full age should be under guardianship, for the common opinion that because of their levity of disposition they are easily deceived and it is only just that they should be subject to the authority of guardians seems to be rather apparent than real; for women of full age transact their own affairs, but in certain cases, as a mere form, the guardian interposes his authority, and he is often compelled to give it by the praetor, though he may be unwilling to do so.

The legal guardianship of parents and patrons is indeed understood to have a certain effect for the reason that they cannot be forced to give their consent to the making of a will, to the alienation of property subject to mancipation, or to the assumption of obligations; unless there should be some urgent reason.... These provisions have been made for their own benefit... [in order that being entitled to the inheritance of their wards should these die intestate] they can neither be excluded from them by will nor have the estate come into their hands diminished in value on account of debts which have been incurred or through the alienation of the most valuable part of the property.

Moreover, a freeborn woman is released from guardianship if she is the mother of three children, and a freedwoman if she is the mother of four, and is under the legal guardianship of her patron. [Gaius, *The Institutes of Gaius*]⁷

A guardian then—unless he was his ward's own father or her former owner if she was a freedwoman—could be got rid of or compelled to allow his ward to manage her affairs as she chose. The institution was falling into disuse.

Because of the weakness of women's judgment, our ancestors wanted them to be subject to guardians, but lawyers have devised a type of guardian who can be kept subject to the women. [Cicero, 'For Murena,' *Orationes*]⁸

4 Marriage and the Family

Marriage is the union of a man and woman forming an association during their entire lives, and involving the common enjoyment of divine and human privileges. [*The Digest*][9]

THE LEGISLATION OF AUGUSTUS

By the end of the Republic, free marriage was the norm. The celebration had lost its religious significance, had dropped all formalities resulting in manus, and was now a purely civil ceremony. There were no divorce courts. Wives could repudiate the marriage but had no punitive action against adulterous husbands. A husband still enjoyed the old patriarchal right to kill an adulterous wife and her lover if caught in the act. Failing this, he divorced her and kept a portion of her dowry. The law did not interfere in family affairs, leaving these, as it always had, to the family itself. However, the old system had ceased to work. Women of the upper class often enjoyed economic independence. A wife could anticipate a husband's punitive action by repudiating him first. Many men preferred to live with mistresses and remain unmarried; many others had been killed during the civil wars. And as Roman citizenship had been greatly extended, a falling birth rate among old citizens, particularly of the ruling class, threatened their submergence. Augustus introduced legislation designed to promote the birth rate in this class and preserve its purity of blood by cracking down on adulterous wives, who might otherwise foist spurious issue on their husbands. The first of these objectives was taken care of by the Lex Julia de Maritandis Ordinibus (19 B.C.), which obliged fathers to dower and marry off their daughters; it also freed all mothers of three or more children from guardianship and debarred childless women from receiving legacies from other than near relatives. The Lex Julia de Adulteriis (18 B.C.) took jurisdiction over adultery away from the family and made it a public crime. A court was set up to hear cases against married women and their lovers. The wronged husband was expected to prosecute, and if he failed to do so, he could himself be prosecuted for connivance. Public informers were encouraged to move such cases, until Constantine restricted the right of pressing such charges to close relatives. A married man was not guilty of adultery simply because he had sexual relations with a woman other than his wife;

but if the woman was not a registered prostitute, he was guilty of vice
(stuprum). *He no longer had the right to kill his adulterous wife,
although in certain cases he could still kill her lover. The punishment for
adultery was banishment of woman and lover to different islands. The
man lost half his property; the woman lost one-third of hers and half her
dowry. Augustus' own daughter, Julia, and his granddaughter were
both punished under this law.*

*Augustus' legislation was not popular, particularly those sections
penalizing celibacy and childless marriages. The historian Dio Cassius
relates that in* A.D. *9, after the knights of Rome had been agitating for an
appeal of the laws, Augustus assembled them in the forum and, having
separated those among them who were fathers, addressed them as follows:*

Though you are but few altogether ... yet for this very reason
I ... praise you the more, and am heartily grateful to you
because you have shown yourselves obedient and are helping to
replenish the fatherland. For it is by lives so conducted that the
Romans of later days will become a mighty multitude. We were
at first a mere handful, you know, but when we had recourse to
marriage and begot us children, we came to surpass all mankind
not only in the manliness of our citizens but in the size of our
population as well. Bearing this in mind, we must console the
mortal side of our nature with an endless succession of generations that shall be like the torchbearers in a race, so that through
one another we may render immortal the side of our nature in
which we fall short of divine bliss. It was for this cause most of all
that that first and greatest god, who fashioned us, divided the
race of mortals in twain, making one half of it male and the
other half female, and implanted in them love and compulsion
to mutual intercourse, making their association fruitful, that by
the young continually born he might render even mortality
eternal....

For is there anything better than a wife who is chaste,
domestic, a good housekeeper, a rearer of children; one to
gladden you in health, to tend you in sickness; to be your
partner in good fortune, to console you in misfortune; to
restrain the mad passion of youth, and to temper the unseason-
able harshness of old age? And is it not a delight to acknowledge
a child who shows the endowments of both parents, to nurture

and educate it, at once the physical and spiritual image of yourself, so that in its growth another self lives again? ... Those are
the private advantages that accrue to those who marry and
beget children; but for the State, for whose sake we ought to do
many things that are even distasteful to us, how excellent and
necessary it is, if cities and people are to exist, and if you are to
rule others and all the world is to obey you, that there should be
a multitude of men, to till the earth in time of peace, to make
voyages, practice arts and follow handicrafts, and, in time of
war, to protect what we already have with all the greater zeal
because of family ties and to replace those that fall by others.
Therefore men—for you alone may properly be called men—
and fathers.... I love and praise you for this; and I not only
bestow the prizes I have already offered but will distinguish you
still further by other honors and offices, so that you may not
only reap great benefits yourselves but may also leave them to
your children undiminished.... [Dio Cassius][10]

AGE AND CONSENT

The Romans ... gave their daughters in marriage as early as
twelve years old, or even under; thus they thought their bodies
and minds alike would be delivered to the future husband pure
and undefiled. [Plutarch, 'Comparison of Numa with Lycurgus,'
Lives][11]

In contracting a betrothal, there is no limit to the age of the
parties, as is the case in marriage. Wherefore, a betrothal can be
made at a very early age, provided [the following proviso is
thought by some scholars to be a post-classical interpolation]
what is being done is understood by both persons, that is to say,
where they are not under seven years of age. [Digest][12]

Where a girl under twelve years of age is married, she will
not be a lawful wife until she has reached that age while living
with her husband. [Digest][13]

A betrothal, like a marriage, is made with the consent of the
contracting parties, and therefore, as in the case of a marriage, a
son under paternal control must agree to it.

A girl who evidently does not resist the will of her father is
understood to give her consent. A daughter is permitted to

refuse to consent to her father's wishes only when he selects someone for her husband who is unworthy on account of his habits or who is of infamous character. [*Digest*]¹⁴

Widows under the age of twenty-five, even though they may have obtained the freedom of emancipation, still cannot marry a second time without the consent of their father. If, however, in the choice of a husband, the desire of the woman is opposed to that of her father and other relatives, it is established (just as has always been decreed with reference to the marriage of virgins), that judicial authority should be interposed for the purpose of examination, and if the parties are equal in family and in morals, he shall be considered preferable whom the woman has selected herself. . . . [A.D. 371].

The wishes of the father are to be considered in case of the marriage of daughters under paternal control. Where, however, a girl is her own mistress, and is under twenty-five years of age, the consent of her father must be obtained. . . . [*Code of Justinian*]¹⁵

If any man who has not previously made a pact with the parents of a girl should ravish this girl against her will, or if he should abduct a girl who was willing, hoping to obtain protection from the consent of the girl, although it was because of the fault of frivolity and the inconstancy of her sex and judgment that a girl was altogether excluded by the ancients from conducting suits in court and from giving testimony and from all matters pertaining to courts, the consent of the girl shall be of no advantage to him, as it would have been under the ancient law, but rather the girl herself shall be held liable as a participant in the crime. . . .

If willing agreement is discovered in the girl, she shall be punished with the same severity as her ravisher, since impunity must not be granted even to those girls who are ravished against their will, when they could have kept themselves chaste at home up to the time of marriage and when, if the doors were broken by the audacity of the ravisher, the girls could have obtained the aid of neighbors by their cries and could have defended themselves by all their efforts. But we impose a lighter penalty on these girls, and we command that only the right of succession to

their parents shall be denied them. [1 April A.D. 320; 326]
[*The Theodosian Code*][16]

ADULTERY

*Although the aim of the Julian law on adultery was to make it a public
crime punishable by the state, some of the old prerogatives of husband
and father were maintained. They were probably rarely enforced. The
following extract is from a pre-Justinian law collation assembled sometime between A.D. 390 and 438. It begins with a discussion of the Lex
Julia de Adulteriis.*

The second chapter enacts that if a father, either at his own
house or at that of his son-in-law who has applied to him in the
matter, has caught anyone committing adultery with his
daughter, she being at the time in his power or having passed,
with his sanction, out of his power into that of her husband, he
is permitted to slay the adulterer without risk of prosecution,
provided that he slays the daughter immediately....

Marcellus [jurist] ... shows that a father has also the sanction
of the law to kill a man of consular rank or his own patron,
should he take him in adultery with his daughter.

But if he does not kill the daughter but only the adulterer, he
is guilty of murder....

The same Paulus [another jurist, died c. A.D. 235] in the same
Single Book and Title:

Certain classes of persons are enumerated whom the husband
may kill when the wife is taken in adultery (with any of them),
though he may not kill her.

Thus the husband, even if he is a *filius familias*, is permitted,
according to the Statutes, to kill a man whom he has taken in
adultery in his house, if the adulterer is a slave, a paid gladiator,
or one who has let out his services to fight with wild beasts, or
has been convicted on a criminal charge, or is a freedman,
whether his own or his father's, and whether a Roman or a
Latin citizen.

Moreover, he is permitted to kill the freedman of his father,
mother, son, or daughter; and this class also includes a freed-

man with the status of an enemy surrendered at discretion [*Collatio Legum Mosaicarum et Romanarum*][17]

[Women] convicted of adultery shall be punished with the loss of half their dowry and the third of their estates, and by relegation to an island. The adulterer ... shall be deprived of half his property, and shall also be punished by relegation to an island; provided the parties are exiled to different islands. [*Opinions of Julius Paulus*][18]

The Lex Julia declares that wives have no right to bring criminal accusations for adultery against their husbands, even though they may desire to complain of the violation of the marriage vow, for while the law grants this privilege to men it does not concede it to women [A.D. 198].

Those are guilty of the crime of pimping who allow their wives taken in adultery to remain in marriage, and not those who merely suspect their wives of committing adultery [A.D. 200]. [*Code of Justinian*][19]

The following law (A.D. *326*) *put an end to the activities of outside informers who must often have extorted blackmail.*

Although adultery is considered a public crime, the right of accusation for which is granted to all persons in common, without any special interpretation of the law, still, lest the right of accusation be rashly entrusted to persons who wish to dishonor marriages, it is Our pleasure that the right of accusation shall be granted only to the nearest and closest of kin, that is, a father or cousins, and especially to consanguineous brothers who are driven by real indignation to accusation. But even upon these persons We impose the law that they shall have the right to suppress the accusation by annulment of the suit. The husband above all ought to be the avenger of the marriage bed, since to him the former Emperors of olden time granted the right to accuse the wife even on suspicion and not to be bound by the bond of inscription within the statutory time limits. [*Theodosian Code*][20]

At present, however, a woman convicted of adultery is placed in a monastery, from which her husband is permitted to remove her within the term of two years. After the two years have expired, without her husband having taken her back, or before that, if he should have died, the adulteress, having had her head shaved, and assumed a religious habit, shall remain there during her lifetime, and her property, if she had any, shall be divided into three parts, two of which shall be given to her children and the third to the monastery.... [*Code of Justinian*][21]

DIVORCE

In one of his letters Cicero reports, as a remarkable bit of gossip, the fact that a woman had just broken up her marriage without any pretext. In the next few centuries, marriages dissolved for trivial reasons ceased to astonish anyone. Augustus brought divorce under state jurisdiction and formalized the procedure but did not limit its availability. The Christian Emperors restricted the grounds for unilateral repudiation, probably in an attempt to protect the woman as the weaker partner. They vacillated in their rulings on divorce by mutual consent, which was first allowed and then condemned by Justinian, only to be revived by Justin II, his successor.

It is our pleasure that no woman, on account of her own depraved desires, shall be permitted to send a notice of divorce to her husband on trumped-up grounds; as, for instance, that he is a drunkard or a gambler or a philanderer, nor indeed shall a husband be allowed to divorce his wife on every sort of pretext. But when a woman sends a notice of divorce, the following criminal charges only shall be investigated, that is, if she should prove that her husband is a homicide, a sorcerer, or a destroyer of tombs, so that the wife may thus earn commendation and at length recover her entire dowry. For if she should send a notice of divorce to her husband on grounds other than these three criminal charges, she must leave everything, even to her last hairpin, in her husband's home, and as punishment for her supreme self-confidence, she shall be deported to an island. In the case of a man also, if he should send a notice of divorce, inquiry shall be made as to the following three criminal charges, namely, if he wishes to divorce her as an adulteress, a sorceress, or a procuress. For if he should cast off a wife who is innocent of these crimes, he must restore her entire dowry, and he shall not marry another woman. But if he should do this, his former wife shall be given the right to enter and seize his home by force and to transfer to herself the entire dowry of his later wife in recompense for the outrage inflicted upon her [A.D. 331]. [*The Theodosian Code*]²²

[The Emperors Theodosius and Valentinian:] We decree that legal marriage may be contracted by consent, but this having once been done, that it cannot be dissolved unless by notice of repudiation, for the favor to which children are entitled demands that its dissolution should be rendered more difficult.

We clearly enumerate the causes of repudiation by this most salutary law . . . for We desire that he or she shall be liberated by Our aid, when this becomes necessary.

Therefore, if a woman should ascertain that her husband is an adulterer, a homicide, a poisoner, or one who is plotting anything against Our government; or has been convicted of perjury or forgery; or is a violator of sepulchers, or has stolen anything from sacred buildings; or is a robber or a harborer of robbers, a cattle thief or a kidnapper; or, in contempt of his house and of her, or in her presence, has consorted with dissolute women (which is especially exasperating to females who are chaste); or if he has attempted to deprive her of life by poison, or by the sword, or in any other way; or if she should prove that he had beaten her (which is not allowed in the case of freeborn women), We then grant her permission to avail herself of the necessary aid of repudiation, and to present legal reasons for divorce. . . .

The husband also is controlled by similar restrictions, for he shall not be permitted to repudiate his own wife, except for reasons which have been clearly designated . . . [A.D. 449].

[The Emperor Anastosius:] Where a marriage has been dissolved by common consent, rather than by the repudiation of the wife, and not on account of any cause included in the most wise Constitution of the Emperors Theodosius and Valentinian of Divine Memory, the woman shall not be required to wait for the expiration of the term of five years, but can contract a second marriage after the lapse of one year [A.D. 497] . . . .

[Extract from Novel 117, Chapter 10] At the present time, a

divorce of this kind [by common consent] cannot take place except where the husband and wife desire to live in chastity, and under such circumstances the dowry, as well as the ante-nuptial donation, shall be preserved for the benefit of the children. If, however, the parties subsequently contract another marriage, or are found to be living in debauchery, their property shall be delivered to their children, and they shall lose control of the same. In case there are no children, it shall be forfeited to the Treasury. Those who are guilty of such offenses shall be subjected to the penalties prescribed by law. . . .

We add the following to the causes specifically enumerated by reason of which repudiation can legally take place; namely, when a husband on account of natural impotence is unable to have coition with his wife for two consecutive years, from the beginning of the marriage, the wife, or her parents, can serve notice of repudiation upon him, without risk of losing the dowry; provided, however, that the ante-nuptial donation is preserved for the benefit of the husband [A.D. 528]. . . .

We add to the causes of divorce of husbands and wives already enumerated by the laws, the following, namely, if the wife should by her own efforts produce an abortion... [A.D. 528]. [Code][23]

If a man should beat his wife with a whip or a rod, without having been induced to do so for one of the reasons which We have stated to be sufficient [i.e., where the woman is blame-worthy enough to justify divorce] ... We do not wish [the marriage] to be dissolved on this account; but the husband who has been convicted of having, without such a reason, struck his wife with a whip or a rod shall give her by way of compensation for an injury of this kind (even during the existence of the marriage) a sum equal in value to the amount of the ante-nuptial donation to be taken out of his other property. [Novels] [24]

WIDOWS

Though a widower might remarry right after his wife's death, a widow was expected to wait at least ten months. This rule may have had a religious origin. But obviously it also served the purpose of ensuring that the woman was not pregnant by the deceased at the time of her remarriage.

Emperors Gratian, Valentinian and Theodosius Augustus to
Entropius, Praetorian Prefect.

If any woman who has lost her husband should hasten to
marry another man within the period of a year (for We add a
small amount of time to be observed after the ten-month period,
although We consider that to be very little), she shall be
branded with the marks of disgrace and deprived of both the
dignity and rights of a person of honorable and noble status.
She shall also forfeit all the property which she had obtained
from the estate of her former husband, either by the right of
betrothal gifts or by the will of her deceased husband. She
shall know also that she shall expect no help from Us through
either a special grant of imperial favor or an annotation
[A.D. 381]. [*Theodosian Code*]²⁵

WANTONS AND MATRONS

*We learn what we know of individual Roman women from the writings of
Roman men, and they, whose taste ran to the monumental, present us with
a gallery of extremes: virtuous civic-minded matrons or wanton jades,
both, preferably, of the upper classes. Clodia—born in 94 B.C.—was
one of the wanton. A consul's wife, she had a love affair with Catullus
and was celebrated by him as Lesbia, mistress of ecstasy. After her
husband's death, she had another affair with M. Coelius Rufus, who was
twelve years younger than she and left her; whereupon she provoked a
court case in an effort to damage his character. Cicero defended him in a
speech which pivots on the double standard. How, he asks, can Clodia
instigate accusations against Coelius when it was improper for her to
know him intimately? If she did so know him, then she is no better than a
whore and need not be believed. If she did not, then the accusations are
groundless. The system was against Clodia, and of course she lost.*

If any woman, not being married, has opened her house to the
passions of everybody, and has openly established herself in the
way of life of a harlot, and has been accustomed to frequent the
banquets of men with whom she has no relationship; if she does
so in the city, in country houses, and in that most frequented
place, Baiae; if, in short, she behaves in such a manner, not only
by her gait, but by her style of dress, and by the people who are

seen attending her; and not only by the eager glances of her eyes
and the freedom of her conversation, but also by embracing
men, by kissing them, at water parties and sailing parties and
banquets, so as not only to seem a harlot, but a very wanton and
lascivious harlot; I ask you, O Lucius Herennius, if a young
man should happen to have been with her, is he to be called an
adulterer, or a lover? Does he seem to have been attacking
chastity, or merely to have aimed at satisfying his desires? I forget, for the present, all the injuries which you have done me,
O Clodia; I banish all recollection of my own distress; I put out
of consideration your cruel conduct to my relations when I was
absent. You are at liberty to suppose that what I have just said
was not said about you. But I ask you yourself, since the accusers
say that they derived the idea of this charge from you, and that
they have you yourself as witness of its truth; I ask you, I say, if
there be any woman of the sort that I have just described, a
woman unlike you, a woman of the habits and profession of a
harlot, does it appear an act of extraordinary baseness, or extraordinary wickedness, for a young man to have had some connection with her? If you are not such a woman—and I would much
rather believe that you are not—then, what is it that they impute
to Coelius? If they try to make you out to be such a woman,
then why need we fear such an accusation for ourselves, if you
confess that it applies to you and that you despise it? Give us
then a path to and a plan for our defense. For either your modesty will supply us with the defense, that nothing has been done
by Marcus Coelius with any undue wantonness; or else your
impudence will give both to him and everyone else very great
facilities for defending themselves. ['For M. Coelius,' *The Orations of Marcus Tullius Cicero*][26]

*Despite their stringency, the Julian laws on adultery left loopholes. Since
extramarital sex was legal only for registered prostitutes, some upper class
women attempted to protect themselves and their lovers from the public
prosecutor by registering as prostitutes.*

An ancient Roman custom revived by Tiberius was the punishment of married woman guilty of improprieties, by the decision
of a family council; so long as a public prosecutor had not

intervened. When one Roman knight had sworn that he would never divorce his wife whatever she did, but found her in bed with his son, Tiberius absolved him from his oath. Married women of good family but bad reputation were beginning to ply openly as prostitutes, and to escape punishment for their adult- eries by renouncing the privileges of their class; and wastrels of both the Senatorial and Equestrian Orders purposely got them- selves reduced in rank so as to evade the law forbidding their appearance on the stage or in the arena. All such offenders were now exiled, which discouraged any similar sheltering behind the letter of the law. [Suetonius, *The Twelve Caesars*][27]

In the same year [A.D. 190] the senate passed stringent decrees against female immorality. The granddaughters, daughters, and wives of Roman gentlemen were debarred from prostitution. A woman of a family that had held the praetorship had advertis- ed her availability to the aediles in accordance with the custom of our ancestors who believed that an immoral woman would be sufficiently punished by this shameful declaration. Her husband was also requested to state why, when his wife was obviously guilty, he had refrained from enforcing the statutory penalty. He alleged, however, that the sixty days allowed him for con- sultation had not expired. It was therefore decided to take action against the woman only, and she was deported to the island of Seriphos. [Tacitus, *The Annals of Imperial Rome*][28]

The funeral inscription from which the following extracts come celebrates a virtuous matron. She was a type. The inscription dedicated by her husband between 8 and 2 B.C., is commonly called the 'laudatio Turiae' (in praise of Turia), although Turia was probably not the anonymous woman's name, and it consists of a long address giving the main facts of her life. She was not only virtuous but tough: when her parents were murdered, she saw to it that the murderers were punished; she defended her inheri- tance from scheming relatives and, later, when her husband was pro- scribed, helped him to escape and went down on her knees to Lepidus to beg for his life.

Few are the long marriages which end not in divorce but death. It was our lot to be harmoniously married for forty-one years. [Description of her virtues follows] ... But why recall your wifely qualities, your goodness, obedience, sweetness, kindness, your diligent spinning and weaving, your piety, the discretion of your clothes and jewelry? Why talk of your affection and devotion to your relatives when you were as thoughtful with my mother as with your own family? ... When I was on the run you used your jewels to provide resources for me. You stripped off your gold and pearls so that I could take them with me; and later, skillfully deceiving our enemies' guards, you kept me supplied during my absence with slaves, money, and provisions.... During the civil war, when a gang of men collected by Milo— I had bought a house of his while he was in exile — attempted to break into our house and pillage it, you successfully repulsed them and defended our home.... Yet I admit that at one point I owed to you the greatest bitterness of my life. When my civil rights had been restored by Caesar Augustus, who was out of Rome at the time, you went to Marcus Lepidus to ask him to honor this decision. You threw yourself on the ground at his feet and not only were you not raised up but you were dragged out like a slave. Your body was covered with bruises. With the greatest courage you told Lepidus of Caesar's edict, begging him to ensure my recall from exile. You were insulted and wounded, and you let your wounds be seen so that people might know who was the cause of my misfortunes. Not long afterward he got into trouble over this matter.... [Later still] you began to be afraid that you might be barren. In your distress at my having no children and not wanting to see me suffer over this or lose hope, you raised the idea of divorce and wanted to go away so as to leave the house to the fertility of another woman; this was your only reason.... I must admit I went wild: almost out of my mind. Your suggestion so horrified me that I could scarcely take hold of myself. The idea that we should divorce ... of your imagining you could cease being my wife, you who had been so utterly faithful to me when I was in exile and almost dead! How could wanting or needing children have mattered to me more than our marriage? But why say more? You stayed. I could not have given in to your proposal without bringing dishonor on myself and misery to us both. [Marcel Durry, ed., *Eloge funèbre d'une matrone romaine*][29]

Juvenal (c. A.D. 60–c. 140), one of the most acerb of Roman satirists, gives this picture of upper-class wives:

The bed that contains a wife is always hot with quarrels
And mutual bickering: sleep's the last thing you get there.
This is her battleground, her station for husband-baiting:
In bed she's worse than a tiger robbed of its young,
Bitching away to stifle her own bad conscience,
About his boy-friends, or weeping over some way-out
Fictitious mistress. She keeps a copious flow
Of tears at the ready, awaiting her command,
For any situation: and you, poor worm, are agog,
Thinking this means she loves you, and kiss her tears away—
But if you raided her desk drawers, the compromising letters,
The assignations you'd find that your green-eyed whorish
Wife has amassed! Suppose, though, you catch her in bed with
A slave or some businessman? 'Quick, quick, Quintilian,
Find me a pat excuse,' she prays. 'I'm stuck,' says the Maestro.
'You can get yourself out of this one.'

[Juvenal, *The Sixteen Satires*][30]

5 Property and Legal Rights

In early Rome a wife's dowry—her contribution to the conjugal fortunes—was absorbed irrecuperably into the husband's property. Under free marriage it was recoverable unless the husband could show grounds for keeping some of it back. As divorces became more frequent, the law began to hedge the dowry with safeguards: husbands might not, for instance, alienate dotal property and must keep up its value.

When a divorce takes place, if the woman is her own mistress, she herself has the right to sue for the recovery of the dowry. If, however, she is under the control of her father, he having joined with her ... can bring the action for the recovery of the dowry....

Portions of a dowry are retained on account of children [i.e., for their keep, since the husband always got custody of them], on account of bad morals, on account of donations or ... articles which have been abstracted.

A portion is retained on account of children, when the divorce took place either through the fault of the wife, or of her father; ... a sixth part of the dowry shall be retained in the name of each child, but not more than three-sixths altogether.

A sixth of the dowry is also retained on the ground of a flagrant breach of morals; an eighth where the offense is not so serious. Adultery alone comes under the head of a flagrant breach of morals, all other improper acts are classed as less serious. [Ulpian, *Rules*][31]

By the Lex Julia, a husband was forbidden to alienate dotal land against the consent of his wife, although the land may have become his own by sale to him as a dowry, or by surrender in court or by usucaption. [Gaius, *The Institutes*][32]

After the time of Augustus, the adulterous wife lost half her dowry.

It is to the interest of the state that women should have their dowries preserved in order that they can marry again.

The cause of the dowry always and everywhere takes precedence, for it is to the public interest for dowries to be preserved for wives, as it is absolutely necessary that women should be endowed for the procreation of progeny and to furnish the state with freeborn citizens. [*Digest*]³³

We order that where anyone has taken a wife with the consent of her parents or, if she had no parents, actuated by true marital affection, even if no dotal instrument were drawn up, nor any dowry given, the marriage ... shall be considered valid ... for marriages are not contracted by means of dowries but through mutual attachment.

When anyone desires to separate from a woman whom he married without a dowry, he shall not be permitted to do so, unless some fault is committed which is condemned by Our laws. If, however, he should reject her without her having been guilty of any fault, or he himself should commit such a fault ... he shall be compelled to give her the fourth part of his own property [A.D. 528]. ... [*Code*]³⁴

We decree by this law that the husband shall not interfere with any of the property which his wife has exclusive of her dowry, and which the Greeks designate as *parapherna*, if she forbids him to do so, nor can he impose any necessity upon her in this respect. For, although it is well that the wife, who entrusts herself to her husband, should also permit her property to be controlled by his judgment, still, as it is only proper that the legislators should comply with the rules of equity, We are not willing (as has already been stated) that the husband should in any way meddle with the property of the wife against her consent. [*Code*]³⁵

LEGACIES

Since a dowry tended to be invested in land, only its income might be enjoyed and would represent no more than a fraction of a rich woman's wealth. Girls had equal rights with brothers to the family patrimony. The Lex Voconia (169 B.C.) restricted women's rights to inherit, but only in the case of very large fortunes and only to the extent that they might not be appointed heirs (meaning heads of families) or receive more than the heir appointed. But a woman could still receive considerable legacies from both her father and her husband; and as girls married very young, the rich

*young widow was no rarity in Rome. Augustus' legislation, which remain-
ed in effect until the fourth century, penalized barren wives. Their
husbands, if aged between twenty-five and sixty, might not leave more
than one-tenth of their estate to wives who were young enough to bear
children but who had failed to do so and thus, apparently, welshed in their
duty toward the state.*

Husband and wife may under a will, take one-tenth of the estate
of either on account of marriage; but if either of them has surviving children by a previous marriage, he or she may, in addition
to the tenth on account of marriage, take as many more tenths
as there are children.

Any son or daughter born to both of them, who dies after the
day when he or she was named, adds another tenth; and two of
them dying after the day when they were named add two-tenths.

In addition to the tenth, either of the parties can take the
usufruct of the third portion of the estate of the other, and when
they have children, the ownership of the said portion as well;
and further, the woman, in addition to the tenth, can take her
dowry if it is left to her. . . .

Sometimes husband and wife can take the entire amount
which one leaves to the other. (There follows a complex of
provisos.) [*Rules of Ulpian*][36]

POLITICAL AND CIVIL RIGHTS

*Women had no political rights, even at the end of the empire. They could
not hold official positions, nor were they allowed to plead in court, despite
the example cited by Quintilian (p. 70). They could, however, give
evidence in court, and under the empire they might claim testamentary
competence.*

Since the Lex Julia de Adulteriis prohibits a woman who has
been convicted of adultery from testifying, it follows that even
women have the right to give evidence in court. (*Digest*)[37]

A woman cannot act as a witness to a will, although she can
be a witness in court, as is established by the Lex Julia de
Adulteriis. [*Digest*][38]

A decree of the Senate was enacted at the instance of the

Divine Hadrian, by which women were permitted to make a will even without the ceremony of coemption; provided, however, they were not under twelve years of age; and if they were not released from guardianship, they were required to execute the wills with the consent of their guardians.

Females therefore appear to be in a better position than males; a male under the age of fourteen cannot make a will, even with the authority of his guardian; but a female obtains the right of testamentary disposition with the consent of her guardian after she has reached her twelfth year. [Gaius, *Institutes*][39]

If mothers who have lost their husbands should demand tutelage over their children to administer their affairs, before confirmation of such an office can legally come to them, they shall state in the public records that they will not proceed to another marriage. Certainly, no woman is forced to make such a choice, but she shall comply of her own free will with the conditions which We have prescribed. For if she prefers to choose another marriage, she must not administer the guardianship of her children.

In order that such a woman may not easily be taken by storm after she has lawfully undertaken the guardianship, We order that, first of all, the property of any man who eagerly seeks the marriage of a woman who is administering a guardianship shall be obligated and held liable for the accounts of the children, so that nothing may be lost to them through negligence or through fraud [A.D. 390]. [*Theodosian Code*][40]

6 Women and Social Class

It is more honorable for a freedwoman to be the concubine of a patron than to become the mother of a family: Ulpian (A.D. 170–228).

When considering women, Roman law distinguished between those worth protecting and those not. The first were of citizen stock and good morals: actual or potential mothers of families who were expected to live unblemished lives, could marry men of the senatorial class, and might not live as concubines. These were the 'matrons.' They and they only had the right to wear the stola (a long tunic with arm slits at the sides) and not the toga which was worn by prostitutes, actresses, disreputable women, and wives repudiated on grounds of adultery. A man who took a matrona for his mistress could be prosecuted for stuprum *(vice) under the Lex Julia, and we have already seen what happened to women who tried to get around this by registering as prostitutes. After Augustus exslaves were permitted to marry any man who was not descended from a senator. Concubinage had no legal effect except in the case of a slave freed by her patron: such a freedwoman did not enjoy a wife's rights, but the law imposed both a wife's duties and the penalties for neglecting them. Slaves could not marry legally but were allowed a de facto union called* contubernium. *The lines between matronae and nonmatronae fluctuated over the centuries and are not easily definable in retrospect, although they were probably clear to Romans: for example, after about the second century* A.D., *matronae did not necessarily lose their status because of leading 'immoral' lives.*

But so that women's honor might find a safeguard in men's respect, it was forbidden anyone suing the mother of a family to lay hands on her; her dress (stola) must not be profaned by the touch of another's hand.... In those days (early Rome) conjugal faith need fear no seducer's glance. One looked on others and was oneself looked on with a religious respect. Reciprocal modesty protected the sexes. [Valerius Maximus, *Facta et Dicta Memorabilia*][41]

By the Lex Julia senators, as well as their children, are forbidden to marry their freedwomen or any woman when either they themselves or their fathers or mothers were professional actors.

The same persons, and others who are freeborn, are forbidden to marry women who were public prostitutes, or procuresses, or any woman manumitted by a procurer or a procuress; or one [who] had been taken in adultery or convicted of a crime or who had belonged to the theatrical profession. [*Rules of Ulpian*]⁴²

It has been decided that adultery cannot be committed [i.e., there is no such thing as adultery] with women who have charge of any business or shop.

Fornication committed with female slaves, unless they are deteriorated in value or an attempt is made against their mistress through them, is not considered an injury. [*Opinions of Julius Paulus*]⁴³

If a woman whom you have carnally known indiscriminately sold herself for money, and prostituted herself everywhere as a harlot, you did not commit the crime of adultery with her [A.D. 290].

Slaves cannot accuse their wives of adultery for violation of conjugal faith.

Although it is established by the contents of certain documents that you are consumed with the lust of immoderate desire, still, as it has been ascertained that you confined yourself to female slaves, and did not have intercourse with free women, it is clear that by a sentence of this kind your reputation suffers rather than that you become infamous [A.D. 291]. [*Code*]⁴⁴

If any woman should commit adultery, it must be inquired whether she was the mistress of a tavern or a servant girl and thus in the performance of her servile duty she herself frequently served the wines of intemperance. If she should be mistress of the tavern, she shall not be exempt from the bonds of the law. But if she should give service to those who drink, in consideration of the mean status of the woman who is brought to trial, the accusation shall be excluded and the men who are accused shall go free, since chastity is required only of those women who are held by the bonds of the law, but those who, because of their mean status in life, are not deemed worthy of the consideration of the laws shall be immune from judicial severity [A.D. 326].

Interpretation: If the mistress of a tavern, that is, the wife of a tavernkeeper, should be found in adultery, she can be accused; but if her maidservant or a woman who gives service in the tavern should be apprehended in adultery, she should be acquitted in consideration of her mean status. But even the wife of the tavernkeeper, if she should perform the duty of such menial service and should be apprehended in adultery, cannot be accused by her husband. [*Theodosian Code*]⁴⁵

[The jurist Ulpian, on the Lex Julia et Papia:] Where a freedwoman is living in concubinage with her patron, she can leave him without his consent, and unite with another man, either in matrimony or in concubinage. I think, however, (despite the letter of this law) that a concubine should not have the right to marry if she leaves her patron without his consent, since it is more honorable for a freedwoman to be the concubine of a patron than to become the mother of a family. . . .

I hold . . . that only those women who are not disgraced by such a connection [i.e., women of low status] can be kept in concubinage without the fear of committing a crime. [*Digest*]⁴⁶

Where a man lives with a free woman, it is not considered concubinage but genuine matrimony, if she does not acquire gain by means of her body. [*Digest*]⁴⁷

Since it was 'intention' or 'marital feeling' which distinguished concubinage from marriage, and this was a difficult condition to prove, the woman's rank—here the fact that she was freeborn—might be the determining circumstance.

We have held that if anyone should live in concubinage with a reputable woman, and have children by her without the exception of any dotal instrument, and should afterward desire to marry her, and a contract should be drawn up to this effect, and he should beget other children, then not only those born after this contract was executed, but also those born previously, will be legitimate. . . .

Another doubt has been raised as to whether this rule is applicable to men living in concubinage with their freedwomen; but Our intention is clear in this respect, and this has already been decided by Us, for marriage with a freedwoman is by no means prohibited, and what We have decided with reference to other persons is also applicable to them.

In order to dispose of all ambiguity on this point, We decree that if anyone who has no legitimate wife or children should entertain affection for his female slave, and have children by her, while she is in servitude, and should afterward manumit her and her children, and confer upon all of them the rank of freeborn persons, and honor them with freedom in accordance with the prescribed formalities, and then should marry the woman, and, after the ceremony, should draw up a nuptial contract; whether any children are born afterward or not ... she shall be his legal wife, and his children shall be under his control, and his proper heirs, as well as his heirs at law, in case of necessity (We refer to those born before the marriage), and by this means all of them will be placed in the rank of freeborn persons, and by the subsequent marriage they will enjoy the privilege of legitimacy [A.D. 536]. [*Novels*][48]

The same license was not granted to free women living with slaves.

Next Claudius proposed to the senate that women marrying slaves should be penalized. It was decided that the penalty for such a lapse should be enslavement, if the man's master did not know, and the status of an ex-slave if he did [A.D. 521]. [Tacitus, *Annals of Imperial Rome*][49]

If any woman is discovered to have a clandestine love affair with her slave, she shall be subject to the capital sentence, and the rascally slave shall be delivered to the flames. All persons shall have the right to bring an accusation of this public crime.... [A.D. 326]. [*Theodosian Code*][50]

The following texts reveal some discomfort in the Christian Emperors with regard to prostitution—and not a little doubt as to what belongs to Caesar, what to God.

If any man should wish to subject to wantonness the women who are known to have dedicated themselves to the veneration of the holy Christian law and if he should provide that such women should be sold to brothels and compelled to perform the vile service of prostituted virtue, no other person shall have the right to buy such women except either those who are known to be ecclesiastics or those who are shown to be Christian men, upon the payment of the proper price [A.D. 343]. [*Theodosian Code*][51]

We have ascertained that, at the present time, a cruel and intolerable fraud has been committed against chastity, which is something greatly revered by Us ... those who profit by the vile profession of prostitutes compel them to swear that they will never abandon their base and wicked life; and these wretched women, influenced in this way, think that they are acting honorably if they remain, and they keep their oaths to the destruction of their chastity, when they should be aware that such transgressions are more agreeable to God than the observance of such oaths. Therefore, even though a woman may have taken such an oath, she shall be permitted to violate it, and to live chastely without danger of prosecution for perjury. . . .

Wherefore We impose the penalty of ten pounds of gold upon anyone who presumes to exact and receive an oath of this kind, as soon as it is tendered. We order that this sum shall be collected by the Governor of the province, and given to the unfortunate woman to assist her in leading a virtuous life. [*Novels*][52]

Funeral inscriptions erected by slaves to their parents or children use the same formulas as those of citizens, and it is thought that their family ties were usually respected, even if they could not legally marry. Not seldom even poor households had a few slaves to do the servile work, and in large households they were trained to do skilled work as well. Inscriptions list slave laundresses, librarians, readers, governesses, midwives, female doctors, dressmakers, hairdressers, and the like. Slave women with such skills might work exclusively for a mistress or partly for the public. If freed, they might go into business for themselves or with a husband, perhaps another ex-slave to whom, once both had obtained their freedom, they could be formally married. Epitaphs reveal cases of freed couples who were in business together. And that is as close a picture as we can get of them unless we turn to literature. Petronius' picture of a freedman who freed his wife and made a fortune, though patronizing, has a likely ring to it:

I walk like a free man. I don't owe any man a thing. I've never been hauled into court. That's right: no man ever had to tell me to pay up. I've bought a few little plots of land and a nice bit of silver plate. I feed twenty stomachs, not counting the dog. I bought my wife's freedom so no man could put his dirty paws on her. I paid a good two hundred for my own freedom.... Forty years, boy and man, I spent as a slave, but no one could tell now whether I was slave or free.... [Petronius, *The Satyricon*][53]

7 Education and Religion

The orator and lawyer, Quintilian (c. A.D. 35–c. 95) approached having an ideal of education for women:

In parents I should wish that there should be as much learning as possible. Nor do I speak, indeed, merely of fathers; for we have heard that Cornelia, the mother of the Gracchi (whose very learned writing in her letters has come down to posterity), contributed greatly to their eloquence; the daughter of Laelius is said to have exhibited her father's elegance in conversation; and the oration of the daughter of Quintus Hortensius, delivered before the Triumviri [pleading for a partial remission of the tax laid on matrons], is read not merely as an honor to her sex. [Quintilian, *Institutes of Oratory*] [54]

Now and then the outstanding woman left her mark, in this case on the historian Sallust (86–35 B.C.):

Well educated in Greek and Latin literature, [Sempronia] had greater skill in lyre-playing and dancing than there is any need for a respectable woman to acquire.... She could write poetry, crack a joke, and converse at will with decorum, tender feeling, or wantonness; she was in fact a woman of ready wit and considerable charm. [Sallust, *The Conspiracy of Catiline*] [55]

Roman unlike Greek women were educated: the poorer ones went to school, the richer stayed at home and had tutors. The advice given by Ovid (43 B.C.–A.D. 18) to women of light morals and to courtesans presupposes a readiness to take an interest in literature. Judging by inscriptions, even women slaves sometimes got an education. But nothing approaching a syllabus is available, unless it be Ovid's:

Read some poets, too, Callimachus, and the Coan,
    All that Anacreon wrote, rollicking drinking-songs.
Study Sappho—what girl could set more alluring example?—
    Read Menander, whose plots tell of the wiles of the slave.
You should be able, I hope, to learn some lines of Propertius,
    Poet of our own time, Gallus, Tibullus as well.

Quote from 'The Golden Fleece,' that masterpiece written by
Varro,
Don't forget Arms and the Man; Virgil's our greatest and
best.
Possibly works of my own may not be considered unworthy. . . .
[Ovid, *The Art of Love*] [56]

Women played an essential part in the celebration of Roman religion. The wife shared responsibility with her husband for supervising the household cult. Apart from the Vestal Virgins, whose function was official and important, the wives of two of the major priests were themselves priestesses. Women had cults and ceremonies from which men were excluded (and vice versa), and some of the speculations to which these secret rites gave rise provided fine fodder for satirists like Juvenal. The Christian practice of keeping women away from the altar was to be a departure from Roman custom.

III   Byzantium

From A.D. 395, the eastern half of the Roman empire had been ruled from Constantinople (Byzantium). When the western half fell (A.D. 476), the Byzantine emperors proclaimed themselves sole heirs to Rome's territories and traditions. Justinian failed to make good the tangible part of this claim when he was unsuccessful in his bid to reconquer the West; but he and his successors gave some reality to their wish to be the spiritual heirs of Rome by retaining and revivifying the body of the Roman law. With time, Byzantine society gave up the use of Latin and grew increasingly isolated from the West.

We begin with a keynote:

For the virgin, her chamber is the only fitting place.... For the virgin ought not to appear publicly at all at a marriage.... If thou wishest to have men in love with thee, this is the part of saleswomen, greengrocers, and handicrafts people.... If then, saith one, neither virgins dance nor the married, who is to dance? No one, for what need is there of dancing.... Art thou desirous of seeing choirs of dancers? Behold the choirs of Angels. [St John Chrysostom, *Homilies on Colossians*] [1]

Dost thou wish to adorn thy face? Do so not with pearls but with modesty and dignity.... These are the tints of virtue. By means of these thou wilt attract angels, not human beings, to be thy lovers. [Chrysostom, *Instructions to Catechumens*] [2]

In Byzantine society, three component elements interact: Eastern custom, Christianity, and Greco-Roman law. The first two favored the veiling and semicloistering of women, a narrowing of their social role, and withdrawal of some of the privileges they had enjoyed in imperial Rome. Christianity was responsible for the law's efforts to strengthen the marriage bond and family stability. Fluctuations aside, post-Justinian legislation tended to treat women as minors who needed controlling and protecting. On the question of divorce, it imposed a double standard countenanced neither by later Roman practice nor by Christian theory.

Of the lawbooks quoted, the first group consists of the Ecloga *or 'first Christian lawbook', the* Ecloga Privata Aucta, *and the* Ecloga ad Procheiron Mutata. *The* Ecloga *was issued by imperial edict in A.D. 726; redacted, like its successors, in Greek, it was based on Justinian's legis-*

lation and intended for use by subjects of the emperor who knew no Latin. The other two books in this group are based on it. The Procheiros Nomos *was issued some time between 867 and 879. Last in time is the legislation of Leo the Wise (886-912). Leo still allowed divorce but gave the church all the power it needed to refuse to remarry divorcees by making the nuptial blessing indispensable for a valid marriage. The tightening up of legislation on marriage from the* Ecloga, *which holds that cohabitation constitutes marriage, to the* Procheiros Nomos, *which demands that concubines be either sent away or 'married according to the proper solemnities', to Leo's final insistence on the nuptial blessing provides examples of the seepage of Christian principle into the Roman legal structure. But we do not know how consistently the law was applied. Our image of Byzantine society is shifting and shadowy, and the few female figures who stand vividly out are saints, empresses, and one or two mothers celebrated in the funeral orations of their sons. The saints and mothers owed their prestige to Christianity. The importance of the empresses is more surprising in that it is out of keeping with the misogynist attitudes that emerge from Byzantine texts and contrasts with the strict background role assigned to the consorts of Roman emperors. Byzantine empresses were associated with their husband's power, and a few actually reigned in their own right. Some—before the tenth century—were of humble, even of disreputable origin; some led untrammeled lives. Others, at least in the accounts of hagiographers, were virtue incarnate. They all, like the actresses and whores at the other end of the social scale, escaped the smothering grid of law and convention which must have pressed most heavily on women of middle rank.*

RIGHTS AND DUTIES

I have never understood how the ancients came to accept women as witnesses or how they could have failed to consider the obvious fact that it is disgraceful for women to expose themselves to the gaze of men and that decency and propriety for a woman consist in avoiding such encounters. How could they permit women to be summoned as witnesses when this often results in their mingling with large crowds of men and using their tongues in an irreverent way totally improper for their sex? This question, as I have said, has always perplexed me. For why should legislators have allowed women's evidence to be valid in business matters and permitted them to testify on the same footing with men, just as the Scythians, we are told, permitted women to bear arms like their husbands? Is there not a paradox here, as well as a confusion and subversion of the natural barriers between the sexes? Do they not thereby betray the natural modesty and decency which are characteristic of women? For women should be approached only in private and then with difficulty, not freely and without restraint. Certainly, to allow them as witnesses opens the way to deplorable license. By bringing them into crowded places, by permitting them to take part in men's affairs, one destroys that submissiveness and modesty which is natural to them and ends up by encouraging brazenness. Moreover, to do this is also, in a certain sense, to wrong men; for what else is it but a wrong, a grievous wrong, to cause the female sex to meddle in matters which pertain uniquely to men?

For these reasons, We uphold the custom which, rectifying the errors of the law, denies women the right to give evidence. We hereby give this custom legal force and forbid women's evidence to be taken in matters connected with contracts. But in purely feminine affairs, where men are not permitted to be present—I refer to childbirth and other things which only the female eye may see—women may testify. [*The Novels of Leo*][3]

The following is from a lawbook based on the Ecloga (726) *but dating from twelfth-century Sicily, where it was used by the Greek community there.*

No magistrate shall cast a woman into a public prison as a result either of a criminal prosecution or of a judgment in a civil action. If a woman is sued according to law in regard to public or private debts, she shall defend the suit either in person or by her husband, or by any other person whom she may select. And if the offense is of the basest kind, she shall be put into a nunnery or seminary for women, to be kept in custody until she makes full disclosure of her crime. [*A Manual of Later Roman Law: The Ecloga ad Procheiron Mutata*][4]

The following law from the Ecloga *illustrates the way in which Christian concern for family stability could work in a woman's favor.*

If the husband predecease the wife and there are children of the marriage, the wife being their mother, she shall control her marriage portion and all her husband's property as becomes the head of the family and household, and she shall carefully make a public record in the form of an inventory of all the goods and possessions of the husband, including property not included in her marriage portion, if any remain, and she shall be responsible to show by satisfactory proof how the same came into her husband's household and what it appeared to consist of at his death. And the children shall not take her place or claim from her the patrimony, but treat her with all obedience and honor according to God's command and, as it were embracing her, she on her part as befits a parent being bound to educate and provide for their marriage and dower portion as she may determine. But if it happens that she marries again, her children shall be entitled to obtain completely and entirely all their patrimony and all the marriage portion which she brought in to their father, and she shall only retain the sum which the father may have given her in augmentation of her marriage portion. [*A Manual of Roman Law: The Ecloga*][5]

MARRIAGE

If anyone takes a free woman into his house and entrusts her with the management of his household and cohabits with her, that shall be a verbal contract of marriage with her. And if upon the pretext that she is childless he attempts to banish her from his house without lawful reason she shall naturally keep her own property and receive a fourth part of her husband's estate. [*Ecloga*][6]

Marriage is constituted not upon cohabitation but upon the mutual consent of husband and wife.

We find that men of old permitted consorting in concubinage to those who so desired. It does not seem right that we should ignore this law, lest our State should be degraded by such unseemly unions. Wherefore we decree that henceforward no one shall be permitted to keep a concubine in his house, since we consider that such a proceeding differs in no way from adultery.

If a man wishes to live in common life with a woman let him marry her according to the accustomed solemnities prescribed by law. If he considers that she is unworthy to rank as a legitimate wife, let him abandon continual concubinage and expel her from his house and choose someone whom he considers to be worthy. If, however, he prefers to live continently, we approve. [*A Manual of Eastern Roman Law: The Procheiros Nomos*][7]

The Procheiros Nomos *was issued by Emperor Basil I some time between 867 and 879. The tendency, illustrated by the above texts, to bring marriage under the increasingly firm control of church and state, was carried further by Leo the Wise.*

. . . We order that marriages shall be confirmed by a nuptial blessing, so that if the future spouses fail to legitimize their union in this way from the beginning, their marriage shall not be valid and shall not produce the effects of matrimony. For there is no intermediary situation between marriage and celibacy which is not open to reproach. Do you aspire to the married state? Then observe the laws of matrimony. Do the worries of matrimony displease you? Then remain celibate and you will neither pervert the rules of marriage nor mendaciously imitate celibacy. [*The Novels of Leo*][8]

Members of the Senate shall not marry low-class women, such as a slave and her daughter, or a freedwoman and her daughter, or a seamstress, or a shopwoman, or their daughters, or the daughter of a brothel keeper or a circus keeper.

. . . And, moreover, girls whose lot it is to be in [domestic] service shall not be taken from their rank and made lawful wives by those who are of superior station and rank; and anyone, who from the present time contracts such a union, makes an unlawful marriage, and the issue born of such a marriage shall be treated as illegitimate. [*Ecloga ad Procheiron Mutata*][9]

DOWRIES AND NUPTIAL GIFTS

The wife contributed her dowry, the husband a pre- (or propter-) nuptial gift to the marriage fund. The nuptial gift was an Eastern importation.

It already figures in Justinian's Code *and* Novels, *where its equality with the dowry is prescribed. This is revoked in the* Ecloga.

A written marriage contract shall be based upon a written agreement providing the wife's marriage portion; and it shall be made before three credible witnesses ... the man on his part agreeing continually to protect and preserve undiminished the wife's marriage portion, and also such additions as he may naturally make thereto.... And a prenuptial gift of equal amount to the wife's marriage portion shall not be demanded of or debited to the man. [*Ecloga*][10]

Dowry and prenuptial gift were preserved intact and reverted to the wife if she was left a widow. An undowered widow could claim one-fourth of her husband's estate.

If the wife provides dower for her husband and the latter either suffers loss or falls into debt either to the State or to a private person and then dies, neither the State nor such person can come into the house and seize anything until the wife's dower has been paid to her.... [*Ecloga*][11]

Property which forms part of a prenuptial gift or dower cannot be alienated or pledged even with a wife's consent, unless after a space of two years the wife agrees to the transaction, and provided she can be indemnified by property of equal value from other sources. Any person who acquires property contrary to this ordinance shall not prejudice the wife but shall be liable to her for it.

If a husband pledges a wife's property without her consent the pledge is void; and moreover the law declares the pledge void even if she consented....

When a marriage has taken place the wife can claim to take the dower for the following reasons: to enable her to maintain her husband or their children; to buy an advantageous estate; to support her father if he is in exile; and her brothers if they are in penury. [*Procheiros Nomos*][12]

The nuptial gift could be punitively withdrawn:

... if there happens to be issue the wife who does not observe twelve month's widowhood shall be guilty of infamy; and she shall forfeit all her right and benefit in the property accruing to her from her first marriage; and also she shall forfeit her propternuptial gifts. And she can bestow no more than a third of her property on her second husband. And she shall not benefit by ... a legacy.... And she shall not be entitled to any inheritance from her relatives.... But if she has children she may by petition to the Sovran obtain a remission of the penalty of infamy; but she shall have none of the aforementioned benefits without the Sovran's permission; and to be freed from other penalties she shall give unconditionally a half of her property as it existed upon her second marriage to the children of her first marriage.... [Procheiros Nomos][13]

ADULTERY

A man who commits adultery with a woman under coverture shall have his nose slit. And also the adulteress; since thenceforward she becomes a whore and is parted from her husband and lost to her children, disregarding the word of the Lord who teaches us that He has made one flesh of man and wife.... And after their noses have been slit the adulteress shall take the things which she brought in to her husband and nothing more. But the adulterer shall not be separated from his own wife though his nose be slit....

Anyone who seduces a woman shall have his nose slit, and he shall not be divorced from his own wife. The adulteress shall have her nose slit and she shall take her own property from her husband....

The husband who is cognizant of, and condones, his wife's adultery shall be flogged and exiled. [A Revised Manual of Roman Law: Ecloga Privata Aucta][14]

Of all other sacrilegious acts, the crime of adultery deserves, to my mind, a punishment not inferior to that for murder.... However, since a lighter sentence was substituted for the old one of death, and since We are ourselves drawn to the more humane solution, We confirm the sentence prescribed by later legislators, that is, that both guilty parties should have their noses slit. So let that remain the punishment for this crime.

But, since the husband should not remain without any compensation, he may retain the dowry as a consolation.... Moreover, the wife must on no account be allowed to make a mock of marriage and receive, together with the slitting of her nose, as though as a reward, the right to mingle thereafter freely with profligates; instead, let her be shut up in a convent on account of her misdeed, and this punishment will be lightened for her by repentance....[*The Novels of Leo*][15]

The Wisdom of God the Maker and Creator of all mankind teaches that the marriage tie binding those who live together in [the fear of] the Lord cannot be dissolved .... And we who follow in His footsteps and obey will not ordain anything else or more than that. But we have determined to include in the present legislation the grounds upon which those bound in marriage can be parted, since many persons habitually live in a way so vicious that they cannot cohabit happily and divorce themselves on many pretexts. [*A Manual of Roman Law: The Ecloga*][16]

The above text, after piously invoking a perfection unlikely to be attained by many, allows the following grounds for divorce: adultery (by the wife), impotence (in the man), plotting to kill one's marriage partner, leprosy, and insanity. Later lawbooks add further grounds. Clearly in Byzantium human frailty was fighting a rear-guard battle against the growing power of the church. The Procheiros Nomos *allows a man to divorce a wife who had conspired against the emperor or himself or, of course, committed adultery. It adds:*

[Divorce may be granted] if contrary to her husband's wish she consorts with strange men, drinking or bathing with them.

If contrary to her husband's wish she stops away from home, unless it be with her parents.

If without her husband's knowledge or against his wish she frequents the hippodrome, theaters, or low resorts.

Should it happen that any husband expels his wife for reasons other than those aforementioned, and, having no parents to go to, she is forced to spend the night out, we command that the husband was not justified in expelling his wife since he was responsible for the occurrence.

Also: if the wife is guilty of deception, or abets murder, or kidnapping, or grave-robbing, or sacrilege, or is an accessory to thieves or theft, or dares to lay hands on her husband, or purposely contrives to procure abortion and so distresses and disappoints her husband by frustrating his hope of offspring.

She could divorce him if he conspired against the sovereign, herself, or her chastity (by abetting adultery).

If a man charges his wife in writing with adultery and fails to convict her, she has, upon that ground, the option of divorcing him, and taking her own dower, and recovering the prenuptial gift; and in consequence of the slander, if she has no children of the marriage, also a sum equal to one-fourth of such gift, from her husband's estate. If there are children then all the husband's estate shall be kept for them, and the prenuptial gift disposed of according to preceding law. So that if the husband fails to convict his wife he shall suffer the same penalties as his wife, if convicted, would have suffered.

If the husband, whether it be in his own home where his wife is, or in any other house in the city, continually consorts with another woman, and being once or twice admonished by his own or his wife's parents or other responsible witnesses, not to persist in such debauchery; in that case the wife can dissolve the marriage and take her dower and prenuptial gift and also, as a penalty for the offense, from her husband's property a share equal to one-third of the antenuptial gift. . . . And also if the wife proves that her husband . . . beats her violently. [*The Procheiros Nomos*][17]

A PLACE FOR PROSTITUTES

Christianity brought in spasmodic attempts to rehabilitate fallen women (attempts unheard of in the ancient world), with what success we can only wonder.

Theodora [508–548] made it her business also to devise punishments for the sins of the flesh. Prostitutes—more than five hundred in all—were rounded up; women who in the middle of the forum sold their services for a shilling a time, just enough to keep body and soul together. They were then dispatched to the mainland opposite and confined in the convent known as Repentance in an attempt to force them into a better way of life. However, some of them from time to time threw themselves down from the parapet during the night, and so escaped being transmogrified against their will. [Procopius, *The Secret History*][18]

Scattered all over the city was a vast multitude of harlots, and without attempting to turn them away from their trade by argument—that class of woman is deaf anyway to all advice that would save them—without even trying to curb their activities by force, lest he earn the reputation of violence, he [Emperor Michael IV, 1034–1041] built in the Queen of Cities a place of refuge to house them, an edifice of enormous size and very great beauty. Then, in the stentorian notes of the public herald, he issued a proclamation: all women who trafficked in their beauty, provided they were willing to renounce their trade ... were to find sanctuary in this building: they were to change their own clothes for the habits of nuns, and all fear of poverty would be banished from their lives forever.... Thereupon a great swarm of prostitutes descended upon this refuge, relying on the emperor's edict, and changed both their garments and their manner of life. [Michael Psellus, *Fourteen Byzantine Rulers*][19]

IV   The Early Hebrews

The first books of the Old Testament indicate that bride purchase and marriage between near relatives were basic to the customs of the early Hebrews. Values centered on the protection of property and perpetuation of the clan. When a man died leaving a childless widow, one of his brothers or even his father was obligated to take her as his wife. Her position within his family was secured by her fertility. Polygamy was common, seen as yet another guarantee of the clan's perpetuity. The right to marry out of the clan came slowly but was still, for example, prohibited in Numbers 36. Thereafter, clan-restricted property was broken up: the clan fell subject to gradual fragmentation and a smaller family cluster emerged, backed up by the appearance of strict laws against incestuous marriage. The nomadic desert life of the early Hebrews had given way, in short, to a more settled existence, and landed property became more and more the individual's to do with as he pleased. As early as Numbers, women began to inherit land in the absence of male heirs, while in Kings it was no longer unusual for daughters to inherit part of the family patrimony even in the presence of brothers. Among at least some Judaic groups polygamy was disappearing by about the time of Tobias. Widows came into their own, disposing fully of their own persons and properties. But a woman with a father or husband remained under his authority and could conclude no contracts without his consent—an incapacity which survived much social change. Again, throughout the biblical period men could repudiate their wives. This was once a relatively simple step; with time, however, it became increasingly difficult to show sufficient legal and moral reason for taking it. Although adultery provided the best grounds by about the second century B.C., the problem of repudiation remained to vex Jewish communities under the Roman Empire and during the Middle Ages. Women, on the other hand, were not allowed to repudiate husbands; in this, as in the forms of worship, women were subject to a permanent disadvantage, afterward to be seen among Christians as well. But the notion of woman's congenital inferiority had not generally prevailed in the Near East: it was not, for example, found in Babylonian law and custom.

The selections that follow are taken from a new translation, The New English Bible, published by the University Presses of Oxford and *of Cambridge 1970, planned and directed by the Protestant churches of Great Britain and Ireland.*

BRIDE PURCHASE AND POLYGAMY

The early Hebrew bought his wife; in return—apart from the presumed bonds of affection—he received labor and assured the continuation of his clan. If his wife was barren, polygamy or repudiation provided solutions. If he was sterile, the proofs were much harder to come by. But if, for example, his 'testicles' had 'been crushed' or his 'organ severed' he could not 'become a member of the assembly of the Lord' (Deuteronomy *23:1*). *The reference, scholars note, is to eunuchs and to the practice of mutilating enemies in wartime, but the connection with sterility seems clear: such a one was on the verge of meriting exclusion from the body of the faithful.*

Now Laban had two daughters: the elder was called Leah, and the younger Rachel. Leah was dull-eyed, but Rachel was graceful and beautiful. Jacob [Laban's nephew] had fallen in love with Rachel and he said, 'I will work seven years for your younger daughter Rachel.' Laban replied, 'It is better that I should give her to you than to anyone else; stay with me.' So Jacob worked seven years for Rachel, and they seemed like a few days because he loved her. Then Jacob said to Laban, 'I have served my time. Give me my wife so that we may sleep together.' So Laban gathered all the men of the place together and gave a feast. In the evening he took his daughter Leah and brought her to Jacob, and Jacob slept with her. . . . But when morning came, Jacob saw that it was Leah and said to Laban, 'What have you done to me? Did I not work for Rachel? Why have you deceived me?' Laban answered, 'In our country it is not right to give the younger sister in marriage before the elder. Go through with the seven days' feast for the elder, and the younger shall be given you in return for a further seven years' work.' Jacob agreed, and completed the seven days for Leah.

Then Laban gave Jacob his daughter Rachel as wife. . . . Jacob slept with Rachel also; he loved her rather than Leah, and he worked for Laban for a further seven years. [*Genesis* 29:16–30]

The sons of Jacob were twelve. The sons of Leah: Jacob's

first-born Reuben, then Simeon, Levi, Judah, Issachar and Zebulun. The sons of Rachel: Joseph and Benjamin. The sons of Rachel's slave-girl Bilhah: Dan and Naphtali. The sons of Leah's slave-girl Zilpah: Gad and Asher. These were Jacob's sons. [*Genesis* 35:23–7]

When a man seduces a virgin who is not yet betrothed, he shall pay the bride-price for her to be his wife. If her father refuses to give her to him, the seducer shall pay in silver a sum equal to the bride-price for virgins. [*Exodus* 22:16–17]

When a man has two wives, one loved and the other unloved, if they both bear him sons, and the son of the unloved wife is the elder, then, when the day comes for him to divide his property among his sons, he shall not treat the son of the loved wife as his first-born in contempt of his true first-born, the son of the unloved wife. [*Deuteronomy* 21:15–17]

David ... said to them, 'Do you think that marrying the king's daughter is a matter of so little consequence that a poor man of no consequence like myself can do it?' Saul's courtiers reported what David had said, and he replied, 'Tell David this: all the king wants as the bride-price is the foreskins of a hundred Philistines, by way of vengeance on his enemies.' The courtiers told David what Saul had said, and marriage with the king's daughter on these terms pleased him well. Before the appointed time, David went out with his men and slew two hundred Philistines; he brought their foreskins and counted them out to the king in order to be accepted as his son-in-law. So Saul married his daughter Michal to David. [1 *Samuel* 18:23–7]

FERTILITY AND BARRENNESS

Lot went up from Zoar and settled in the hill-country with his two daughters, because he was afraid to stay in Zoar; he lived with his two daughters in a cave. The elder daughter said to the younger, 'Our father is old and there is not a man in the country to come to us in the usual way. Come now, let us make our father drink wine and then lie with him and in this way keep the family alive through our father.' ... In this way both Lot's daughters came to be with child by their father. [*Genesis* 19:30–6]

Abram's wife Sarai had borne him no children. Now she had

an Egyptian slave-girl whose name was Hagar, and she said to Abram, 'You see that the LORD has not allowed me to bear a child. Take my slave-girl; perhaps I shall found a family through her.' Abram agreed to what his wife said; so Sarai, Abram's wife, brought her slave-girl, Hagar the Egyptian, and gave her to her husband Abram as a wife [or concubine]. When this happened Abram had been in Canaan for ten years. He lay with Hagar and she conceived; and when she knew that she was with child, she despised her mistress. Sarai said to Abram, 'I have been wronged and you must answer for it. It was I who gave my slave-girl into your arms, but since she has known that she is with child, she has despised me. May the LORD see justice done between you and me.' Abram replied to Sarai, 'Your slave-girl is in your hands; deal with her as you will.' So Sarai ill-treated her and she ran away. [*Genesis* 16:1–6]

When brothers live together and one of them dies without leaving a son, his widow shall not marry outside the family. Her husband's brother shall have intercourse with her; he shall take her in marriage and do his duty by her as her husband's brother. The first son she bears shall perpetuate the dead brother's name so that it may not be blotted out from Israel. But if the man is unwilling to take his brother's wife, she shall go to the elders at the town gate and say, 'My husband's brother refuses to perpetuate his brother's name in Israel; he will not do his duty by me.' At this the elders of the town shall summon him and reason with him. If he still stands his ground and says, 'I will not take her,' his brother's widow shall go up to him in the presence of the elders; she shall pull his sandal off his foot and spit in his face and declare: 'Thus we requite the man who will not build up his brother's family.' [*Deuteronomy* 25:5–9]

There was a man ... named Elkanah ... and he had two wives named Hannah and Peninnah. Peninnah had children, but Hannah was childless. This man used to go up from his own town every year to worship and to offer sacrifice to the LORD of Hosts in Shiloh.... On the day when Elkanah sacrificed, he gave several shares of the meat to his wife Peninnah with all her sons and daughters; but, although he loved Hannah, he gave her only one share, because the LORD had not granted her children.

Further, Hannah's rival used to torment and humiliate her because she had no children. Year after year this happened when they went up to the house of the LORD; her rival used to torment her.... [Hannah then made a vow, promising the wished-for child to the LORD–Ed.] 'and no razor shall ever touch his head.' For a long time she went on praying before the LORD.... Elkanah had intercourse with his wife Hannah, and the LORD remembered her. She conceived, and in due time bore a son, whom she named Samuel, 'because,' she said, 'I asked the LORD for him.' [1 Samuel 1:1–20]

THE GOOD WIFE

Her virtue is measured by her devotion and by the material value of her productive labor: such is what the imagery of the following verses affirms, whatever the parabolic or symbolic overtones.

> She chooses wool and flax
> and toils at her work.
> Like a ship laden with merchandise,
> she brings home food from far off.
> She rises while it is still night
> and sets meat before her household.
> After careful thought she buys a field
> and plants a vineyard out of her earnings....
> She sees that her business goes well,
> and never puts out her lamp at night.
> She holds the distaff in her hand,
> and her fingers grasp the spindle.
> She is open-handed to the wretched....
> She makes her own coverings,
> and clothing of fine linen and purple....
> She weaves linen and sells it,
> and supplies merchants with their sashes.
> She is clothed in dignity and power....
> When she opens her mouth, it is to speak wisely....
> She keeps her eye on the doings of her household
> and does not eat the bread of idleness....
> Charm is a delusion and beauty fleeting;

it is the God-fearing woman who is honored.
Extol her for the fruit of her toil,
and let her labors bring her honor in the city gate.
[*Proverbs* 31:13–16, 18–20, 22, 24–27, 30–31]

CHASTITY AND IMPURITY

When a man takes a wife and after having intercourse with her
turns against her .. saying, 'I took this woman and slept with
her and did not find proof of virginity in her,' then the girl's
father and mother shall take the proof of her virginity [a blood-
stained garment–Ed.] to the elders of the town, at the town
gate. . . . If, on the other hand, the accusation is true and no proof
of the girl's virginity is found, then they shall bring her out to the
door of her father's house and the men of her town shall stone
her to death. She has committed an outrage in Israel by playing
the prostitute in her father's house: you shall rid yourselves
of this wickedness.

When a man is discovered lying with a married woman, they
shall both die, the woman as well as the man who lay with her:
you shall rid Israel of this wickedness.

When a virgin is pledged in marriage to a man and another
man comes upon her in the town and lies with her, you shall
bring both of them out to the gate of that town and stone them
to death; the girl because, although in the town, she did not cry
for help, and the man because he dishonored another man's
wife: you shall rid yourselves of this wickedness. If the man
comes upon such a girl in the country and rapes her, then the
man alone shall die because he lay with her. You shall do
nothing to the girl, she has done nothing worthy of death: this
deed is like that of a man who attacks another and murders him,
for the man came upon her in the country and, though the girl
cried for help, there was no one to rescue her.

When a man comes upon a virgin who is not pledged in marriage and forces her to lie with him, and they are discovered,
then the man who lies with her shall give the girl's father fifty
pieces of silver, and she shall be his wife because he has dishonored her. He is not free to divorce her all his life long.
[*Deuteronomy* 22:13–29]

When a woman has a discharge of blood, her impurity shall last for seven days; anyone who touches her shall be unclean till evening. Everything on which she lies or sits during her impurity shall be unclean. Anyone who touches her bed shall wash his clothes, bathe in water and remain unclean till evening. . . . If he is on the bed or seat where she is sitting, by touching it he shall become unclean till evening. If a man goes so far as to have intercourse with her and any of her discharge gets on to him, then he shall be unclean for seven days, and every bed on which he lies down shall be unclean. [*Leviticus* 15:19–24]

You shall not approach a woman to have intercourse with her during her period of menstruation. [*Leviticus* 18:19]

The LORD spoke to Moses and said, Speak to the Israelites in these words: When a woman conceives and bears a male child, she shall be unclean for seven days, as in the period of her impurity through menstruation. On the eighth day, the child shall have the flesh of his foreskin circumcised. The woman shall wait for thirty-three days because her blood requires purification; she shall touch nothing that is holy, and shall not enter the sanctuary till her days of purification are completed. If she bears a female child, she shall be unclean for fourteen days . . . and shall wait for sixty-six days because her blood requires purification. [*Leviticus* 12:1–6]

INHERITANCE AND CONTRACTS

A claim was presented by the daughters of Zelophehad son of Hepher. . . . They appeared at the entrance of the Tent of the Presence before Moses, Eleazar the priest, the chiefs, and all the community, and spoke as follows: 'Our father died in the wilderness. . . . Is it right that, because he had no son, our father's name should disappear from his family? Give us our property on the same footing as our father's brothers.'

So Moses brought their case before the LORD, and the LORD . . . said: 'The claim of the daughters of Zelophehad is good. . . . When a man dies leaving no son, his patrimony shall pass to his daughter. . . . This shall be a legal precedent for the Israelites.' [*Numbers* 27:1–11]

No patrimony in Israel shall pass from tribe to tribe, but every

Israelite shall retain his father's patrimony. Any woman of an Israelite tribe who is an heiress may marry a man from any family in her father's tribe. Thus the Israelites shall retain each one the patrimony of his forefathers.... [Thus–Ed.] every tribe in Israel shall retain its own patrimony. [*Numbers* 36:7–9]

Then Moses spoke to the heads of the Israelite tribes and said, 'This is the LORD's command: When a man makes a vow to the LORD or swears an oath and so puts himself under a binding obligation, he must not break his word. Every word he has spoken, he must make good. When a woman, still young and living in her father's house, makes a vow to the LORD or puts herself under a binding obligation, if her father hears of it and keeps silence, then any such vow or obligation shall be valid. But if her father disallows it when he hears of it, none of her vows or obligations shall be valid; the LORD will absolve her, because her father has disallowed it. If the woman is married when she is under a vow or a binding obligation rashly uttered, then if her husband hears of it and keeps silence ... her vow ... shall be valid. If, however, her husband disallows it ... then the LORD will absolve her. Every vow by which a widow or a divorced woman has bound herself shall be valid. But if it is in her husband's house that a woman makes a vow or puts herself under a binding obligation by an oath, and her husband ... does not disallow it, then every vow and obligation under which she has put herself shall be valid; but if her husband clearly repudiates them when he hears of them, then nothing that she has uttered, whether vow or obligation, shall be valid.' [*Numbers* 30:2–12]

REPUDIATION

When a man has married a wife, but she does not win his favor because he finds something shameful in her, and he writes her a note of divorce, gives it to her and dismisses her; and suppose after leaving his house she goes off to become the wife of another man, and this next husband turns against her and writes her a note of divorce which he gives her and dismisses her, or dies after making her his wife—then in that case her first husband who dismissed her is not free to take her back to be his wife again after she has become for him unclean. [*Deuteronomy* 24:1–4]

Keep watch on your spirit and do not be unfaithful to the wife of your youth. If a man divorces or puts away his spouse, he overwhelms her with cruelty, says the LORD of Hosts the God of Israel. [*Malachi* 2:15–16]

V   The Early Middle Ages

*We turn next to the barbarian peoples who overran the Roman Empire.
They came of Germanic stock and lived by differing customs. Their
tribal laws were redacted between the late fifth and ninth centuries,
issuing in the codes from which most of the selections below are taken.
In general the northern tribes put more restraints upon women than
tribes to the south, where the Burgundian and Visigothic codes, owing
partly to Roman influences, show a greater liberality with regard to
matters of inheritance, property, and guardianship. Exceptionally, the
barbarians who conquered northern Italy in the later sixth century, the
Lombards, long retained their 'purity.' Up to the eleventh century or later
no Lombard woman was ever allowed to be her own guardian: she was a
perpetual minor.*

*The following texts apply to free and semifree women only. In a book
of historical readings, it is hard enough to catch the voices of ordinary men
(not to speak of women), harder still to record the faint voices of the en-
slaved and those subject to degrees of serfdom. Sources, moreover, are
meager for the Dark Ages, when effective centralized authority all but
vanished and the impact of Christianity on tribal customs was feeble.
Laws aimed more at remedying chaotic situations than at providing a
watertight system of legislation.*

GUARDIANSHIP

If any woman, Burgundian or Roman, voluntarily give herself
to a husband in marriage, we order that the husband have the
property of that woman. Just as he has the power over
her, also is he to have it over all her possessions. [*Leges
Burgundionum*][1]

*Burgundian law was compiled by King Gundobad (474–516). An east
German tribe, the Burgundians, had been in contact with the Romans
since the third century. They received land west of the Rhine from the
Emperor Honorius and could be more open-handed than the above law
suggests, as in their recognition of women as guardians:*

If a mother should want to be guardian [over her children]
no other relative shall precede her in this. [*Leges Burgundionum*][2]

The Visigothic code had a similar provision;

If a father dies leaving his sons as minors, let the mother, if she is willing, assume their guardianship while she remains a widow. [*Leges Visigothorum*][3]

On the question of guardianship the Saxon code, redacted in 785, was stricter and set down a full circle of restraints :

If any man die and leave a widow, let his son by another wife be her guardian; failing him, let the brother of the dead man be guardian, and if he had no brother, then the nearest of the husband's kinsmen.

When a man dies leaving no sons but only daughters, the inheritance shall go to them, but the guardianship over them shall pass to their father's brother or nearest kinsman.

If a widow with a daughter remarries and has a son, the guardianship over the daughter goes to the said son; if, however, having a son, she then marries and has a daughter, the guardianship over the daughter goes not to the son by her first marriage but to the father's brother or nearest kinsman. [*Leges Saxonum und Lex Thuringorum*][4]

Guardianships bearing upon marriage may be seen in the ninth-century codes of the Thuringians and Frisians :

If a free woman marry anyone without the consent of her father or guardian, she shall lose any property she had or should have had. [*Leges Saxonum und Lex Thuringorum*][5]

If anyone marries a free woman without the consent of her parents or of those who have authority over her, he shall make a settlement to her guardian of twenty solidi, that is of forty denarii.

If, however, the woman was noble, thirty solidi. [*Lex Frisionum*][6]

INHERITING

The exclusion of women from the right to inherit land and immovables —though the Burgundian and Visigothic codes allow it—should be seen in the light of military service. That is to say, originally much conquered land had been doled out in return for military service due to a chieftain, lord, or prince; and that land long bore the marks, real or vestigial, of the obligation. This explains the precedence of spear over spindle, but the custom persisted, artfully, long after true military obligations had utterly lapsed.

On the death of the father or mother the inheritance goes to the son, not the daughter.

When a man has a son and a daughter and the son marries, has a son, and then dies, the inheritance belongs to the son's son, that is to the grandson, not to the daughter. [*Leges Saxonum*][7]

The son of the deceased father, not the daughter, succeeds to the inheritance [of freehold land].

If the deceased had no son, the daughter inherits the money and movables but the land goes to his nearest male relative. If, however, he had no daughter, his sister gets the money and movables, and the nearest male relative in his line inherits the land. If he had neither son nor daughter nor sister but his mother survives, she shall inherit the daughter's or sister's share, that is to say, the money and movables. And if he is survived [by none of these], his nearest male relative shall succeed as heir to everything—money, movables, and land.

A dying mother shall leave the land, movables, and money to her son; to her daughter go the spoils of her neck, which is to say necklaces, ornaments, jewels, earrings, clothes, bracelets, and whatever personal ornaments it turns out she had. . . .

Down to the fifth generation the males in the paternal line shall succeed [to the inheritance of property]. After the fifth, however, the daughter shall succeed to everything coming both from her father's and mother's side; not until then does the inheritance pass from the spear to the spindle. [*Lex Thuringorum*][8]

The earliest Salic law text (c. 500) denies women the right to inherit real property (i.e., land and immovables):

Salic land is no inheritance for a woman; rather, all the land goes to the male sex—the brothers. [*Pactus Legis Salicae*][9]

Chilperic I, King of Neustria (561–584), brought in a change:

In the same way it is resolved and agreed that if a deceased man leave sons or daughters... the sons shall hold the land as long as they live, in accordance with Salic law. And if the sons die prematurely, the daughters shall receive the land in the same way as the sons would have if they had lived. And if a brother dies and another one survives him ... he shall get the land. And if a brother has an early death, leaving no surviving brother, then the sister shall succeed to the inheritance of the land. [*Pactus Legis Salicae*][10]

In the absence of males, girls could now inherit land. But the systematic precedence of the male sometimes caused marked discomfort, as is clear from this eighth-century Frankish formulary:

That a daughter may succeed with her brothers to her father's freehold land. My dearest daughter so and so. A long-standing but wicked custom of our people [Lex Salica, tit. 59] denies sisters a share with their brothers in their father's land; but I consider this wrong, since my children came equally from God.... Therefore, my dearest daughters, with this letter I hereby make you an equal and legitimate heir with your brothers, my sons, so that you may divide and share the family freehold land, as well as the movables and buildings, or whatever else we leave on our death, equally with the spear-side (my sons and your brothers), and you are not to receive a lesser share in anything but divide all things equally among yourselves. [*Textes relatifs aux institutions privées et publiques aux époques mérovingienne et carolingienne*][11]

The Burgundian laws (redacted c. 500) had these pertinent provisions:

Among Burgundians we wish it to be observed that if anyone does not leave a son, let a daughter succeed to the inheritance of the father and mother in place of the son.

Concerning those women who are vowed to God and remain in chastity, we order that if they have two brothers they receive a third portion of the inheritance of the father, that is, of that land which the father, possessing by the right of allotment [*sic*], left at the time of his death. Likewise, if she has four or five brothers, let her receive the portion due to her.

The mother's ornaments and vestments belong to the daughters without any right to share on the part of the brother or brothers; further, let this legal principle be observed concerning those ornaments and vestments in the case of girls whose mothers die intestate. But if the mother shall have made any disposal of her own ornaments and vestments, there shall be no cause for action thereafter.

But if an unmarried girl who has sisters dies, and she has not declared her wish in writing or in the presence of witnesses, let her portion after her death belong to her sisters and, as has been stated, let her brothers have no share therein.

However, if the girl dies and does not have a blood sister, and no clear disposition has been made concerning her property, let her brothers become her heirs. [*The Burgundian Code*] [12]

Of all the collections the Visigothic code, compiled in the fifth and sixth centuries, is perhaps the most favorable to women:

Let sisters have an equal share with their brothers in their parents' inheritance. If a father or a mother should die intestate, sisters shall succeed without any hindrance to the inheritance of their parents' wealth, sharing it equally with their brothers. [*Leges Visigothorum*] [13]

BRIDE PURCHASE

The entries under guardianship, and those below, indicate that the Germanic peoples of western and central Europe—like the early Hebrews—observed the custom of bride purchase. Here possibly is the best example we have of an institution which reveals the free woman in her incarnation as property or material value. Far from seeing rape or sexual violence as an expression of moral turpitude, the Germanic law codes treat it as a form of theft, as an invasion of property: property belonging to the guardians or husband or overlord of the woman involved. Consequently, the sexual thief had to make amends by paying the wittimon or wergeld (terms defined below) of the stolen or violated woman.

The bridegroom shall give the bride's kinsmen three hundred solidi; if, however, he has married her against their wishes but with her consent, he shall pay double the sum. And if indeed neither the kinsmen nor the girl consented, that is to say, if she was taken by force, he shall pay three hundred solidi to her kin, two hundred and forty solidi to the girl herself, and he shall restore her to them.

Whoever wants to marry a widow shall, if her relatives are in agreement, offer her guardian the bride price for her; if her guardian refuses, let him turn to her next of kin and, with their consent, take her, having the money ready to pay out, that is, the three hundred solidi, if the guardian should want to protest. [*Leges Saxonum*] [14]

Burgundian law also called for the purchase of brides. Normally the father received the bride price or wittimon. In his absence, it was divided among the girl's relatives.

If a girl be given in marriage and has an uncle and sisters, but no father or brothers, the uncle shall take a third of the wittimon, and be it known to the sisters that they also may claim a third.

If she marries and is in fact fatherless and brotherless, it is well that her mother should take a third of the wittimon and that the nearest relatives should have another third.

And if she have no mother, her sisters are to get that third. [*Leges Burgundionum*] [15]

In each case the above provisions account for no more than two-thirds of the total bride price. The assumption is that the bride received a third for herself, doubtless as a sort of dower.

Brides were also purchased in seventh-century Britain, as is revealed by the Laws of Wessex. Thus a law (c. 690) from the reign of King Ine:

If anyone buys a wife and the marriage does not take place, he [the bride's guardian] shall return the bridal price and pay [the bridegroom] as much again, and he shall compensate the trustee of the marriage according to the amount he is entitled to for infraction of his surety. [*The Laws of the Earliest English Kings*] [16]

REPUDIATION

If any woman leaves (puts aside) her husband to whom she is legally married, let her be smothered in mire.

If anyone wishes to put away his wife without cause, let him give her another payment such as he gave for her marriage price, and let the amount of the fine be twelve solidi.

If by chance a man wishes to put away his wife, and is able to prove one of these three crimes against her, that is, adultery, witchcraft, or violation of graves, let him have full right to put her away: and let the judge pronounce the sentence of the law against her, just as should be done against criminals.

But if she admits none of these three crimes, let no man be permitted to put away his wife for any other crime. But if he chooses, he may go away from the home, leaving all household property behind, and his wife with their children may possess the property of her husband. [*The Burgundian Code*][17]

Originally, in Germanic law, repudiation was the prerogative of the husband only, but subsequently Roman influence made way temporarily for divorce by mutual consent.

ADULTERY AND VARIETIES OF VIOLENCE

The town of Le Mans had a priest who was extremely depraved, mad for women, devoted to the pleasures of the belly, to fornication, and to every other sort of indecency. Often debauching himself with a woman of free status and good family, he cropped her hair, dressed her up as a man, and led her off to another town, hoping to dispel the suspicion of adultery by going to live among strangers. When, some time afterward, her relatives discovered what had happened, they rushed to revenge the family's disgrace. Having found the priest, they tied him up and took him prisoner. The woman they burned alive, but being driven by the greed for gold, they decided to ransom the priest.... Hearing of the case, Bishop Aetharius took pity on the man and snatched him from certain death .by paying twenty solidi of gold for him. [Gregory of Tours (538-594), *Historia francorum libri decem*][18]

Interestingly, the family's honor was restored by the woman's death and the bishop's gold. The Burgundians of Gregory's time had tough laws on the subject:

If adulterers are discovered, let the man and the woman be killed.

This must be observed: either let him [the injured party] kill both of them, or if he kills only one of them, let him pay the wergeld [see below] of that one according to that customary wergeld which has been established in earlier laws.

[Under another title.] If indeed a native girl unites voluntarily with a slave, we order both to be killed. [Other things aside, how could a slave pay her wittimon?]

But if the relatives of the girl do not wish to punish their own relative, let the girl be deprived of her free status and delivered unto servitude to the king. [In Salic law, all her property went to the royal treasury.]

[Another title.] Whatever woman, barbarian by nation, enters into union with a man willingly and secretly, let her wedding price be paid in fee simple to her relatives; and he to whom she has been joined in an adulterous union may be united afterward in marriage to another if he wishes. [*The Burgundian Code*][19]

The presumption in the last of these laws is that the girl and her paramour were single; hence there is no conflict with the first law in the series, where the crime is adultery proper. The following law, although included in a thirteenth-century Spanish code, was labeled 'an ancient law,' had long since lost its force, and had its origins in an earlier Visigothic collection (but a Roman or southern influence is present):

If a woman's adulterous relations with the husband of another can be proved, let her be put under the power of the adulterer's wife, that the wife may revenge herself as she wishes. [*Fuero Jusgo*][20]

Wergeld was the price or fee due for killing a person. The wergeld due for women was generally equal or superior to that of men. A woman's wergeld was highest in south German law. Saxon law, in the case of a virgin, put it at double the amount due for a man, the reason being that her bride price could normally fetch a fair sum for her clan. Frisian law attached a higher price to a murdered embroideress or ribbon maker—she had been worth more—than to other women, whose wergeld was generally on a par with men's. Women of childbearing age had a triple wergeld in the Salic and Ripuarian codes.

If anyone shall steal a girl, let him be compelled to pay the price set for such a girl ninefold, and let him pay a fine to the amount of twelve solidi.

If a girl who has been seized returns uncorrupted to her parents, let the abductor compound six times the wergeld of the girl; moreover, let the fine be set at twelve solidi.

But if the abductor does not have the means to make the above-mentioned payment, let him be given over to the parents of the girl that they may have the power of doing to him whatever they choose. [*The Burgundian Code*][21]

If any free virgin [as opposed to one of servile status], on her way between two farms, is stopped by someone and he violently uncovers her head, he shall make amends by paying six solidi. And if he lifted her dress up to the knee, he must pay six solidi. And if he uncovered her genitals or backside, he shall pay twelve solidi. But if he raped her, he must pay forty solidi in compensation. [*Leges Alamannorum*][22]

The Burgundians brought in a law against the wives of thieves:

Although in former laws it has been established by what means the crimes of robbers should be repressed, nevertheless, because so far neither by corporal punishments nor by losses of property has it been possible to bring an end to the cruel acts of robbers, we decree in the present law: if any native freeman, barbarian as well as Roman, or a person of any nation dwelling within the provinces of our kingdom, takes horses or oxen in theft, and his wife does not immediately reveal the committed crime, let her husband be killed, and let her also be deprived of her liberty and given in servitude without delay to him against whom the deed was committed; because it cannot be doubted, and is often discovered, that such women are sharers in the crimes of their husbands. [*The Burgundian Code*]²³

THE KENTISH LAWS

In 597 Pope Gregory the Great sent a mission to Britain to convert its people. Shortly thereafter the king of Kent, Ethelbert, ordered a compilation of the Kentish laws (c. 604–614), which show an obvious kinship with Germanic codes and few traces of Christian influence. Following are some of the laws regarding women.

10   If a man lies with a maiden belonging to the king, he shall pay 50 shillings compensation.

11   If she is a grinding slave he shall pay 25 shillings; if she is of the third class, 12 shillings.

14   If a man lies with a nobleman's serving maid, he shall pay 12 shillings compensation.

16   If a man lies with a commoner's serving maid, he shall pay 6 shillings [to the protector or guardian, here and in the articles above].

31   If [one] freeman lies with the wife of [another] freeman, he shall pay [the husband] his [or her] wergeld, and procure a second wife with his own money, and bring her to the other man's home.

73   If a freeborn woman, with long hair [sign of her free status], misconducts herself, she shall pay 30 shillings as compensation.

74   Compensation [for injury] to be paid to an unmarried woman shall be on the same scale as that paid to a freeman.

75   The compensation to be paid for violation of the *mund* [meaning unclear] of a widow of the best class [nobility] shall be 50 shillings. For violation of the *mund* of a widow of the second class, 20 shillings; of the third class, 12 shillings; of the fourth class, 6 shillings.

76   If a man takes a widow who does not [of right] belong to him, double the value of the *mund* shall be paid.

77   If a man buys a maiden, the bargain shall stand, if there is no dishonesty. If, however, there is dishonesty, she shall be taken back to her home, and the money shall be returned to him.

78   If she [the said maiden] bears a living child, she shall have half the goods left by her husband, if he dies first.

79   If she wishes to depart with her children, she shall have half the goods.

80   If the husband wishes to keep [the children], she shall have a share of the goods equal to a child's.

81   If she does not bear a child, [her] father's relatives shall have her goods, and the 'morning gift' [the husband's present to his wife, a kind of dower, on the morning after their marriage night].

82   If a man forcibly carries off a maiden, [he shall pay] 50 shillings to her owner, and afterward buy from the owner his consent.

85   If a man lies with the woman of a servant, during the lifetime of the husband, he shall pay a twofold compensation. [*The Laws of the Earliest English Kings*][24]

VI Islam

Islam, now a 'third world' religion, was a European one when Muslim culture was at its peak. Muslims reigned for seven centuries over much of Spain (Granada, their last stronghold, fell in 1492), while Sicily was a center of Arab culture for more than two centuries before the coming of the Normans (1070). This culture was particularly influential in scientific matters. The Arab doctors had inherited the learning of the Nestorian Greeks, including Aristotelian thought and Galenic anatomy, and had themselves developed the science of chemistry as applied to medicine. Europe went to school to them. When Toledo fell to the Christians (1085), a college was set up to translate Arabic works into Latin and, through the pages of Arabists like Guy de Chauliac (1300–1368) and Michael Scot (c. 1175–c. 1230), the Arabs exercised an influence on European medieval science. A few words of Arabic origin—alchemy, elixir, algebra—and our system of numbers indicate the points of impact. Europe was then the 'third world.'

In view of Islam's contacts with Europe, the status of Muslim women must interest us. Our representations will be necessarily skeletal. As with the early Jews, who influenced Mohammed (570–632), so also with Muslims law and religion are fused. The basis for the law is fourfold: the Koran, traditions concerning what Mohammed said or did, the consensus of the Muslim community, and reasoning by analogy. The Koran is not itself a code—we should bear this in mind—and is not directly referred to by Muslim judges. They refer instead to interpretations previously rendered by learned Muslim jurists. In questions of family law, however, the Koran provides the fiqh—*Muslim jurisprudence—with a broad base, and therefore we shall draw upon it, fine distinctions falling beyond our scope. The other sources used belong to the Maliki law system, observed in Muslim Spain.*

Quite unsurprisingly—given our preceding chapters—women in Muslim law occupy a subject status. Yet historically Islam brought protection and safeguards not to be found in earlier Arab customs. It forbade the elimination by burial of infant girls, and polygamy was a measure designed to keep superfluous women—inevitable in a warrior society—from want. Moreover, as is often pointed out, in matters of property Muslim women were more emancipated than European women. A daughter inherited half the share of a son. When she married, her property remained her private possession, and she was not required to draw from it for household expenses. She could sell, alienate, or pledge up to one-third of it without marital consent.

We use the J. M. Rodwell translation of the Koran (2d edn, 1871). The selections have been modernized wherever it seemed fitting.

MARRIAGE AND REPUDIATION

Men are superior to women on account of the qualities with which God hath gifted the one above the other, and on account of the outlay they make from their substance for them. [*Koran*, Sura IV, verse 38]

[Of] ... women who seem good in your eyes, marry but two, three, or four; and if ye still fear that ye shall not act equitably, then one only; or the slaves whom ye have acquired: this will make justice on your part easier. [*Koran*, IV, 3)

You may decline [to sleep with] any [of your wives or female slaves] and take to bed whichever one you choose, even if you had already refused her. This is no crime. [*Koran*, XXXIII, 51]

Zaid has related to me on the authority of his father who heard it from his grandfather who heard it from Ali—may salvation be his: 'When a man gives his daughter in marriage while she is small and then she reaches puberty, the marriage is valid and she may not refuse it; but if she has already reached puberty and the marriage is repugnant to her, then it is not binding.'

Zaid has related to me ... that Ali said: 'Nobody can legally impose marriage on children who have not reached puberty except their father and grandfather'. [*Majmu'al-Fiqh*][1]

Zaid was allegedly the great-grandson of Ali, the Prophet's son-in-law, and hence the Majmu *is one of the oldest texts of Muslim jurisprudence.*

A woman who has already been married cannot be given in marriage except at her own demand; a virgin can only be given in marriage after she has been asked for her consent.—'And how, O Prophet, will she signify consent?' asked the faithful.— 'By her silence', replied the Prophet. [*Sahih* of al-Bukhari, *Les Traditions Islamiques*][2]

And when you divorce [repudiate] your wives, and they have

waited the prescribed time, hinder them not from marrying their husbands when they have agreed among themselves in an honorable way. [*Koran*, II, 232]

But if a husband divorce her a third time [i.e., verbally repudiate her three times; no ritual or witnesses required], it is not lawful for him to take her again, until she shall have married another husband; and if he also divorce her, then shall no blame attach to them if they return to each other, thinking that they can keep within the bounds fixed by God. [*Koran*, II, 230]

The preceding verse is assumed to be a check, to keep husbands from repudiating their wives in a fit of temper or even as a warning. The second marriage, which must intervene before the couple can get together again, had to be consummated. There was no faking allowed.

O believers! when you marry believing women, and then divorce them before you touch them, you have no term prescribed you which you must fulfill toward them: provide for them, and dismiss them with a reputable dismissal. [*Koran*, XXXIII, 48]

O Prophet! when you divorce women, divorce them at their special times [menstrual period]. And reckon those times exactly, and fear God your Lord. Do not put them out of their houses, nor let them depart, unless they have committed a proven indecency. [*Koran*, LXV, 1]

A woman had no legal way of initiating divorce, but if the husband was willing and she had the money or property, she could pay him to repudiate her. Here is a reported ninth-century eyewitness account:

The man said to the judge: 'Sir, order this woman to come home with me.'

Whereupon the woman, prostrating herself on the floor, swore that she would not go one span with her husband and told the judge: 'In the name of the one and only God, if you make me go with this man I shall kill myself and you will be responsible for my death.'

When the judge heard these words, he turned to the counselor beside him and asked: 'What do you think of this case?'

The counselor replied that if it was not clear to the judge that the man in question was mistreating his wife, he should compel her to go with him whether she wished it or not, unless the husband agreed to let her go because of an indemnity or something else that she might offer him. But if he chose, the husband could refuse to agree to the separation unless she offered to pay an indemnity. Such a refusal was perfectly legal, for a husband can strip his wife of her very earrings if he has not harmed or ill-used her.

On hearing the counselor say this, the husband interjected: 'But good Lord! She's poor and hasn't got anything.'

'And if she thought,' inquired the judge, 'that she could free herself from you by paying you an indemnity, would you then let her go?'

'In that case I certainly would, with great pleasure.' ...

The judge then turned to me [to Nasir, the judge's steward, who is telling the story] and asked: 'Did you bring provisions along on this trip?'

'I brought only a measure of wheat and two measures of barley,' I told the judge. At that moment I could see him making some calculations.

'Provisions enough,' said the judge, 'for nine months and then some.'

He turned to the husband, saying: 'Take what remains of my crop in the grange [i.e., the provisions brought by the steward] and leave your wife in peace. In this way you shall be rid of her.'

'I would accept the offer,' the husband replied, 'if those provisions were in Córdoba' [his home].

'I see,' said the judge, 'that you are a man who doesn't miss a trick.'

The judge then got up, went off to another part of the house, brought back a piece of white woolen fabric, and handed it to the husband, saying: 'This cloth was made here in my house and I was to make use of it this winter. Actually, I can do without it. Take it and sell it, and the price you get for it will give you enough to cover the costs of transporting my crop from here to your house.'

The man took the cloth and let his wife go free. The judge

ordered me to turn over the supplies of wheat and barley. [Aljoxani, *Historia de los Jueces de Córdoba*]³

DOWER AND CONJUGAL RELATIONS

The dower is analogous to a purchase price and may consist in a female slave to be chosen by the bride and not by the bridegroom....

When the dower consists in a specified sum of goods or capital, it must be made over to her; if not, the wife ... may refuse her husband access to her; or, if access has taken place, she may refuse to have sexual intercourse with him or to accompany him on a journey until he has handed over what he owes....

The entire dower is due: (1) after consummation of the marriage, even if it takes place under forbidden conditions; (2) after the death of one of the marriage partners; (3) after a year of living together. [*Mukhtasar* of Khalil Ben Ishak]⁴

Freely give women their dower; but if of themselves they give any of it to you, then enjoy it....

You may seek out wives by means of your wealth, modestly and without fornication. Give a dower to those with whom you have lived. This is the law....

And any one of you who is not rich enough to marry free believing women, let him marry those believing maidens which have fallen into your hands as slaves.... Marry them with the consent of their people and give them a fair dower. [*Koran* IV, 3, 28–29]

Abu Horaira relates that the Prophet said: 'Woman is like a rib: if you want to straighten her out, you will break her, and if you want to use her, you must use her with her curve.' [*Sahih* of 'al-Bukhari']⁵

Virtuous women are obedient and careful during their husband's absence.... But scold those who you fear may be rebellious; leave them alone in their beds and beat them. [*Koran* IV, 38]

Abdallah Ben Zem 'a relates how the Prophet declared: 'Let no one among you beat his wife the way one beats a slave, when he may perhaps have intercourse with her before the end of the day.' [*Sahih* of 'al-Bukhari]⁶

They will question you as to the periods of women. Say: they are a pollution. Separate yourselves therefore from women and approach them not, until they be cleansed. But when they are cleansed, go in unto them as God hath ordained for you....

Your wives are your field: go in, therefore, to your field as you will. [*Koran*, II, 222–223]

ILLICIT INTERCOURSE

If any of your women be guilty of whoredom, then bring four witnesses against them from among themselves; and if they bear witness to the fact, shut them up within their houses till death release them, or God make some way for them. [*Koran*, IV, 19]

The penalty of immurement later gave way to stoning for a married woman and one year's exile, as well as flogging (100 stripes), for an unmarried girl.

The whore and the fornicator: whip each of them a hundred times....

The fornicator shall not marry other than a whore or an idolatress; and the whore shall not marry other than a fornicator or an idolater. Such alliances are forbidden to the faithful.

They who defame virtuous women, and fail to bring four witnesses, are to be whipped eighty times; and receive not their testimony forever, for these are perverse persons. [*Koran*, XXIV, 2–4]

If the guilty pair are unmarried, let them be whipped. Both the man and the woman will be exiled. Give a hundred strokes of the whip to each; do not let pity soften you when God's religion is at stake.... Let a group of believers be present at the punishment, for the shame of the chastisement is more impressive than the chastisement itself. A man guilty of adultery may marry only an adulterous woman or a polytheist. An adulterous woman may marry only a man guilty of the same crime or a polytheist. [*Sahih* of 'al-Bukhari]⁷

The rich Muslim had enough latitude with concubines and slaves so that the foregoing penalties quite likely weighed most heavily on the classes of poorer Muslims.

PROPERTY AND INHERITANCE

Men who die and leave wives behind shall bequeath to them a year's maintenance. . . .

And let there be a fair provision for women divorced. This is a duty in those who fear God.

But if you divorce them before consummation and have already settled a dower on them, you shall give them half of what you have settled, unless it be returned to you by them or the guardian. [*Koran*, II, 241, 242, 238]

Half of what your wives leave shall be yours, if they have no issue; but if they have issue, then a fourth of what they leave shall be yours, once you have paid the fees and debts.

And your wives shall have a fourth part of what you leave, if you have no issue; but if you have issue, then they shall have an eighth part, once they have paid the fees and debts. . . .

O believers! it is not allowed you to be heirs of your wives against their will; nor to hinder them from marrying, in order to take from them part of the dower you had given them, unless they have been guilty of undoubted lewdness. [*Koran*, IV, 13, 14, 23]

In matters of inheritance, pre-Islamic Arab custom seems to have excluded women and descendants from the distaff side in favor of agnates. The Prophet brought about a change. Henceforth men were still favored but provision was made for women:

With regard to your children, God commands you to give the male the portion of two females; and if there be more than two females, then they shall have two-thirds of what their father leaves; but if there be one daughter only, she shall have the half. [*Koran*, IV, 12]

AGAINST INFANTICIDE

The following passage refers to idolatrous Arabians who regarded angels as females and the daughters of God, but for themselves preferred sons.

And they assign daughters to God! Glory be to Him! But they desire them not for themselves.

For when the birth of a daughter is announced to any one of them, dark shadows settle on his face, and he is sad.

He hides himself from the people because of the ill tidings: shall he keep it with disgrace or bury it in the dust? Are not their judgments wrong?

To whatever is evil may they be likened. [*Koran*, XVI, 59–62]

Kill not your children for fear of want: for them and for you will we provide. Verily, the killing of them is a great wickedness....

> When the sun shall be folded up ...
> And when the female child that has been
>   buried alive shall be asked
> For what crime she was put to death ...
> Then every soul will know what it did.
>   [*Koran*, LXXXI, 1, 8–9, 14]

VII Biological and Medical Views

In the next few pages we try to catch some of the essential biological views concerning women. The texts presented span the 2,100 years or so between the fifth century B.C. and the seventeenth century of our era. During all this time serious views on the subject changed little.

PROCREATION

The writings attributed to Hippocrates of Cos (c. 460–c. 375 B.C.), the most distinguished of all early Greek physicians, greatly influenced the leading biologists and physicians who came after him.

Men produce female as well as male seed. So do women. Male seed is stronger than female seed.... This is what happens: if the stronger seed comes from both sides, the product is male; if the weaker, then the product is female. The [sex of the] product is determined by whichever of the two [kinds of seed] prevails quantitatively. Thus if the weaker seed is much more abundant, the stronger is overcome and, mingling with the weaker, is transformed and becomes female. If the stronger is more abundant, then the weaker is overcome and becomes male. [Hippocrates, *Oeuvres Complètes*][1]

People on the upper tiers of a hierarchy are more at ease if their inferiors seem inferior by nature. It is therefore not surprising that when scientists came to study the female of their own species, they should have looked at once for evidence of her inferiority. Aristotle (384–322 B.C.) was particularly prone to this, not only because his thinking was teleological but also because his interests were much broader than those of most medical researchers. Hippocrates held that the female, like the male, produced seed and that fertilization came about by a mixture of the two. But Aristotle preferred to conclude that the female's contribution was merely a kind of raw material (the menses), while the male, by giving the principle of life or soul, contributed the essential generative agency.

The contribution which the female makes to generation is the *matter* used therein; and this is to be found in the substance constituting the menstrual fluid....

There are some who think that the female contributes semen during coition because women sometimes derive pleasure from it comparable to that of the male and also produce a fluid secretion. This fluid, however is not seminal; ... the female, in fact, is female on account of an inability of a sort, viz., it lacks the power to concoct semen out of the final state of the nourishment (this is either blood, or its counterpart in bloodless animals) because of the coldness of its nature.... No, what happens is what one would expect to happen. The male provides the 'form' and the 'principle of the movement', the female provides the body, in other words the material. Compare the coagulation of milk. Here, the milk is the body, and the fig juice or the rennet contains the principle which causes it to set....

Thus, if the male is the active partner, the one which originates the movement, and the female *qua* female is the passive one, surely what the female contributes to the semen of the male will not be semen but material. And this is in fact what happens; for the natural substance of the menstrual fluid is to be classed as 'prime matter.'

Taking, then, the widest formulation of each of these two opposites, viz., regarding the male *qua* active and causing movement, and the female *qua* passive and being set in movement, we see that the one thing which is formed is formed *from them* only in the sense in which a bedstead is formed from the carpenter and the wood, or a ball from the wax and the form. [Aristotle, *Generation of Animals*][2]

The above work, issued in Arabic at Bagdad in the early ninth century, was translated (c. 1215) from the Arabic into Latin by Michael Scot, then resident in Spain, and his translation was much used in thirteenth-century Europe. Aristotle goes on in the same work to make an observation which was very widely echoed from the thirteenth to the sixteenth centuries:

In human beings the male is much hotter in its nature [hence more capable of generation] than the female. On that account male embryos tend to move about more than the female ones,

and owing to their moving about they get broken more ...
females are weaker and colder by nature; and we should look
upon the female state as being as it were a deformity, though
one which occurs in the ordinary course of nature. [Aristotle,
Generation of Animals][3]

*Galen (A.D. 131–201), one of the greatest biologists of antiquity, was the
principal authority in the medical schools of medieval and Renaissance
Europe. He mastered the Hippocratic writings and the works of Aristotle,
dissected monkeys, and discussed the ovaries, which he called 'testes'.*

The female's testicles are located on each side of the uterus and
reach down as far as its horns. [It was thought that the uterus
contained seven cells and came to two points or 'horns'. Down
to the sixteenth century the belief lingered that males were gene-
rated on the right, females on the left, and hermaphrodites in
the middle.] They [the female testicles] are much smaller and of
a different appearance and substance than in men.... The
seed vessels issuing from the testicles clearly contain seed just as
men's do. These vessels are wide as they leave the testicles and
contain a considerable cavity; farther on they narrow ... then
near the horns they dilate again at the point where they enter
the uterus. These connections were unknown to Aristotle.
[Galen, *De Uteri Dissectione*][4]

Galen put his findings into a more general context:

The female is more imperfect than the male. The first reason
is that she is colder. If, among animals, the warmer ones
are more active, it follows that the colder ones must be more
imperfect....

Just as man is the most perfect of all animals, so also, within
the human species, man is more perfect than woman. The cause
of this superiority is the [male's] superabundance of warmth,
heat being the primary instrument of nature....

The male's testicles are all the stronger because he is warmer.
The sperm born there, on reaching the final degree of concoction, is the formative principle of the animal. From a single principle wisely imagined by the Creator — that whereby the female

is less perfect than the male—follow all the conditions useful for the generation of the animal: the impossibility for the female genitalia to emerge externally, the accumulation of a superfluity of useful nourishment, an imperfect sperm, a hollow organ capable of receiving perfect sperm. In the male, instead, everything is the reverse: an elongated member suitable for copulation and emitting sperm, and an abundance of this same thick warm sperm. . . .

Do not therefore be surprised if the right [side] of the womb and the right testicle are much warmer than the left [side] of the womb and the left testicle. [This is] not only because of their nourishment humoral but also because of their position in a straight line with the liver, Now, if this is established and it is agreed that the male is warmer than the female, it is no longer illogical to assert that the right sides must engender males and the left sides females. [*Oeuvres de Galen*][5]

Historians speak of medicine marking time for a thousand years after Galen. The death of his contemporary, Soranus of Ephesus (second century A.D.), was followed by a similar fate for practical obstetrics. Greek biological and medical treatises were studied by Persian and Arab physicians and reached Europe through translations from the Arabic. Medieval and Renaissance physicians and thinkers were pleased with the Aristotelian image of woman as a deformity in nature and accepted the Greek and Galenic humoral notion, according to which woman was cold, too dry or too moist, insufficiently decocted, and weak. But Galen's crediting her with testicles was less pleasing. The Italian anatomist Borgarucci had this to say (1564):

Nature placed the female testicles internally. . . . [The deeper significance of this follows.] Woman is a most arrogant and extremely intractable animal; and she would be worse if she came to realize that she is no less perfect and no less fit to wear breeches than man. . . . I believe that is why nature, while endowing her with what is necessary for our procreation, did so in such a way as to keep her from perceiving and ascertaining her sufficient perfection. On the contrary . . . to check woman's continual desire to dominate, nature arranged things so that every time she thinks of her supposed lack, she may be humbled and shamed [P. Borgarucci, *Della contemplatione anatomica sopra tutte le parti del corpo umano*][6]

Eight years earlier the Spanish anatomist Valverde had expressed a similar view:

I would have preferred to omit this chapter [on female testicles], that women might not become all the more arrogant by knowing that they also, like men, have testicles, and that they not only suffer the pain of having to nourish the child within their bodies ... but also that they too put something of their own into it. [I. de Valverde, *Historia de la composicion del cuerpo humano*][7]

In 1651 William Harvey (1578–1657), discoverer of the circulation of the blood, published his Exercitationes de Generatione Animalium. *There, advancing a neo-Aristotelian theory of generation, he promotes an ingenious concoction of idealism and masculine pride:*

It is to the uterus that the business of conception is chiefly entrusted: without this structure and its functions conception would be looked for in vain.... The woman, after contact with the spermatic fluid in coitu, seems to receive influence, and to become fecundated without the cooperation of any sensible corporeal agent, in the same way as iron touched by the magnet is endowed with its powers and can attract other iron to itself. When this virtue is once received the woman exercises a plastic power of generation, and produces a being after her own image; not otherwise than the plant, which we see endowed with the forces of both sexes....

[Since] ... the substance of the uterus, when ready to conceive, is very like the structure of the brain, why should we not suppose that the function of both is similar, and that there is excited by coitus within the uterus a something identical with, or at least analogous to, an 'imagination' (phantasma) or a 'desire' (appetitus) in the brain, whence comes the generation or procreation of the ovum? For the functions of both are termed 'conceptions' and both, although the primary sources of every action throughout the body, are immaterial, the one of natural or organic, the other of animal actions; the one (viz., the uterus)

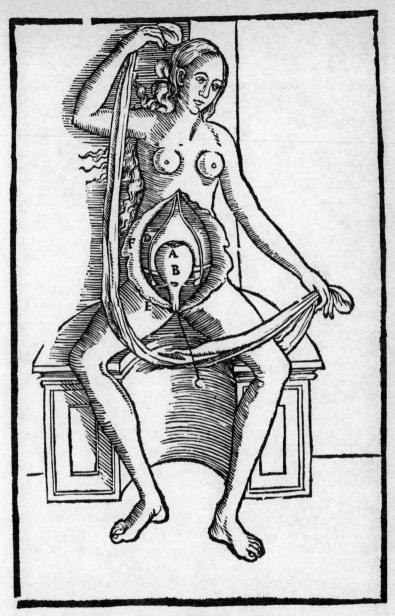

5　The essential woman
From *Anatomia Mundini* by I. Dryander

6   Combing, carding and spinning wool
From an early 15th-century royal manuscript

the first cause and beginning of every action which conduces to the generation of the animal, the other (viz., the brain) of every action done for its preservation. And just as a 'desire' arises from a conception of the brain, and this conception springs from some external object of desire, so also from the male, as being the more perfect animal, and, as it were, the most natural object of desire, does the natural (organic) conception arise in the uterus, even as the animal conception does in the brain.

From this desire, or conception, it results that the female produces an offspring like the father. For just as we, from the conception of the 'form' or 'idea' in the brain, fashion in our works a form resembling it, so, in like manner, the 'idea', or 'form', of the father existing in the uterus generates an offspring like himself with the help of the formative faculty, impressing, however, on its work its own immaterial 'form.' [On Conception, in *The Works of William Harvey*][8]

COITUS

The biology of intercourse is pertinent here because theory presupposed a vital relationship between coitus and good health in women. It was suggested that women need or use men for reasons of health. Thus Hippocrates:

The woman feels pleasure from the beginning and throughout intercourse. . . . If she has an orgasm, she ejaculates before the man does and ceases to feel the same degree of pleasure; if she does not have an orgasm, her pleasure ceases at the same time as the man's. . . . Woman's sensation of heat and pleasure comes to a climax at the moment when the sperm falls into the matrix [used by the ancients to mean both vagina and uterus], then everything stops. If one throws wine on a flame, the flame flares and is momentarily increased by this affusion, then it dies way; in the same fashion, the [woman's sensation of] heat is intensified by the contact of the male sperm, then dies away. In intercourse women feel a great deal less pleasure than men do, but they feel it longer. If men feel a more intense pleasure, it is because the discharge of liquid is brusquer in their case and provoked by a more acute excitement than that experienced by women. Another point should be borne in mind: if women are having sexual intercourse, their health is better for it.... One reason for this is that during intercourse the matrix becomes moist and ceases to be dry. Now, when the matrix is dry it contracts sharply and this contraction causes pain. A second reason is that intercourse, by heating and moistening of the blood, makes it easier for the menstrual blood to flow; and when menstrual blood does not flow, women become sickly. [Hippocrates, *Oeuvres*][9]

The encyclopedic and influential thinker Albertus Magnus (1193?–1280), like other leading contemporaries and his greatest disciple (St Thomas), took over many of the biological views of Greek antiquity. A probable work of his on the subject of women and sex, occasionally attributed to Roger Bacon and others, was much quoted and cited:

Chap. XIII. [Speaking of men:] Too much ejaculation dries out the body because the sperm has the power of humidifying and heating. But when warmth and moisture are drawn out of the body, the system is weakened and death follows. This is why men who copulate too much and too often do not live long, for bodies drained of their natural humidity dry out and the dryness causes death.

Chap. IX. The womb is frequently subject to suffocation [*sic*]. Suffocation is the name doctors give to a constriction of the vital breathing caused by a defect in the womb. This hinders the woman's breathing. It happens whenever the womb moves from its proper place. [It was believed in antiquity and down to the sixteenth century that the womb could move about in the body, lodge in the throat, and cause choking.] Then, as a result of a chill in the heart, women sometimes swoon, feel a weakness in the heart, or suffer dizziness....

This illness befalls women when they are full of spoiled and poisonous menstrual blood. It would therefore be good for such women, whoever they be, whether young or old, to have frequent sexual intercourse so as to expel this matter. It is particularly good for young women, as they are full of moisture. This is why young women, when they begin to have sexual intercourse, grow very fat before conceiving and feel little anxiety about children.... Young women, when they are full of such matter, feel a strong desire for sex just because this matter abounds in them. It is therefore a sin, in nature, to keep them from it and stop them from having sex with the man they favor, although [their doing so] is a sin according to accepted morality. But this is another question. [Albertus Magnus, *De Secretis Mulierum*][10]

Thus we move, as if by a natural process, from the biology of intercourse to the question of feminine maladies. A link between the two was presupposed by both Hippocrates and Albertus, as well as by many other writers on the subject. Hippocrates made this additional observation:

Women who have not had children are particularly prone to all mishaps; but those who have are not immune either. These [malfunctions] are serious ... usually acute, intense, and hard to diagnose, for women also suffer from illnesses [common to both sexes]. Sometimes they do not themselves know what ails them until they grow older and acquire experience of the disorders caused by their menstrual periods.... Often the maladies are incurable by the time the patient has told a doctor of the source of her trouble. Indeed, even when they do know, women often keep silent from modesty. Ignorance and inexperience make them imagine such things are shameful. Moreover, doctors make the mistake of failing to inquire precisely into the cause of the illness, and they prescribe as they would for a masculine illness. I have seen more than one woman succumb in this way. [Hippocrates, *Oeuvres*][11]

And no doubt 'modesty' – that is to say, a particular set of absorbed values – was for centuries the chief obstacle to more effective or more informed means of contraception.   The second-century (A.D.) physician and gynecologist Soranus of Ephesus long remained one of the leading authorities.

Bk. I, xix, 60   A contraceptive differs from an abortive, for the first does not let conception take place, while the latter destroys what has been conceived....

61   [To keep from conceiving], at the critical moment of coitus when the man is about to discharge the seed, the woman must hold her breath and draw herself away a little, so that the

seed may not be hurled too deep into the cavity of the uterus. . . .
It also aids in preventing conception to smear the orifice of the
uterus all over before with old olive oil or honey or cedar resin
or juice of the balsam tree, alone or together with white lead;
[prescribes more ointments]; or to put a lock of fine wool into
the orifice of the uterus; or, before sexual relations to use vaginal suppositories which have the power to contract and to con-
dense. [There follows a long series of potions, as well as applica-
tions and suppositories of dried fruit and peels, barks, oils, alum,
and herbs.] . . .

63   . . . Others, however, have even made use of amulets on
grounds of antipathy . . . such are uteri of mules and the dirt in
their ears and more things of this kind which according to the
outcome reveal themselves as falsehoods.

64   Yet if conception has taken place, [then prescribes strenuous exercises]. . . . [Moreover] she should use diuretic decoc-
tions which also have the power to bring on menstruation, and
empty and purge the abdomen with relatively pungent clysters
. . . . If this is without effect, one must also treat locally by having her sit in a bath of a decoction of linseed, fenugreek, mallow,
marsh mallow, and wormwood. She must also use poultices of
the same substances. . . .

65   For a woman who intends to have an abortion, it is necessary for two or even three days beforehand to take protracted
baths, little food, and to use softening vaginal suppositories; also
to abstain from wine; then to be bled and a relatively great
quantity taken away. [Quotes Hippocrates:] 'A pregnant
woman, if bled, miscarries.' [Then again prescribes strenuous
movements and continues with remedies involving sitz baths,
suppositories, and potions.] [Soranus of Ephesus *Gynecology*][12]

VIII   *The Later Middle Ages*

1 The Christian Context

The Middle Ages stretch from roughly 500 to 1300 or even 1500, depending upon whether the emphasis is on northern or southern Europe, rural society or cities, popular culture or the accomplishments of an elite. The final and the opening phases of periods overlap confusingly. Having treated the period before 1000 in Chapter V, we turn here mainly to the period after 1000 and begin with the religious context of our story.

NOT IN GOD'S IMAGE: THE DOUBLE CURRENT

Christian theory was egalitarian. Imperial Rome had seen a good deal of emancipation for women. The church fathers were not, however, metropolitan Romans but provincials whose thinking reflected their own social milieux and Jewish accents on the religious and legal incapacity of women. Texts from the Roman law, many obsolete, were used to justify the Greco-Jewish bent for keeping women away from public functions (e.g., the priesthood) and subordinate to the male. Yet since women had to be acknowledged as spiritual equals—their souls were not less worthy than men's—some discomfort came forth. A double current is discernible in the thinking of Christian writers and sometimes in that of a single writer. St Paul is illustrative and instructive (here the translation is from the Authorized Version):

There is neither Jew nor Greek, there is neither bond nor free, there is neither male nor female: for ye are all one in Christ Jesus. [*Galatians* 3:28]

The head of the woman is the man.... For a man indeed ought not to cover his head, forasmuch as he is the image and glory of God: but the woman is the glory of the man. For the man is not of the woman; but the woman of the man. Neither was the man created for the woman; but the woman for the man. [1 *Corinthians* 11: 3, 7–9]

Let your women keep silence in the churches: for it is not permitted unto them to speak; but they are commanded to be under obedience.... And if they will learn anything, let them ask their husbands at home: for it is a shame for a woman to speak in the church. [1 *Corinthians* 14: 34–5]

I suffer not a woman to teach, nor to usurp authority over

the man, but to be in silence. For Adam was first formed, then
Eve. And Adam was not deceived, but the woman being deceived was in the transgression. Notwithstanding she shall be saved
in childbearing, if they [women] continue in faith and charity
and holiness with sobriety. [1 *Timothy* 2: 12–15]

Wives, submit yourselves unto your own husbands, as unto
the Lord. For the husband is the head of the wife. . . . Husbands,
love your wives, even as Christ also loved the church, and gave
himself for it. . . . So ought men to love their wives as their own
bodies. He that loveth his wife loveth himself. For no man ever
yet hated his own flesh; but nourisheth and cherisheth it, even
as the Lord the church: for we are members of his body, of his
flesh, and of his bones. For this cause shall a man leave his
father and mother, and shall be joined unto his wife, and they
two shall be one flesh. [*Ephesians* 5: 22–3, 25, 28–31]

*The paradox in Paul's words elicited gloss without end. Woman was not
perhaps made in God's image, but was she man's equal? Well, spiritually
yes, she must be equal but—the notion oozes persistently through the
subtleties—her spirituality is meshed more intimately with the flesh. It is
borne down, more earthy, somehow more animal. St John Chrysostom
(345?–407), a leading church father, drew out the childbearing theme:*

The woman taught once, and ruined all. On this account . . .
let her not teach. But what is it to other women that she suffered
this? It certainly concerns them; for the sex is weak and fickle.
. . . The whole female race transgressed. . . . Let her not, however, grieve. God hath given her no small consolation, that of
childbearing. . . . By these means women will have no small
reward on their account, because they have trained up wrestlers
for the service of Christ. [*Works of Chrysostom*][1]

*The greatest of the church fathers, St Augustine (354–430), confronted
the paradox in this fashion:*

. . . What then? Have women not this renewal of the mind in
which is the image of God? Who would say this? But in the sex
of their body they do not signify this; therefore they are bidden
to be veiled. The part, namely, which they signify in the very

fact of their being women, is that which may be called the concupiscential part. [Augustine, *Of the Work of Monks*][2]

But we must notice how that which the apostle says, that not the woman but the man is the image of God, is not contrary to that which is written in Genesis, 'God created man: in the image of God created He him; male and female created He them.'.... For this text says that human nature itself, which is complete [only] in both sexes, was made in the image of God; and it does not separate the woman from the image of God which it signifies.... The woman together with her own husband is the image of God, so that the whole substance may be one image; but when she is referred to separately in her quality of helpmate, which regards the woman herself alone, then she is not the image of God; but as regards the man alone, he is the image of God as fully and completely as when the woman too is joined with him. [Augustine, *On the Holy Trinity*][3]

The call to give woman a separate definition persisted, indeed haunts us still, even with the veil of theological terminology torn away. That the problem was formulated at all—as if women somehow had a destiny different from men—is itself revealing. And the discourse was not significantly altered by the intellectual awakening of the twelfth century. We catch the familiar strains in the first enduring systematization of church law, the Decretum (c. 1140), the work of Gratian, a jurist from Bologna:

Women should be subject to their men. The natural order for mankind is that women should serve men and children their parents, for it is just that the lesser serve the greater.

The image of God is in man and it is one. Women were drawn from man, who has God's jurisdiction as if he were God's vicar, because he has the image of the one God. Therefore woman is not made in God's image.

Woman's authority is nil; let her in all things be subject to the rule of man.... And neither can she teach, nor be a witness, nor give a guarantee, nor sit in judgment.

Adam was beguiled by Eve, not she by him. It is right that he whom woman led into wrongdoing should have her under his direction, so that he may not fail a second time through female levity. [*Corpus Iuris Canonici*][4]

Forbidden to teach, to enter the priesthood, or even to touch the sacred vessels (Decretals, *III, ii, 1*), *women were left with a choice between virginity and marriage. The first, like martyrdom, was ideally for the select; the second was woman's normal function. This was of course the old Greek idea and therefore raises the question of Christianity's contribution to the advancement of women. St Thomas Aquinas* (*1225–74*), *the church's most authoritative thinker, combined traditional notions with Aristotelian biology:*

As regards the individual nature, woman is defective and misbegotten, for the active force in the male seed tends to the production of a perfect likeness in the masculine sex; while the production of woman comes from a defect in the active force or from some material indisposition, or even from some external influence.... On the other hand, as regards human nature in general, woman is not misbegotten, but is included in nature's intention as directed to the work of generation. Now the general intention of nature depends on God, Who is the universal Author of nature. Therefore, in producing nature, God formed not only the male but also the female.

[Takes up question of woman's being made from man.] When all things were first formed, it was more suitable for the woman to be made from the man than ... [as happens] in other animals. First, in order thus to give the first man a certain dignity consisting in this, that as God is the principle of the whole universe, so the first man, in likeness to God, was the principle of the whole human race.... Secondly, that man might love woman all the more, and cleave to her more closely, knowing her to be fashioned from himself.

[Takes up image question.] The image of God, in its principal signification, namely the intellectual nature, is found both in man and in woman. Hence after the words, 'To the image of God He created him,' it is added, 'Male and female He created them' (*Genesis* i. 27). Moreover it is said 'them' in the plural ... lest it should be thought that both sexes were united in one individual. But in a secondary sense the image of God is found in man, and not in woman: for man is the beginning and end of woman; as God is the beginning and end of every creature. [Aquinas, *Summa Theologica*][5]

THE DEVIL'S GATEWAY

The early Christians were ascetic. For a man trying to be chaste a woman was, in the church's words, 'an occasion of sin'; in Tertullian's words, 'the devil's gateway'. One of the founders of ecclesiastical Latinity, the influential and austere Tertullian (c. 160–230) had this to say about women:

And so a veil must be drawn over a beauty so dangerous as to have brought scandal into heaven itself, so that before God, in whose eyes it is guilty of the angels' fall, it may blush in the presence of the remaining angels and give up the license to show itself and hide even from the eyes of men. [Tertullian, *De Virginibus Velandis*][6]

If our faith here below were on the scale of the wages awaiting it in heaven, not one of you, my dear sisters, once she had come to know God and her own condition—I am speaking of her condition as a woman—would be hot after pleasure and finery. Rather would she wear rags and mourning, weep and show an Eve plunged in penance, trying to expiate by her contrite appearance the disgrace of that first crime and the shame of having brought ruin to humanity. In pain shall you bring forth children, woman, and you shall turn to your husband and he shall rule over you. And do you not know that you are Eve? God's sentence hangs still over all your sex and His punishment weighs down upon you. You are the devil's gateway; you are she who first violated the forbidden tree and broke the law of God. It was you who coaxed your way around him whom the devil had not the force to attack. With what ease you shattered that image of God: man! Because of the death you merited, the Son of God had to die. And yet you think of nothing but covering your tunics with ornaments? [Passage on fineries: silk, dyes, precious gems, gold, mirrors.] . . . If Eve now hopes to live again, let her not long for, nor even know, things that she neither had nor knew when she was alive. For all this baggage, encumbering a woman already dead and sentenced, adds up to hardly more than the trappings of her funeral procession. [Tertullian, *De Cultu Feminarum*][7]

Clement of Alexandria (c.150–c. 220), probably born in Athens, struck the same keynote:

But women ... aiming at the graceful ... throw back their heads and bare their necks indecently ... and gulp down the liquor as if to make bare all they can to their boon companions. ... Nothing disgraceful is proper for man, who is endowed with reason; much less for woman, to whom it brings shame even to reflect of what nature she is.... By no manner of means are women to be allowed to uncover and exhibit any part of their person, lest both fall—the men by being excited to look, they by drawing on themselves the eyes of men. [*The Writings of Clement of Alexandria*][8]

MARRIAGE AND THE CHURCH

The medieval church claimed jurisdiction over questions relating to marriage and divorce (i.e., annulment). In principle a uniform marriage law came to prevail throughout Europe. The aims of matrimony were held to be reproduction and the remedying of incontinence; the relationship was also dignified by the Pauline comparison with the union between Christ and the church. Adultery by the husband—no crime in Roman law until very late—was punished by canon law, which aimed, with no success, to base separation and divorce upon the same grounds for both parties. The church succeeded in making consent of the parties a necessary condition for valid matrimony. Proof of constraint was supposed to invalidate the contract. Parental consent as a necessary condition was dropped in the twelfth century, but practice stifled theory. Parents and feudal overlords easily brought irresistible pressures on children of both sexes, and girls—whose consent was valid from the age of twelve, two years earlier than boys— were in the weaker position.

Following are two papal letters on specific cases; they inadvertently point up the limitations of the church's power. Marriage had impediments of consanguinity: the prohibition to marry was extended to the seventh generation of descendants from a common ancestor (reduced to the fourth generation by the Lateran Council of 1215). Pope Alexander III to the Bishop of St Asaph in England (c. 1179):

M, a noble lady, has sought the mercy of the apostolic see and stated in her petition to us that when she was a little girl she was given by her parents to be the wife of R, knight, son of R. After three or four years the marriage was called in question both by her relations and her husband's as being within the fourth or fifth degree or nearer. The aforesaid R, disturbed by this, fetched home the said M who hitherto had remained at her parents' house, and kept her for three years as if she were a prisoner. At length when she had returned to her own home those who were raising the question of the relationship between them had both her and the man summoned before the Bishop of Lincoln. . . . But the man went to . . . the Archbishop of Canterbury, legate of the apostolic see . . . and asked that the aforesaid woman . . . be restored to him by ecclesiastical judgment. And when the Archbishop had committed the case to be investigated . . . and subsequently came into their district both parties appeared before him, and R, urgently demanding his wife, she constantly replied that she could not and ought not to return to him, as well because she often feared schemes against her life as that she was, as she constantly asserted, related to him in close line of consanguinity, and showing herself to be pregnant and near to childbirth she added that she now had to face a greater danger in that by the injuries which she suffered from certain of her husband's relations and attendants she might bring forth prematurely and scarcely escape death. But the man persisted with his petition and asserted that neither by himself nor by anyone else at his command, desire, or approval had any schemes or injuries been prepared against her, and that no consanguinity could be reckoned between them. The Archbishop, because the woman was near to childbirth and he wished to take care for the life and safety of both her and her child, arranged for her to stay with some neighboring nuns or other honest women until she had borne her child and could fittingly plead the case against her husband. And when he had several times enjoined the man to provide the necessary equipment for his wife and to await the expected birth, the latter refusing to do so unless he was allowed to place her where he wished, appealed to the apostolic see. . . . She then returned to Lincoln to prepare herself to prosecute the appeal, and when she thought that the man would come with an armed band to her she took refuge in the church of St Margaret, and after she had clung to the door of the church for some time, appealing and having the Archbishop's letters in her hands, a certain dean, scorning the appeal, had the doors of the church opened. The man entered and dared to pursue her with drawn sword to the altar, and at length compelled her to promise that she would accept and observe whatever should be decided in this matter by two men chosen on her side and two on his, and that she would no longer compel him to go to the judgment of the church.... We command your discretion by letters apostolic to inquire into the truth of the matter, and if it appears to you lawfully that the said man, after the appeal had been made, pursued the said woman with naked sword in the church and compelled her to promise to accept the judgment in this case of four friends whom they both should choose, you shall, without appeal, absolve her from the observance of the promise, and then you shall carefully hear the case about the relationship and bring it to a canonical end without appeal. And as the woman seems to allege a just fear as well for her inheritance which she is unwilling to lose as for other reasons which we have stated above, we do not wish the man to have any pretext for seeking her again before the opening of the case. [*Papal Decretals Relating to the Diocese of Lincoln in the Twelfth Century*][9]

Canon law made it difficult for adulterers to remarry when a legitimate partner died. Dispensations were, however, granted, except in cases in which the adulterer had given his or her accomplice a sworn promise to marry after a spouse's death. In such cases, fearing that the adulterers might be tempted to murder the obstacle to their union, the church forbade any marriage between them. This comment throws light on the following letter from Pope Celestine to the Bishop of Lincoln (c. 1195):

Whereas John, bearer of these presents, had a lawful wife, Alice by name, he committed the crime of adultery with Maxilla, which he himself unfolded to you in public confession, as your letters directed to us have shown, and when he was summoned to law in this matter he abjured the said M in court as an adulteress but afterwards he set aside and scorned his oath, and during the lifetime of his lawful wife he dared to contract a form of marriage with the said M and for long lived with her in adultery. Then, the abovementioned Alice having died, the said John nevertheless remained with the said adulteress for ten years and begot ten sons by her. Because, therefore, you ask whether the said John and M may remain together, or if they ought to be separated whether it is lawful for them to contract other marriages, we reply to your consultation that they ought to be separated altogether, and when a suitable penance has been enjoined perpetual continency should be imposed upon them, particularly as they are both advanced in years and by knowingly continuing for so long in public adultery and perjury have disturbed the church by grave scandal. For you know that Pope Leo decreed that no one should marry a woman whom he had defiled with adultery, and this case has gone further than a promise to the adulteress to marry her on the death of the lawful wife, for even during the latter's lifetime the adulterer dared to cleave to the adulteress as if in marriage and presumptuously violate his oath. Both Pope Gregory and the Council of Tribur condemn such a marriage in which there is no bond of oath, and decree that both parties to such a union be put to public penance and remain for ever unmarried. Nor is it any extenuation which would allow J and M to remain together that they lived together for ten years and begat ten sons, since the multiplicity of offspring thus begotten rather exaggerates the crime, and the length of time increases rather than reduces the sin. It shall, however, be part of your care to see that they both provide for their children and supply what is necessary for their support in so far as their means allow. [*Papal Decretals*][10]

2 Virginity

The ideal of virginity has an illustrious and stubborn history, especially in its bearing upon the formation of the cardinal feminine virtue (chastity). Constantly associated with purity and transcendent athleticism, as well as with treasure hoards, precious stones, private property, special and even magical effects, virginity occasioned a whole mode of mystification. It was reified: converted to a grab bag of values. There men saw the pure and the valuable, the abstract and the tactile; they saw their own honor and virility on the day of marriage; they saw the opposite of their own 'lust', and 'carnality'; and they saw that a chaste wife was property. Women, the vessels of virginity, nurtured on the mystification, readily accepted it— that stick wherewith to beat all who were not virginal or chaste and modest. Virginity was woman's particular security, supremely so on the day of marriage. A woman who was not a virgin on that day could scarcely, it was thought, remain chaste thereafter; and this sort of thing made paternity uncertain, mongrelized the family, and endowed the unworthy with property.

VIRGINITY ABOVE MARRIAGE

It is good for a man not to touch a woman.... I say therefore to the unmarried and widows, it is good for them if they abide even as I. But if they cannot contain, let them marry: for it is better to marry than to burn.... The unmarried woman careth for the things of the Lord, that she may be holy both in body and in spirit: but she that is married careth for the things of the world, how she may please her husband. [Paul, 1 *Corinthians* 7:1, 8–9, 34]

Now we are speaking to virgins: in them is the flower of the church, the honor and masterpiece of spiritual grace, a happy blossoming of nature ... the most brilliant portion of Christ's flock.... When the world was half formed and uninhabited, the race had to be propagated and human kind increased by generation. Now that the world is peopled and filled, those who can remain continent become eunuchs for the sake of the kingdom of heaven. The Lord does not demand it.... But when he says that there are many mansions in his father's house, he means that some places there are better than others. Those places are for you, virgins. [St Cyprian, *De Habitu Virginum*]¹¹

Scarcely had they [Adam and Eve] turned from obedience to God than they became earth and ashes and, all at once, they lost the happy life, beauty and the honor of virginity: thereupon God took virginal chastity from them.... Then they were made serfs, stripped of the royal robe ... made subject to death and every other form of curse and imperfection; then did marriage make its appearance with the mortal and servile garment of human nature.... Do you see where marriage took its origin? How it had of necessity to be preceded by the breaking of the divine commandment, by malediction and death? For where there is death, there too is sexual coupling; and where there is no death, there is no sexual coupling either. But virginity is not accompanied by such things. [Chrysostom, *Della Verginità*]¹²

Similar echoes are strikingly combined in a poem written for two Frankish nuns by the poet Fortunatus (530–609), Bishop of Poitiers:

Consider Him who chose to be born of a virgin.... Happy virginity found worthy of giving birth to a God, and of creating its Creator. The chaste limbs of virgins are his temples: therein He dwells and is at ease. Freely He penetrates viscera known only to Himself and with greater joy enters paths where none has ever been. These limbs, he feels, are His own: unsoiled and unshared by any man. Tenderly and with affection He kisses the breast.... He wants to live alone in the house of virgins. There he is king....

Happy virgin!.... She does not weigh down sluggish limbs with an imprisoned embryo; she is not depressed and worn out by its awkward weight....When the belly swells from its wound and sensual dropsy grows, the woman's exhausted health hangs by a hair. The raised skin is so distent and misshapen that even though the mother may be happy with her burden, she becomes ashamed.... How describe the tears shed at the moment when the muscles relax to release the prisoner and procure relief for the viscera? A way is forced violently through the passage and a being, perhaps lifeless, brought to life. The mother painfully

7 Jealous husband beating wife
From a 15th-century manuscript

8 Woman bleeding a pig
From an early 16th-century Flemish calendar

turns her dull glance toward him. What does she see? An infant stretched motionless....so that she no longer deserves to be called either mother or virgin. [Fortunatus, *Opera Poetica*][13]

Virgins are 'the more honored portion of Christ's flock and their glory more sublime' [quoting St Cyprian] in comparison with widows and married women. The hundredfold fruit is ascribed to virginity, according to St Jerome, on account of its superiority to widowhood, to which the sixtyfold fruit is ascribed, and to marriage, to which is ascribed the thirtyfold fruit....

The error of Jovian consisted in holding virginity not to be preferable to marriage. This error is refuted above all by the example of Christ Who both chose a virgin for His mother and remained Himself a virgin. [Aquinas, *Summa Theologica*][14]

CONSECRATED VIRGINITY : NUNS

Having no doubts about the superior merits of the celibate life, the medieval church had no scruples about forced vocations.

If a woman, become the spiritual bride of Christ, should afterwards openly marry, she may not be admitted to do penance unless her marriage partner withdraws from the world [to a monastery]. For if men reckon one who marries a second time, while her first husband still lives, to be an adulteress debarred from doing penance until one of the two men die, how much truer must this be of the woman who, being united to an immortal spouse, turns afterwards to human marriage [*Corpus Iuris Canonici*][15]

For all the emphasis on spiritual ties, the bond between virgin nun and Holy Spouse was invariably represented by the poetics of physical union. The point surely was better made that way. Germany furnished the best terrain for the aims of consecrated virginity, for ascetic women and their susceptibility to ecstatic visions. The outstanding names are Jutta of Spanheim (fl. 1100), Hildegard of Bingen (1099–1179), Elizabeth of Schönau (c. 1128–65), and Mechthild of Magdeburg (c. 1212– c. 1285): noblewomen all, ascetic, tough, mystical, and hallucinative. Their ideal pervades a thirteenth-century poem on the life of Mary.

The poem was very popular in fourteenth- and fifteenth-century convent circles. We select a passage in which the imagery of family is directly transformed into the imagery of physical love. The 'holy and pure' Mary speaks to God:

You are my father, you are my brother, you are my sister and my mother. You are my husband, you are my lord, you are my king and all my honor. You are my sustenance and comfort; in you I shall not perish. You are my beloved bridegroom; to you I give my maidenhood. You are my handsome husband; I long to be with you always. You are my lover and my friend: I'm set on fire by your love. [Philip the Carthusian, *Marienleben*][16]

Jacques de Vitry (1180–1240), a French cardinal legate, visited many convents and drew the following picture:

You saw, banded together, many holy virgins who despised the attractions of the flesh and the riches of the world for the sake of the kingdom of heaven. Clinging in poverty and humility to their heavenly Spouse, they earned a meager living with the labor of their hands, yet they came from very rich families. . . .

You saw mothers of families, fervent and modest, desiring only their celestial Spouse; wives, leading an angelic and celibate life with the consent of their husbands; widows, serving the Lord through prayers, vigils, manual labor, tears, supplications, and often remembering the words of the apostle 'the widow that liveth in pleasure is dead'. . . .[1 *Timothy* 5:6]

You saw women so utterly melted by a singular and marvelous love of God that they seemed to succumb as if from the weight of desire, so that for many years they rarely got up from their beds. Their only infirmity was in the desire of their melted souls. Resting sweetly with the Lord, they became infirm of body according as they were comforted and strengthened in spirit; although crying out in their hearts, in modesty they murmured something else: 'Stay me with flowers, comfort me with fruits, for I languish of love' [*Vulgate*, Cant. 2:11]. . . .

Many of these women had the actual taste of honey on their lips, as it welled up richly from the sweet spiritual honeycomb

in their hearts, drawing forth sweet tears and maintaining the
mind in devotion....

Others, again, were seized by such a drunkenness of the spirit
that they would pass into a state of holy silence for the whole
day, while 'The king was on his couch' [*Vulgate*, Cant. 1:7];
and they heard or felt nothing around them, the peace of God
having so overwhelmed and buried their senses, that no clamor
could wake them and they felt no corporal injury, however violently they might be struck. I saw one who guarded her Spouse
for nearly thirty years with so much zeal that no one could make
her come out of her cell, not even a thousand men trying to pull
her out by the hand. I saw another who was often possessed
by a kind of ecstasy twenty-five times in a day, and in that state
she remained perfectly motionless. A hand of hers might hang
in the air, immobile, in the position taken when going into the
trance. Then, returning to her senses, she was filled with such
intense pleasure that she had to express her joy by means of
violent dancing movements, like David leaping before the
Ark. [Jacques de Vitry, *Vita B. Mariae Ogniacensis*][17]

CHASTITY AND SPECIAL PROPERTIES

Women have one great advantage: it is enough for them to cultivate a single virtue if they wish to be well thought of. Men,
however, must have several if they wish to be esteemed. A man
must be courteous, generous, brave and wise. But if a woman
keeps her body intact, all her other defects are hidden and she
can hold her head high. [Philippe de Navarre, *Les Quatre Ages
de l'Homme*][18]

Every good quality is obscured in the girl or woman whose
virginity [or chastity] falters.... This is why women of sense
avoid not only the sin itself but also the appearance of it, so as
to keep the good name of virginity [and chastity].... Know
too that riches, beauty, and all other virtues are lost and as nothing in the woman so stained. For a woman need only be once
suspected for all to be utterly lost, ruined, and effaced without
hope of recovery.... So you see in what peril a woman places
her honor and that of her husband's lineage and of her children

when she does not avoid the risk of such blame. [Anon. moral treatise, 1393, *Le Ménagier de Paris*][19]

The age ascribed special and even magical properties to virginity:

The unicorn is a proud beast with a horse's body, an elephant's foot, a stag's neck, and a horn in the middle of his forehead.... And know that the unicorn is so wild and proud that none may reach him by any wile; he can be killed but not taken alive. And yet hunters send a virgin maid to the unicorn's hiding place, for it is in his nature to go straight to the maiden and, setting aside all wildness, to sleep on her lap. Such is how the hunters trick him. [Brunetto Latini, *Li Livres dou Tresor*][20]

Latini above was retailing common belief. Not surprisingly the unicorn came to symbolize Christ, and artists sometimes depicted the theme. There were some roundabout ways to ascertain virginity:

On jade. This stone gives proof of a person's virginity, for whoever drinks pulverized jade will not piss it out if he or she is a virgin; but if they are not, they piss it out at once, whether they want to or not. [Bartholomaeus Anglicus, *Les Propriétés des Choses*][21]

Virgins' urine is quite unclouded, bright, thin, and almost lemon color when healthy. The urine of the woman who has lost her virginity is very muddy and never bright or clear, save exceptionally when she is more than three months pregnant. [Michael Scot, *Physonomia*][22]

And note that there are great differences in women's urine. For the urine of virgins is a bit reddish and clear and very thin, and this is healthy. The urine of the woman who is not a virgin is always dense and a bit greasy and never clear. [Zuane Saraceno, *Recetario de Galeno Optimo*][23]

COUNTERFEITING VIRGINITY

Trotula, an eleventh-century woman doctor from Salerno, had remedies for damaged maidenheads. The prescriptions were compiled by a later Salernitan doctor, probably in the thirteenth century.

This remedy will be needed by any girl who has been induced to open her legs and lose her virginity by the follies of passion, secret love, and promises.... When it is time for her to marry, to keep the man from knowing, the false virgin may stop up [the passage] as follows. Let her take ground sugar and the white of an egg and mix them in rainwater in which alum, fleabane, and the dry wood of a vine have been boiled down with other similar herbs. Soaking a soft and porous cloth in this solution, let her keep bathing her private parts with it. The vagina ought to be fully washed. Or let her mix rainwater with well-ground fresh oak bark and make a suppository which she should insert in the vagina shortly before she expects to have intercourse. Or as follows: plantain, sumac ... oak galls, large black bryony, and alum cooked in rainwater and the private parts fomented with the mixture as above.... But best of all is this deception: the day before her marriage, let her put a leech very cautiously on the labia, taking care lest it slip in by mistake; then she should allow blood to trickle out and form a crust on the orifice; the flux of blood will tighten the passage. Thus may a false virgin deceive a man in intercourse. [*Collectio Salernitana*][24]

The Belgian physician Johann Wier (1516–88) observed:

It is very common in Spain for brides to preserve the linen showing the blood smears of their deflowering. There too certain women, greedy for money, are in the custom of selling girls several times over as virgins by falsifying the hymen with trickles of blood and other materials. [*De Praestigiis Daemonum*][25]

3 The View of the Law

A variety of legal systems characterized the different parts of medieval Europe; Roman and German influences, as well as local custom, competed in their formation. Generally speaking, the legal capacity or competence of women in law was limited. Until the seventeenth century, when the Courts of Equity devised ways of allowing married women to hold separate property, English law quite possibly put the greatest restraints upon women. Throughout Europe the appropriate body of law sought to preserve property in the family and for children. Thus widows, whether their livelihood was guaranteed by dower or dowry, tended to have only the usufruct thereof if they had children. But whatever the specific legal condition of property in marriage, the variations in practical terms must have been slight: the husband administered matters and took decisions. The one notable exception to this occasionally involved married tradeswomen. In Spain and parts of Italy wives sometimes administered their own possessions during marriage, at least in principle; and in the north wives had a claim to dower. Much, however, depended upon the ascendancy of the husband, who could persuade his wife to sign property away, or upon the power and willingness of her family to intervene. The succeeding pages will draw upon a variety of legal collections; the resulting sketch will be suggestive and generalized.

LEGAL RIGHTS AND INCAPACITIES

There is no reason to parade readings on the exclusion of women from public office. The fact is well known. By her exceptional status, the queen or female regent had so little to do with any discernible norm that any document centering upon her immediately loses all representativeness. Medieval queens were not freakish, but their effective authority was. Again, a female lawyer would have been impossible. How could women, by nature hasty, inconstant, and indiscreet—such the language of certain laws – fill the high office of advocate? Indeed, there were restrictions on woman's competence in courts of law:

France, 1270. No married woman can go to court ... unless someone has abused or beaten her, in which case she may go to court without her husband. If she is a tradeswoman, she can sue and defend herself in matters connected with her business, but not otherwise. [*Les Etablissements de Saint Louis*][26]

An English lawyer put things a little more colorfully:

Every Feme Covert [married woman] is a sort of infant....

It is seldom, almost never that a married woman can have any action to use her wit only in her own name: her husband is her stern, her prime mover, without whom she cannot do much at home, and less abroad.... It is a miracle that a wife should commit any suit without her husband. [*The Lawes Resolutions of Womens Rights*][27]

The autonomous cities of medieval Italy had similar laws:

City of Pesaro. No wife can make a contract without the consent of her husband. [E. Rodocanachi, *La Femme italienne*][28]

Florence, 1415. A married woman with children cannot draw up a last will in her own right, nor dispose of her dowry among the living to the detriment of her husband and children. [*Statuta Florentiae*][29]

Lucca. No married woman ... can sell or give away [anything] unless she has the agreement of her husband and nearest [male] relative. [Rodocanachi, *La Femme italienne*][30]

But the city of Belluno (1424) allowed her to give up to one-fourth the value of her estate as a bequest for the good of her soul, and Rome (statutes, 1580) allowed up to one-tenth.

German customary law was more strict in its restraints on women. The most famous and authoritative of all German regional codes, the Mirror of Saxony *(c. 1230), heavily traditional, declared:*

When a man takes a wife, he also takes all her goods into his power by right of guardianship. [*Der Sachsenspiegel*][31]

The reference above is to the old and enduring institution of Vormundschaft, *which put all German women under the guardianship of the father or husband or nearest male relative. In court cases he represented her, and all lawsuits or summonses involving her were addressed to him. Similarly, in Spain, the most authoritative late medieval code,*

Las Siete Partidas *(compiled 1256–65), reveals a strong distaste for having women appear in court, particularly women of property, wives, widows, and young girls (III, vii, 3).*

In England, generally, married women owned nothing and could not incur debts. Thus Chief Justice Fineux in 1506:

A married woman cannot make a contract to her husband's loss or prejudice but can if it is to his profit. Thus I can give a married woman a gift and the husband agree to it, but if a married woman make a contract or buy something in the market, this is not valid since the cost may be a burden to her husband. But my wife can buy something for her own use and I can ratify the purchase. If I order my wife to buy necessaries and she buys them, I shall be held responsible because of the general authorization given her. But if my wife buys things for my household, like bread, etc., without my knowledge, I shall not be held responsible for it even if it was consumed in my household. [*Year Book 21, Henry VII*][32]

But Fineux's words did not cover all circumstances. Under the traditional blanket of restraining laws, in England as on the Continent, economic and social change was making gradual alterations in the law. Businesswomen and tradeswomen were the principal benefactors. During the later Middle Ages, they begin to appear in the courts both as plaintiffs and as defendants. At Magdeburg, Cologne, and other German cities certain married women acceded to the right to retain particular movables as their exclusive property disposable at will. Childless widows often regained full rights over property in France, Italy, and Spain. In such cases we may say that the death of one partner was the legal liberation of the other. But even where the general thrust of the law contained women, as in England, certain cities, drawing upon proviso or local custom, made allowances for increasing the legal capacity of married tradeswomen. The example of London must suffice and conclude (act dated 1419):

Where a woman coverte de baron [i.e., married] follows any craft within the said city by herself apart, with which the husband in no way intermeddles, such a woman should be bound as a single woman in a Court of Record, she shall have her law and other advantages by way of plea just as a single woman. And if she is condemned she shall be committed to prison until she shall have made satisfaction; and neither the husband nor his goods shall in such case be charged or interfered with. If a wife, as though a single woman, rents any house or shop within the said city, she shall be bound to pay the rent ... and shall be impleaded [prosecuted] and sued as a single woman, by way of debt if necessary, notwithstanding that she was coverte de baron, at the time of such letting, supposing that the lessor did not know thereof. [Alice Clark, *Working Life of Women in the Seventeenth Century*][33]

SUCCESSION AND INHERITANCE

Succession and inheritance might be determined by the military exigencies of feudal right. Hence noblemen were apt to live by one law, burghers and rustics by another. Moreover, as the law also had regional variations, we shall illustrate only a few representative solutions. Brothers preceded sisters in feudal law, as in this text from Philippe de Beaumanoir (1246–96), a French lawyer:

Where an inheritance descends to children and there is a male heir, the firstborn male takes the principal manor and, over and above that, two parts of each fief. The remaining third shall then be shared out equally among the younger children, both male and female.

Sisters in the direct line of inheritance take one-third of fiefs but no share of those left by collaterals if there is a male heir of the same degree of relationship to the deceased; in the absence of such a male heir, they may, however, inherit.

It has been stated that sisters take no share of fiefs left by collaterals, but if the inheritance is leasehold land, then they share equally with the males, for no matter what its origin, leasehold land is equally shared between males and females. [*Coutumes de Beauvaisis*][34]

Something like the foregoing principle, more restrictive, once obtained in English law:

Because women lose the name of their ancestors, and by

marriage usually are transferred into another family, they participate seldom in heirship with males. Bracton [English jurist, d. 1268] is bold to say, 'A woman is never called to succeed as long as there is a male,' but to this rule he subjoineth exception. [*The Lawes Resolutions of Womens Rights*][35]

Another solution preserved the privilege of males by dowering daughters and thereby excluding them from the major inheritance. The Italian cities favored this solution:

But the sister may ask for no share of her father's inheritance if her brother procures a decent match for her and gives her a dowry. Milan, 1216.

Married daughters or granddaughters may not inherit with the males; they must be content with their dowries. Venice, 1232.

If a woman has received anything from her brother, let her be content and let her not be able to inherit anything more. Pistoria, 1296. [A. Pertile, *Storia del diritto italiano*][36]

Spanish law treated the sexes as equals in matters of inheritance:

A woman should succeed equally with her brothers to the estate of the father and mother; also to the estate of the brothers and sisters. Moreover, she should succeed [as an equal with her brothers] to the estate of her uncles, aunts, and children. For it is right that those whom nature has made equal in kinship [to the deceased] should succeed equally to the estate. (*Fuero Jusgo*)[37]

PROPERTY

Woman's role as perpetuator ('the vessel of life') was most vital and beset by risks when her family had property. This power base, a tangible and almost sacramental manifestation of family identity, had to be passed on to true lineal descendants ('heirs of the body'). When she obtained title to property, she had to be watched; and if barren, she was perhaps no more than a caretaker. Some German cities made it possible for a husband and wife to draw up a contract which could issue in the woman's absolute title to ownership:

Date, 1264. Lambert, the road builder, and his wife, Aleida, agreed in the presence of the officials of the Holy Apostle's parish [in the city of Cologne] that whichever survives the other will have the right to alienate their properties to whomsoever it may be: namely, the house with yard in front of the old sheep gate and the bakehouse with yard nearby [proviso attached].

27 August, 1395. Be it known that the lord magistrates of Cologne witnessed and have the following instrument: that the barber Henry Loeff and his legitimate wife, Metza [now deceased], drew up an agreement to this effect, that if the couple was childless, the last living of the two will have the right to dispose of all their personal goods and immovables, present or future, according as he or she shall see fit. [*Die Kölner Schreinsbücher des 13. und 14. Jahrhunderts*][38]

The dominant norms for France and England were as follows:

A husband cannot sell his wife's property, nor burden it with perpetual expenses, without her consent or unless she has expressly given him power of attorney. [*Grand Coutumier de France*][39]

If it should happen that a man sells his property during his wife's lifetime and ... dies before she does, she takes her dower [from the property]; but as soon as she dies, the property reverts to the buyer....

As long as they live together, the husband is the administrator and the wife must obey and allow him to decide everything with regard to movables. [*Coutumes de Beauvaisis*][40]

Movables are by custom bestowed upon the husband. [*Très Ancienne Coutume de Bretagne*][41]

England. The very goods which a man giveth to his wife, are still his own, her chain, her bracelets, her apparel, are all the goodman's goods.... A wife however gallant soever she be, glittereth but in the riches of her husband, as the moon hath no light but it is the sun's....

For thus it is, if before marriage the woman was possessed of horses ... sheep, corn, wool, money, plate and jewels, all manner of movable substance is presently ... the husband's to sell, keep or bequeath if she die. [*The Lawes Resolutions*][42]

England. The manner is, that the land which the wife bringeth to the marriage or purchaseth afterwards, the husband cannot sell or alienate the same, no, not with her consent, nor she herself during the marriage, except that she be alone examined by a judge at the common law: and if he have no child by her and she die, the land goeth to her next heirs at the common law: but if in the marriage he have a child by her, which is heard once to cry, whether the child live or die, the husband shall have the usufruct of her lands [that is the profit of them during his life] and that is called the courtisie of England. [Thomas Smith, *De Republica Anglorum*][43]

An English husband could alienate the third of his properties due to his wife as dower, but only if he got her consent. The anonymous legal adviser to women was not greatly impressed:

What cannot men get their wives to do.... She shall be barred and forever excluded from a great many acres for a few kisses and a gay gown. [*The Lawes Resolutions*][44]

Dower: that portion of a husband's property over which his widow had the right of enjoyment during her lifetime. In principle the following norms obtained in France and Spain.

France. The general custom of dower is for the wife to take half of what her husband owned on their wedding day. [*Coutumes de Beauvaisis*][45]

If the husband owned nothing and his father or grandfather who held the land was present and agreed [to the marriage], then the woman shall have dower on all their possessions. [A. Loisel, *Institutes Coustumiers*][46]

A noblewoman receives one-third of her husband's lands in dower. But her husband may give her any acquests [c. 1270]. [*Les Etablissements de Saint Louis*][47]

Spain, 1240–65. If a husband gives something to his wife and after his death she lives in chastity, or if she remarries properly, she may do as she pleases with the gift, provided she bore him no children. [*Fuero Jusgo*] [48]

What portion of the possessions of a rich husband can a poor woman legally inherit if she should marry without a dowry and has nothing to live from? In this case she can inherit up to one-fourth, provided she has children, but not more than the value of 100 pounds gold, however large the estate. But if the woman has enough to keep her decently, she can claim nothing. [*Las Siete Partidas*][49]

SEPARATION AND DIVORCE

Although European civil law had much to say about the status of married women, the bonds of marriage were beset by uncertainty. Ecclesiastical efforts to achieve uniformity failed. Marriage often went unsolemnized, bastardy was rampant, and attested legitimacy not seldom turned out to be dubious. All the more were questions of separation and divorce (i.e., annulment) likely to be flanked by doubt. Extreme brutality occasionally ended in legal separation. But generally speaking, consanguinity, adultery, impotence, and leprosy were the effective grounds for separation or divorce. In Spain, exceptionally, owing to the significant presence and 'crossing over' of Jews and Muslims, apostasy or heresy could also provide reason for divorce.

France. Should a husband be or become of so cold a nature as to be unable to have carnal relations with his wife of the sort proper between husband and wife, then the prelate grants perpetual divorce to the couple and the woman may remarry according to her will and pleasure.

Divorce comes about by adultery when the husband discovers and can prove that his wife has been committing adultery. Know that this divorce is not perpetual: the law always hopes for a reconciliation.... If the divorce does take place, know that the wife has a right to a portion sufficient to keep her in accordance with her condition. If, however, the wife left of her own free will without being forced to do so by her husband, or if the husband caught her in the act of fornication and for this reason turned her out of the house, know that in such circumstances the wife has no claim to any subsistence money and that if she has a dowry, she shall lose it. Some laws, however, provide that the wife should even then be allowed money enough to keep her. [Jean Boutillier, *Somme Rurale*][50]

A decent woman has to suffer and endure a great deal before leaving her husband. But she may be excused for leaving him in certain cases. If the husband threatens to kill her, or refuses to give her food, drink, or clothes ... or when the husband wants to sell his wife's property or dower by force and maltreats her unbearably when she refuses to agree, or when he throws her out for no fault of her own; or when he keeps another woman in the house in the sight and knowledge of neighbors ... in such cases a woman may be excused for leaving and may have recourse to justice to request that subsistence be paid to her out of their common property.... [But] if her husband should wish to take her back and should agree to give her no further grounds for leaving, and she should refuse to return, then she shall not be granted subsistence.... And if the judge has granted her subsistence and she leads an immoral life while separated from her husband—sleeping with men or keeping a bad house or bad company—the subsistence granted by the judge shall be cut off. [*Coutumes de Beauvaisis*][51]

The annulment of marriage because of impotence took this form:

If one or both members of a married couple appear before an ecclesiastical judge to request a separation because of this obstacle [sexual impotence], he shall give them another three years to live together and make them swear to try to have intercourse. If, after three years, intercourse between them is still impossible and one of the partners again takes legal action, the obstacle shall be ruled a permanent one ... [but not before each is again examined and questioned: he by seven men and she by seven women]. Then the marriage may be dissolved and each shall have the right to remarry. [*Las Siete Partidas*][52]

The following statute (two actually, one intercalated) from the city of Perugia had equivalents in other Italian city-states.

Date, 1342. We [the collegiate government of Perugia] state and ordain that if a man be denounced ... for expelling his wife or if indeed he no longer lives with her, the examining magistrate shall conduct a secret and summary investigation ... among the neighbors, male and female, of the couple. If he finds, through local consensus or by other means, that she left or no longer lives with her husband, owing to some fault of his, he shall compel the husband, if the woman so desires, to provide her and any children she may have had by him with the means of life. A sworn statement from her will certify for how long she has been banished from the house, provided the dowry has been paid to the husband. [But if she is proved guilty of adultery, she forfeits her dowry, can be run out of the house, and has no claim to separate maintenance. If she had no dowry, all her possessions become his. But if he committed adultery, he is subject to a fine of 50 pounds Perugian, provided the deed was done] in his own house ... and provided there is public knowledge of it. [*Statuti di Perugia*][53]

4 Working Women

The 'weaker sex' was not too weak for hard physical labor. An illustrious history of technology has called woman 'man's first beast of burden'. Medieval women labored at every manner of job in town and country, at plow and spindle, mines and fine craft. Laboring alongside men, they could do the heaviest fieldwork; in towns they might work at highly skilled trades. Rarely inscribed in craft guilds but never as full-fledged members, they held no guild offices and had no voice in the guild's regulation of the trade. They received lower wages for the same work, the assumption being that they produced and ate less. Not infrequently they were admitted to only the lowest-paying skills and jobs.

German cities opened a large variety of crafts and jobs to women. At Strasbourg, for example, between 1445 and 1453, the following women were licensed to assist in the trades indicated:

Frau Nese Lantmennyn, blacksmith; Katherine, widow of Andreas Kremer, gardener; Katherine Rebestoeckyn, goldsmith; Agnes Broumattin, widow of Hans Hirtingheim, waggoner; Katherine, widow of Helle Hensel, grain dealer; Else von Ortemberg, Oberlin Rulin's daughter, tailor; Katherine, widow of Heinrich Husenboltz, cooper. [*Le Livre de la Bourgeoisie de la Ville de Strasbourg: 1440-1530*][54]

Throughout much of Europe the detailed regulation of the different trades and crafts was often in the hands of the appropriate guild. The example from an Italian city may be taken as paradigmatic:

Siena, 1297–1309. Statutes of the guild of wool merchants. No one subject to the guild can or should lend any money to any spinster [woman who spins], nor pay for any wool or carded wool until she has done the work. Whoever violates this rule must pay 5 soldi in deniers to the guild.

No one subject to the guild can or should receive any wool or spun carded wool from any spinster not in his employ; and if he does, he must turn it over within three days to the man who put it out [to be worked on] if he knows him; if not, he must

9 Allegorical picture from Christine de Pisan's *Cyte of Ladyes*

10 Presentation
of Christine de
Pisan's *Cyte of
Ladyes*

surrender it to the officials of the guild [penalties otherwise].

The guild consuls ... must see to it that all weavers, male and female, keep their combs well set.... They should do this by appointing three able men to go around and check once a month.

No one subject to the wool guild of the city of Siena can or should buy wool floss from any spinster or female weaver [a directive aimed at fighting alleged pilfering and fraud]. [*Statuti senesi scritti in volgare ne' secoli xiii e xiv*][55]

Paris had about 150 trades and crafts, mainly under royal and municipal regulation; in six of the métiers women predominated. Craft ordinances compiled by a provost of Paris (1254–71) offer a glimpse of skilled workwomen in the silk industry. These owned or hired their own spindles and took on apprentices but were employed by silk merchants, who 'put out' silk to be spun, woven, and finished.

Any woman who wishes to be a silk spinster on large spindles in the city of Paris—i.e., reeling, spinning, doubling and retwisting —may freely do so, provided she observe the following customs and usages of the craft:

No spinster on large spindles may have more than three apprentices, unless they be her own or her husband's children born in true wedlock; nor may she contract with them for an apprenticeship of less than seven years or for a fee of less than 20 Parisian sols to be paid to her, their mistress. The apprenticeship shall be for eight years if there is no fee, but she may accept more years and money if she can get them....

No woman of the said craft may hire an apprentice or work-girl who has not completed her years of service with the mistress to whom she was apprenticed. If a spinster has assumed an apprentice, she may not take on another before the first has completed her seven years unless the apprentice die or forswear the craft forever. If an apprentice spinster buy her freedom before serving the said seven years, she may not herself take on an apprentice until she has practiced the craft for seven years. If any spinster sell her apprentice, she shall owe six deniers to the guardians appointed in the King's name to guard the [standards of the] craft. The buyer shall also owe six deniers....

If a working woman comes from outside Paris and wishes to practice the said craft in the city, she must swear before two guardians of the craft that she will practice it well and loyally and conform to its customs and usages.

If anyone give a woman of the said craft silk to be spun and the woman pawn it and the owner complain, the fine shall be 5 sols.

No workwoman shall farm out another's silk to be worked upon outside her own house.

The said craft has as guardians two men of integrity sworn in the King's name but appointed and changed at the will of the provost of Paris. Taking an oath in the provost's presence, they shall swear to guard the craft truly, loyally, and to their utmost, and to inform him or his agents of all malpractices discovered therein.

Any spinster who shall infringe any of the above rules shall pay the King a fine of 5 sols for each offense ... [from which the craft guardians deduct their own expenses]. [Etienne Boileau, *Livre des Métiers*] [56]

Other snapshots from the same code:

Makers of cotton and silk laces. No man of this craft who is without a wife may have more than one apprentice; and if he has a wife who does not practice the craft, he may still have one apprentice only; if, however, both husband and wife practice the craft, they may have two apprentices and as many journeymen as they wish.

Makers of coral or shell rosary beads. If any woman who was the wife of a man in this craft marry a second husband who is not of this craft, she may continue in the craft but may not assume apprentices.

Glasscutters and gemworkers. No master's widow who keeps working at this craft after her husband's death may take on apprentices, for the men of the craft do not believe that a woman can master it well enough to teach a child to master it, for the craft is a very delicate one. [Boileau, *Livre des Métiers*] [57]

English cities had similar trade ordinances. Normally, women were

*allowed into some of the more specialized crafts only if they were the
wives or daughters of masters inscribed in the craft. At Bristol, in 1461,
they were accused of contributing to unemployment among weavers:*

For as much as divers persons of the weavers' craft of the said
town of Bristol put, occupy and hire their wives, daughters and
maidens, some to weave in their own looms and some ... to
work with other persons of the said craft, [because of which]
many people—likely men to do the King service in his wars and
in the defense of this his land, and sufficiently learned in the said
craft—go vagrant and unoccupied and may not have their labor
to their living, therefore that no person of the said craft of
weavers [in Bristol] from this day forward, set, put or hire, his
said wife, daughter or maid to such occupation of weaving in the
loom ... upon pain of 6s. 8d. to be levied, half to the use of the
Chamber of Bristol aforesaid, and half to the contribution of the
said craft. Provided always and except that this act stretch not
to any man's wife ... now levying at the making of this act.
[*The Little Red Book of Bristol*] [58]

ILLUSTRATIVE SCENES AND CASES

*On a Sunday in August 1520, the artist Albrecht Dürer witnessed a
religious procession in Antwerp:*

The whole city was there, all the guilds and trades, each man
dressed according to his rank and most richly.... The procession also included a large troop of widows, who keep themselves
by the work of their hands and live by a special rule. They were
dressed in white linen from head to foot—a moving thing to see.
Among those women I saw some of very high estate. [Dürer,
Tagebuch der Reise in die Niederlands] [59]

Three cases offer a fleeting view of several women:

Paris, 1399, 22 October. People who have no workshop may not
have apprentices ... Poncette, wife of Cardinot Aubry, a linen
draper, was summoned before us [the court] at the request of
her apprentice, Perrette la Maugarnie, who asked to be freed

from her contract [of apprenticeship] on the grounds that the said Poncette had no workshop and only did occasional work here and there. Poncette confessed that in truth she had no workshop, did only occasional work in one place and another, and had been a long time without working or teaching anything of the said craft to Perrette. After considering the matter, we freed Perrette from her contract and condemned Poncette to pay costs.

1399 ... the officers of the craft of chandlers [makers of candles] of the city of Paris against Guillemette, widow of Regnaut Olivier, engaged in a lawsuit against them because they refuse to allow her to exercise the said craft or keep a workshop on the grounds that she is not skilled enough.... We [the Châtelet court], to put an end to this case and so that the woman and her children may have a means of livelihood ... order that the said widow may work and keep a workshop during her lifetime, on condition that she not go to work or put others to work in other people's houses ... or take any apprentices other than the one she now has ... moreover, that if she remarry someone not in the craft ... she may neither teach the craft to him nor to any children he may have had by another wife.

1415, 12 February. [Alison la Jourdain is appealing against the provost of Paris; the King's attorney speaks for the provost]. The appellant says that she is of respectable parentage, a good decent woman and clean-living, that she was born in Senlis and was formerly married to Regnaut Jourdain. But fearing that marriage as a state might not suit everyone, she took up hat-making, from which craft, along with what she got from her parents, she put together [a certain sum of money].... Since then she has been engaged in weaving and the cloth trade and by these crafts has made a good and honest living. She has had girl apprentices and has lived at [various addresses] and bought herself a good house with her own money. One day, as she was walking in town, the constables ordered her to go and have a talk with the provost at the Châtelet. She went and was reprimanded because she was wearing a sort of tunic with some fur and a belt [i.e., in violation of sumptuary laws]. Then she was sent home and sometime later summoned again by the provost, who told her that she must leave the street [where she lived]. She refused, whereupon he would not see her again and sent an order saying that she had two weeks in which to clear out. She appealed. . . .

The King's attorney, on the contrary, on the basis of information collected here and there, submits that Alison is a sexy young woman and a bit of a tart, who left her husband to go and live in Conroirie, where she was kept by a priest of that town, and that thereafter she was kept by an Italian, who caught her with a manservant and was displeased [*sic!*]. He broke off relations with her for about six months, but she was pregnant and gave the child to the Italian, who took her back and gave her a house to live in at the Pierre au Let. Her door there was broken in three times at night, and there are witnesses who say not only that she has intimate relations with a lot of people but also that she acts as procuress for her two sisters. Others say that since she doesn't take any money this isn't really procuring but just good company. He [the King's attorney] says she then moved to Arsis Street, where she has carried on her business on a large scale, for she has twelve boarders, as she herself has confessed, and one man says he knows of forty guildsmen who have known her intimately. Finally, because of a scandal which arose out of this, a request was made to the provost that he command her to clear out, etc. . . . It was agreed that the court should examine the letters, consider the arguments and deliberate. [G. Fagniez, *Documents relatifs à l'histoire de l'industrie et du commerce en France*][60]

In 1455, reacting to sharp foreign competition, the 'silk women, of London petitioned to have an embargo put on all finished silk entering England from abroad. The petition—granted, save for the entry of Genoese girdles—reveals that 'gentlewomen' were much engaged in silk working.

1455 [Petition from] the silk women and throwsters of the crafts and occupation of silk work within the city of London ... [hitherto, thanks to the silk industry] many a woman lived full honorably, and therewith many households kept, and many gentlewomen and others in great number like as there now be more than a thousand, have been drawn under them in learning the same crafts and occupation. . . . [But] lately divers

Lombards [Italians] and other alien strangers imagining to
destroy the same crafts and all such virtuous occupations for
women within this land, to the intent to enrich themselves and
put such occupations to other lands, bring now daily into this
land wrought silk, thrown ribbons, and laces falsely and deceiv-
ably wrought, and no silk unwrought, to the great hurt of all
such as shall wear or occupy the same and the utter destruction
of all the same crafts and occupations: The sufferance whereof
hath caused and is like to cause great idleness amongst gentlewomen and other women of worship. . . . In reformation whereof [they ask Parliament to get the King to ban all finished silk
from coming into] this land from beyond the sea. [*Rotuli Parliamentorum*][61]

RURAL WOMEN

*This theme receives more ample treatment in Chapter X, later sources
being richer and more accessible. The aim here will be to convey a rough
idea of the different wage scales between men and women, the range of
rural chores, and the restraints of bondage. We begin with England:*

Domesday Book, 1086. [Of men's board and women's board].
To a bondservant belong for board 12 pounds of good corn and
2 sheep carcasses and a good meat cow, and wood, according to
the custom of the estate. To unfree women belong 8 pounds of
corn for food, one sheep or 3*d.* for winter fare, one sester of beans
for Lent fare, in summer whey or 1*d.* [*English Economic History*][62]

*In matters concerning physical labor or the payment of fines, bondage
and the manorial system drew no distinctions between the weaker and the
stronger sex:*

[A widow's obligations in the manor of Frocestor, 1265–7.]
Margery, the widow, holds half a virgate of land which contains
24 acres and she renders 3*s.* every year at two terms, 12*d.* at
Christmas and 2*s.* at Michaelmas. And from Michaelmas to the
Feast of St Peter in Chains she must plow half an acre every
week, and one day's plowing is worth 3*d.* And from the Feast of
St John the Baptist until August she must perform manual

service 3 days every week and the day is worth three farthings. The fourth day she carries on her back to Gloucester or elsewhere at the bailiff's will and that is worth three-halfpence. She shall mow the lord's meadow for at least 4 days and the day is worth $1\frac{1}{2}d$., which is counted as manual service estimated above at three farthings. And she must lift the lord's hay for at least 4 days at her expense, this not being counted as a task, and it is worth altogether $3d$. She shall weed 2 days apart from the work due which is worth three-halfpence. And from the Feast of St Peter in Chains until Michaelmas she must perform manual service with a man 5 days a week and the day is worth three-halfpence.

And every second week during the same period she must perform carrying service for one day, this being counted as one day's task.

And furthermore she performs 8 boon works with a man in autumn which is worth altogether $12d$. And she gives $2s.$ $2\frac{1}{4}d.$ for aid. She performs all the untaxed customs [for king and manorial lord]. And she performs a harvest boon work in autumn fed by the master which is worth, apart from the food, a halfpenny. And she must plow one day, fed by the master with half a plow. And she shall give eggs at Easter at will. [G. Duby, *Rural Economy and Country Life in the Medieval West*] [63]

[Fines, 1350s.] Agnes Chilyonge of Manningham, the lord's bondwoman, came here in Court and made fine of $12d.$ with the lord for her leywrite [fine for bearing an illegitimate child] ... and the fine is not more because she is very poor and has nothing.

Isabel, daughter of William Childyong, the lord's bondwoman, has married one William Cisson, a free man, without license. And Alice, daughter of John Gepson, the lord's bondwoman, has married one William de Hale, a free man at Beston, without license; let them be distrained to make fine with the lord for their merchet [servitude's fine for the right to marry]. [*English Economic History*] [64]

Some French rural wages (Paris, 1350) :

Laborers working in vineyards shall be paid ... from the end of wine harvest until mid-February: cutters no more than 18 deniers a day without food or drink, diggers no more than 16 deniers a day without food or drink, and, from mid-February until the end of April, the best cutters no more than 2 sols and 6 deniers [sol: 12 deniers] of Parisian money a day, and the diggers 2 sols, and everyone else less. . . .

Up to Candlemas [February 2] the best women workers [in vineyards] are to get no more than 8 deniers without food or drink for a day's work on the vines, and the rest less; and from Candlemas to August, they may get up to 12 deniers at the most. [*Les Edits et Ordonnances des Roys de France depuis l'an 1226*][65]

Some English wages (12 Richard I, 1388):

It is agreed that the bailiff for husbandry take 13*s.* 4*d.* a year and his clothing once a year at most, the master hind 10*s.*, the carter 10*s.*, the shepherd 10*s.*, the oxherd 6*s.* 8*d.*, the swineherd 6*s.*, the woman laborer 6*s.*, the dairymaid 6*s.*, the plowman 7*s.* at most. [*The Statutes of the Realm*][66]

SERVANTS

The schedule of French wages will mean more if we note that a two-denier loaf of brown bread weighed 16 ounces if of the best flour, 26 ounces if of the cheapest. A sol equaled 12 deniers.

Paris, 1350. Serving maids . . . now in service may not leave before serving out their time; and if they were promised more [sums specified], they shall not have it. Anyone breaking this rule shall be fined.

Serving maids in service to Paris burgesses . . . shall not take more than 30 sols a year and their shoes, and, if they are worth less shall take less. Wet nurses shall take 50 sols at the most. . . .

Wet nurses who nurse children [away from the children's home] . . . shall be paid 100 sols a year at the most, and those already engaged shall go on working at that price and be compelled to serve out their time. . . .

Agents [women] who find employment for maids and wet nurses shall take 18 deniers at most for placing a maid, and for a wet nurse 2 sols from each party. They may not place the same

person more than once in the year. [An agent who does so] . . .
shall be put in the pillory. [*Les Edits et Ordonnances des Roys de
France*][67]

*The next selection comes from a thirteenth-century Latin compendium
by an English Franciscan. The work was popular all over Europe, translated first into French in 1372, then into English, Dutch, and Spanish.*

A chambermaid is a servant employed by the master or mistress
of the house to do the heaviest and foulest jobs. She is fed coarse
food, clad in the meanest cloth, and bears the burden of servitude. If she has children, they are the master's serfs. If she is a
serf herself, she may not marry whom she chooses, and anyone
who does marry her, falling into servitude, can be sold like an
animal by the master. If freed, the serving maid can be recalled
to serfdom for ingratitude. Chambermaids are frequently beat-
en, abused, and tormented, and scarcely given a chance to
console themselves by laughter or distractions. . . . Rabanus
says that chambermaids have this characteristic: they rebel
against their masters and mistresses and get out of hand if
they are not kept down. . . . Serfs and that sort are kept in place
only through fear. [Bartholomaeus Anglicus, *Les Propriétés des
Choses*][68]

[On employing and managing servants, 1393.] Don't hire a
maidservant without first finding out where she was before.
Then send someone from your household to make inquiries
there, to find out whether she was too talkative or drank too
much, how long she stayed, what work she did or can do,
whether she has rooms or acquaintances in town, from what
village or family she comes, and why she left her last place. For
you can find out, by what she did before, what to expect from
her in the future. And know that women who come from another
village have often lost their reputation there, which is why they
left it. If there weren't something against them, they would be
mistresses instead of servants. . . . And if it seems from the report
of the [former] masters or mistresses or neighbors that she will
suit you, then, on the day you engage her and in her presence,
get your steward to write down in his account book her name,

her father's and mother's name, the names of several of her relatives, the addresses where they live and where she was born, and the names of her referees. For servants will be more careful to avoid bad behavior when they realize that you are writing all this down because if they run off without permission or commit some other offense, you can then write to their friends or to the authorities in their hometown.... Remember that if you take on a proud or bold-faced maidservant, she will wrong you in every way she can; and if she is the opposite, flattering and full of blandishments, don't trust her, for she is somehow set to cheat you; but if she blushes and holds her tongue and is ashamed when you correct her, love her like a daughter....

If you have maids aged between fifteen and twenty, which is an age when they are silly and know nothing of the world, have them sleep near you, in some closet or room without a window giving onto the street, and have them go to bed and rise at the same time as you do, and keep an eye on them. [*Le Ménagier de Paris*][69]

England in 1536, reacting to 'sturdy beggars,' extensive 'vagrancy,' and rural disorder—in short, an upsurge of poverty—saw the institution of a law which press-ganged girls and women into domestic service:

Two justices of peace, the mayor or other head officer of any city ... may appoint any such woman as is of the age of 12 years and under the age of 40 years and unmarried and out of service ... to be retained or serve by the year or by the week or day for such wages and in such reasonable sort as they will think meet; and if any such woman shall refuse to serve, then it shall be lawful for the aforesaid justice [etc.] to commit such woman to ward until she shall be bounden to serve as aforesaid. [*English Economic History*][70]

MEDICAL PRACTITIONERS

For reasons of modesty, medical attendance on women was left largely to women, many of whom were merely herbalists, wise women, or, at best, midwives. But occasionally they had more serious qualifications, and a few like Trotula (p. 142) may even have got to the medical school at

Salerno. The following license was granted by Charles, Duke of Calabria:

Charles, etc . . . : Francesca, the wife of Matteo de Romana of Salerno, has explained to the Royal Court that she is reputed to be proficient in the art of surgery, wherefore she begged us to deign to grant her the license to practice that art. Accordingly, it has been ascertained, through a certificate presented to the same Royal Court by the University of Salerno, that the said Francesca is a member of the faithful and born of a family of the faithful. Moreover, she has been examined and found competent by our own royal physicians and surgeons, even though it be unusual and unseemly for women to appear among assemblies of men, lest this affront womanly decency. . . . Since, however, the law permits women to practice medicine and because it is better, out of consideration for morals and decency, for women rather than men to attend female patients, we grant her the license to heal and to practice, having first received the usual oath from the said Francesca to the effect that she will loyally abide by the traditions of the said art. . . . Naples, 10 September 1321. [*Collectio Salernitana*][71]

Until Charles VIII of France withdrew their right in 1485, women practiced as surgeons in Paris and elsewhere in France. It should be noted, however, that medieval surgeons were often grouped with barbers and received their training via apprenticeship, not at universities.

Paris, c. 1270.   As there are some men and women in Paris who practice surgery without being fit to do so . . . the provost of Paris, on the advice of the masters of this craft, has appointed three of the best and most honest surgeons of Paris, who have sworn on the saints . . . that they will examine all those whom they consider unworthy to practice the craft. . . . And the names of those found unfit to do so will be recorded, and we [the provost] shall forbid them to practice. [Boileau, *Livre des Métiers*][72]

England gave evidence of the same sort:

London, 1390.   [An ordinance provides that master surgeons shall examine the work both of men and] women undertaking cures or practicing the art of surgery. [S. Young, *Annals of the Barber Surgeons of London*][73]

York, 1572.   Isabell Warwicke hath skill in the science of surgery and hath done good therein. It is therefore agreed by these present that she upon her good behavior shall use the same science within this city without let [hindrance] of any of the surgeons of the same. [*A History of Yorkshire*][74]

5 Conduct and Misconduct

The law responds to social demand by setting up external curbs, but oral tradition and manuals of conduct directly express the internal taboos, and these are more constantly at work. The following texts deal mainly with questions of decorum and deportment but conclude with three documents whose realities serve as a foil to the abstract advice.

Franco-Italian source, c. 1420. At parties or gatherings, let them [girls and young widows] not venture in among the men but hang back with their mothers and other women, and let them have a sedate expression and be sober of speech, bearing, and smile; moreover, let their glance be reluctant, decided, neither wandering nor unsure but direct and simple. [Christine de Pisan][75]

Paris, 1393. Keep your head straight, your eyelids lowered and unflinching and your glance directed straight in front of you, eight yards ahead and towards the ground, without moving it about. [*Le Ménagier de Paris*][76]

France, thirteenth century. Women should not learn to read or write unless they are going to be nuns, as much harm has come from such knowledge. For some men will dare to send or give or drop letters near them, containing indecent requests in the form of songs or rhymes or tales, which they would never dare convey by message or word of mouth. And even if the woman had no desire to err, the devil is so crafty and skillful in tempting that he would soon lead her on to read the letters and answer them. . . .

[Illicit intercourse] is different for men. For they . . . preen themselves vaingloriously when it is known that they have a young or pretty or monied mistress. Men's families are not affected, but women shame and dishonor themselves and their children when they incur blame for the like. [Philippe de Navarre, *Les Quatre Ages de l'Homme*][77]

The French Book of the Knight of La Tour Landry (*1371*), *translated into English and published by Caxton in 1484, became very popular in France, England, and Germany. The knight speaks to his daughters:*

Fair daughters, when you get up in the morning, start at once to serve the Great Lord ... and say your prayers with all your heart before breakfasting, for a gorged heart is never humble or devout. Afterwards, hear all the Masses you can, as this will bring you great benefit. . . .

Throughout your married life you ought to fast three days a week to keep your flesh down and yourselves chaste. . . . And if this is too much, fast on Fridays in memory of Christ's passion ... and if you can't keep to bread and water, at least eat nothing that has to be killed ... and it is good to fast on Saturdays for love of Our Lady and reverence for her virginity, praying her to keep you chaste. . . .

Women who fall in love with ... married men, priests, servants, and such ... are worse than whores in a brothel. For many women have been brought to the sin of lechery by need or poverty or the trickery of pimps, but a gentlewoman who has enough to live on and yet takes a lover among the kind of men we have mentioned ... does it from nothing but the carnal heat of lust. [*Le Livre du Chevalier de la Tour-Landry*][78]

Paris, 1393. [How to hold a husband.] Cherish your husband's person and make sure you keep him in clean linen, this being your office. For men have to look after things outside the house and husbands have to go abroad in all sorts of weather, at times getting soaked in rain, at times dry, and sometimes bathed in sweat. . . . But he puts up with it all and takes consolation from thinking about the good care he will have from his wife when he gets home, as she warms him by a good fire, washes his feet, fetches fresh shoes and stockings for him, good food and drink, gives him plenty of attentions, a comfortable bed, white sheets, a nightcap, fur covers, and the cheer of other delights, privy frolics, lovings, and secret matters which I shan't mention.

Indeed, fair sister, these are the services that make a man wish for home and long to return to it. . . . Remember the rustic saying that there are three things which chase a good man from home: a roofless house, a smoking chimney, and a quarrelsome wife ... and don't be quarrelsome but sweet, gentle, and amiable. In the summertime make sure that there are no fleas in your bed or bedroom. There are six ways of getting rid of them [recipes follow] ... and if you do all this, he will keep his heart for you and for the loving service you render him and he will care nothing for other houses or other women. [*Le Ménagier de Paris*][79]

In addition to giving advice to women, which after all expressed half a world view, our moralists, remembering the more important half, also had advice for men. Thus Paolo da Certaldo (fl. 1330–70), a family man, a Florentine, and a small-time entrepreneur, in his Handbook of Good Customs (*c. 1360*):

The female is an empty thing and easily swayed: she runs great risks when she is away from her husband. Therefore, keep females in the house, keep them as close to yourself as you can, and come home often to keep an eye on your affairs and to keep them in fear and trembling. Make sure they always have work to do in the house and never allow them to be idle, for idleness is a great danger to both man and woman, but more to the woman....

If you have a female child, set her to sewing and not to reading, for it is not suitable for a female to know how to read unless she is going to be a nun.... Teach her to do everything about the house, to make bread, clean capons, sift, cook, launder, make beds, spin, weave French purses, embroider, cut wool and linen clothes, put new feet onto socks, and so forth, so that when you marry her off she won't seem a fool freshly arrived from the wilds. [*Libro di buoni costumi*][80]

Certaldo's rough-and-ready realism provides a natural passage to the next two memoirs. In 1403 Giovanni Morelli, a Florentine merchant, made an entry in the family diary recording the financial ruin of his sister (Sandra) at the hands of her husband (Jacopo):

[Sandra's financial undoing] came about through Jacopo's fault, because of the bad state of his business affairs, but also through Sandra's fault and foolishness in being too obedient to her husband. Seeing him in need, she went too far in her obedience and pledged several farms that were in her name, without saying a word of this to us, her brothers, or to any other friend or relative. This too was Jacopo's fault. Knowing how obedient and sweet-tempered she was, he used not to warn her in advance but like a culprit would take her by surprise, arriving with a notary and witnesses, his face looking very upset, and would keep saying, 'Say yes! Say yes!' Through fear and obedience and because she was shamed to deny her husband in the presence of others, she did what she was told, although she suspected that she was making a mistake. The outcome is that she has been living in our house for some time now [about two years] as a young widow with a twelve-year-old son and no dowry, and if God doesn't send us some remedy, she is likely to be here another long while.

I decided to write this down for the benefit of whoever reads it [a memoir intended for his family] as a warning that no one, man or woman, should ever divest himself of his property or rights either from fear, flattery, or any other motive. [G. Morelli, *Ricordi*][81]

We follow with a condensation from the ledger cum *diary of another Florentine merchant, Gregorio Dati (b. 1362). Our selection comprises the entries concerning his four wives and a slave. The laconism—which should not be taken to signify lack of affection—does show the woman's role with skeletal simplicity: she brings a dowry, gives birth, and sometimes dies in childbearing:*

My beloved wife, Bandecca, went to Paradise after a nine-month illness started by a miscarriage, July 1390.

I had an illegitimate male child by Margherita, a Tartar slave whom I had bought. He was born in Valencia on 21 December 1391.

We [business associates] renewed our partnership on 1 January 1393, when I undertook to invest 1,000 [gold] florins. I did not actually have the money but was about to get married —which I then did—and to receive the dowry which procured me a larger share and more consideration in our company.... I married my second wife, Betta, on 22 June.... On the 26th of that same June I received a payment of 800 gold florins from the bank of Giacomino and Co. This was the dowry.

11   Pregnant Madonna, by Piero della Francesca

12 Savonarola preaching to divided male-female congregation
Florentine woodcut, dated 1495

13 Witches hanged at Newcastle—mid 17th-century
From *England's Grievance Discovered* by R. Gardiner

On Sunday, 17 May 1394, Betta gave birth to a girl. . . .

On Friday evening, 17 March 1396, the Lord blessed our marriage with a male son.

12 March 1397, Betta gave birth to our third child. . . .

27 April 1398, Betta gave birth to our fourth child.

1 July 1399, Betta had our fifth child.

22 June 1400, Betta gave birth for the sixth time.

On Wednesday, 13 July 1401 . . . the Lord lent us a seventh child.

On 5 July 1402 . . . Betta gave birth to our eighth child.

After that my wife Betta passed on to Paradise. . . .

The [business] partnership is to start on 1 January 1403 and to last three years. . . . I have undertaken to put up 2,000 florins. This is how I propose to raise them: 1,370 florins . . . are still due to me from my old partnership. . . . The rest I expect to obtain if I marry again this year, when I hope to find a woman with a dowry as large as God may be pleased to grant me. . . .

I record that on 8 May 1403, I was betrothed to Ginevra, daughter of Antonio Brancacci. . . . The dowry was 1,000 florins: 700 in cash and 300 in a farm at Campi.

On Sunday morning at terce, 27 April [1404], Ginevra gave birth to our first-born son. . . .

Altogether Ginevra and I had eleven children: four boys and seven girls. . . .

After that it was God's will to recall to Himself the blessed soul of my wife Ginevra. She died in childbirth after lengthy suffering. . . . God bless her and grant us fortitude.

I then took another wife, Caterina, the daughter of Dardano Guicciardini [30 March 1421]. . . . The dowry was 600 florins.

Caterina, my fourth wife, miscarried after four months.

On 4 October 1422 . . . Caterina gave birth to a daughter. . .

On Friday, 7 January 1424, Caterina gave birth to a fine healthy boy. . . .

20 March, 1425, Caterina had another healthy and attractive child. . . .

26 July 1426, Caterina had a fine little girl. . . .

Monday, 28 August 1427, Caterina gave birth to a fine little girl. . . .

2 June 1431, Caterina gave birth to a girl.... [At this point, with about nine of his children still alive, he stops keeping his diary and dies in 1435.] [G. Brucker, ed., *Two Memoirs of Renaissance Florence*][82]

The next selection takes us to England and some family letters that show us a daughter 'demeaning' herself by a secret marriage to the family steward. Although her husband, Richard Calley, continued as steward, the girl, Margery Paston, was never again received by her family. Her tenacity is the more striking because an earlier letter in the collection reveals that another Paston girl, who resisted her parents' choice of a husband for her, was for three months 'beaten once in a week or twice, sometimes twice in one day, and her head broken in two or three places'.

[Letter 87, John Paston to his elder brother Sir John Paston, 1469.] Sir ... I conceive by your letter that ye have heard of Richard Calley's labor which he maketh by our ungracious sister's assent. But whereas they write that they have my good will ... saving your reverence, they falsely lie ... for they never spoke to me of the matter. Lovell asked me once ... whether I understood how it was betwixt Richard Calley and my sister. Wherefore, to the intent that he nor they should pick no comfort of me, I answered him that ... he should never have my good will for to take my sister to sell candles and mustard at Framlingham.

[Letter 88, Calley to Mistress Margery Paston, 1469.] Mine own Lady and Mistress, and, before God, very true wife, I with heart full sorrowful recommend me to you.... This life that we lead now is neither pleasure to God nor to the world, considering the great bond of matrimony that is betwixt us and also the great love ... wherefore I beseech Almighty God comfort us as soon as it pleaseth him, for we that ought of very right to be most together are most asunder.... I want you to know that I sent you a letter by my lad from London, and that he told me he could not speak with you ... he told me John Thresher came to him and said that you had sent him (to my lad) for a letter or a token which I should have sent you, but he did not trust him.... I conceive since by my lad that it was not of your sending; it was by my Mistress and Sir James' advice. Alas, what mean they? I suppose ... that if you gravely tell them the truth [that we are married], they will not damn their souls for us; though I tell them the truth, they will not believe me as they do you, and therefore, Good Lady, be plain to them. . . . Mistress, I am afraid to write to you ... let no creature see this letter, as soon as you have read it let it be burnt.

[Letter 89, much condensed here, to Sir John Paston from his mother, Margaret Paston, 1469.] I greet you well, etc. . . . My mother and I were with the Lord of Norwich [the bishop], and desired him that he would do no more in the matter of your sister till you and my brothers might be here together. He said plainly that he had been required so often to examine her that he might not nor would no longer delay it ... and charged that she should be at liberty to come when he sent for her; and he said by his troth that he would be as sorry for her, if she did not well, as he would if she were right near of his kin, for he knew that her demeaning had stuck sore in our throats. . . . On Friday the bishop sent for her and put her in remembrance how she was born, what kin and friends she had, and should have more if she were ruled and guided after them; and said that he had heard say, that she loved such one that her friends were not pleased with and therefore he bade her be right well advised how she did; and said that he would decide from the words that she had said to him [to Calley], whether it made matrimony or not, and she rehearsed what she had said to him, and said, if those words made it not sure, that she would make it surer, for she said she thought in her conscience she was bound whatsoever the words were. These lewd words grieveth me. . . . And then Calley was examined apart by himself, that her words and his accorded, and the time, and where it should have been done. . . When I heard say what her demeaning was, I charged my servants that she should not be received in my house; I had given her warning, and I sent to one or two more that they should not receive her if she came; and so my Lord of Norwich hath set her at Roger Best's, to be there [till after Michaelmas]. I am better satisfied that she is there for the while than she had been in other place, because she shall not be suffered there to play the brothel. I pray you and require you that ye take it not pensily for I know well it goeth right near your heart, and so doth it to mine and to others, but remember you, and so do I, that we have lost of her but a frail one, and set it the less to heart, for if he [Calley] were dead at this hour, she should never be at mine heart as she was; as for the divorce that ye write to me of, I charge you upon my blessing that ye do not, nor cause none other to do, that should offend God and your conscience. [And for the rest] know it well, she shall full sore repent her lewdness hereafter, and I pray God she might. [*Original Letters*][83]

6 Punishment

Attitudes toward punishment reveal the values that society takes most seriously. A wife's lord in medieval Europe was her husband. If she killed him, this could be treason in English law and she could be burned like a traitor. From Naples to northern Europe, if he caught her in adultery and killed her there and then, he might go free: society encouraged and condoned his wrath. Logically enough, in more ordinary circumstances, he had the moral and legal right to inflict corporal punishment on her: all law systems agreed on this. If she beat him, popular feeling in France could be so astonished and upset by his abdication that anger and humor merged:

To sit backwards on an ass and hold its tail ... was the penalty formerly inflicted ... on men who showed cowardice and particularly on husbands whose wives used to beat them [cases cited, 1375, 1383]. [C. Du Cange, *Glossarium Novum ad Scriptores Medii Aevi*][84]

France, late thirteenth century.   In a number of cases men may be excused for the injuries they inflict on their wives, nor should the law intervene. Provided he neither kills nor maims her, it is legal for a man to beat his wife when she wrongs him— for instance, when she is about to surrender her body to another man, when she contradicts or abuses him, or when she refuses, like a decent woman, to obey his reasonable commands. In all these and similar cases, it is the husband's office to be his wife's chastiser. [*Coutumes de Beauvaisis*][85]

The power of the English husband was also exalted:

Justice Brooke ... affirmeth plainly that if a man beat or outlaw a traitor, a pagan, his villein, or his wife, it is dispunishable, because by the Law Common these persons can have no action: God send to Gentlewomen better sport or better company.

But it seems to be very true that there is some kind of castigation which law permits a husband to use ... and that he shall neither do nor procure to be done to her any bodily damage, otherwise than pertains to the office of a husband for lawful and reasonable correction. . . .

A woman for committing either grand or petty treason shall be burned. The latter part of the Statute 25 of Edward 3 ca. 2 is [1352], that if any servant kill his master, any woman kill her husband . . . this is treason. [Case]: A woman compasseth with her adulterer the death of her husband, they assailed him riding on the highway, beating, wounding, leaving him for dead, and then they fled. The husband got up, levied hue and cry, came before the justices, they sent after the offenders, which were gotten, arraigned, and the matter found by verdict, the adulterer was hanged, the woman burned to death, the husband living, the intention being taken for the act. [*The Lawes Resolutions*][86]

The medieval Jew was also lord of his wife. The Rabbi R. Perez, who died in France before 1300, proposed the following decree to a synod of rabbis. Somewhat revolutionary in that it would have sanctioned legal separation and payment of maintenance by the husband, the proposal does not seem to have been adopted:

The cry of the daughters of our people has been heard concerning the sons of Israel who raise their hands to strike their wives. Yet who has given a husband the authority to beat his wife? Is he not rather forbidden to strike any person in Israel? Moreover R. I(saac) has written in a responsum that he has it on the authority of three great Sages, namely R. Samuel, R. Jacob Tam and R. I(saac), the sons of R. Meir, that one who beats his wife is in the same category as one who beats a stranger. Nevertheless have we heard of cases where Jewish women complained regarding their treatment before the Communities and no action was taken on their behalf.

We have therefore decreed that any Jew may be compelled on application of his wife or one of her near relatives to undertake by a *herem* [oath] not to beat his wife in anger or cruelty or so as to disgrace her, for that is against Jewish practice.

If anyone will stubbornly refuse to obey our words, the Court of the place to which the wife or her relatives will bring complaint, shall assign her maintenance according to her station and according to the custom of the place where she dwells. They shall fix her alimony as though her husband were away on a distant journey.

If they, our masters, the great sages of the land agree to this ordinance it shall be established. [L. Finkelstein, *Jewish Self-Government in the Middle Ages*][87]

The Rules of Marriage *compiled by Friar Cherubino of Siena sometime between 1450 and 1481 issue from the Italian city-state environment, but Cherubino's tone catches an aspect of the quality of life among the middle and humbler classes. The wives of the Medici, the sisters of cardinals, and the women of the princely courts were treated with less unction and bluster.*

When you see your wife commit an offense, don't rush at her with insults and violent blows: rather, first correct the wrong lovingly and pleasantly, and sweetly teach her not to do it again so as not to offend God, injure her soul, or bring shame upon herself and you. . . .

But if your wife is of a servile disposition and has a crude and shifty spirit, so that pleasant words have no effect, scold her sharply, bully and terrify her. And if this still doesn't work . . . take up a stick and beat her soundly, for it is better to punish the body and correct the soul than to damage the soul and spare the body. But notice, I say, that you shouldn't beat her just because she doesn't get things ready exactly as you would like them, or for some other unimportant reason or minor failing. You should beat her, I say, only when she commits a serious wrong: for example, if she blasphemes against God or a saint, if she mutters the devil's name, if she likes being at the window and lends a ready ear to dishonest young men, or if she has taken to bad habits or bad company, or commits some other wrong that is a mortal sin. Then readily beat her, not in rage but out of charity and concern for her soul, so that the beating will redound to your merit and her good. [Cherubino da Siena, *Regole della vita matrimoniale*][88]

When women's evils were summed up, the chronicle of time and literature make clear that, next to murder, sexual waywardness was a woman's worst crime:

Spain, 1240.   If a woman and her adulterer are killed by her husband or fiancé, he shall pay no fine for the homicide, nor be sentenced to death. [*Fuero Jusgo*][89]

Italy, Perugia, 1342.   If [the city's magistrates] find that a woman is having adulterous relations with a married man, be their liaison open or secret, they must have her severely flogged through the city streets and suburbs and then exile her for three years. As evidence against women of this sort, let public opinion and their reputation suffice. [*Statuti di Perugia*][90]

IX   The Renaissance and Reformation

An age of cultural and religious renewal—and high-minded fanaticism—the Renaissance and Reformation brought major shifts in viewpoints and values. La Querelle des Femmes (the dispute about women), a fashionable preoccupation with the pros and cons of women's capabilities, revealed the inroads of Renaissance humanism and new notions of education. From the Italian princely courts there came a class-based idea of social style as an existential end: a certain kind of woman, the court lady, suddenly advanced to a less submissive and less confined role. In the north the Protestant Reformers plumped for marriage against the life of the convent and thereby emphasized the social function of women. In other ways, however, the old social restraints reserved for women persisted; indeed, the velocity of changing values went to heighten preexisting tensions, with results to be seen in the craze for witch-hunting and the penchant for 'ecstatic' or 'heretical' states of mind. When an age is in the grip of serious social maladies, we do well in our studies to look to women first, particularly if their lot seems to be improving, for their special burdens are apt to issue in hysterias that will brand or victimize some of them.

1 The Dispute About Women

Polemics against women abounded during the late Middle Ages. The writers were mostly clerics, the language Latin. With the coming of the Renaissance, as upper-class women became increasingly literate and the influence of humanism spread, writers began to produce works and apostrophes in defense of women. Thus the origins of a literary controversy lasting three centuries, La Querelle des Femmes, which led, despite the fluff, to one major conquest—education for women.

CHRISTINE DE PISAN (C. 1363–C. 1431)

Perhaps the first woman to enter the lists in the dispute, Christine de Pisan, daughter of an Italian physician and astrologer at the court of France, was one of the most learned women of her time. Broaching the question of educating girls, she made some moderate and sensible statements in her book Cyte of Ladyes.

If it were customary to send little girls to school and to teach them the same subjects as are taught to boys, they would learn just as fully and would understand the subtleties of all arts and sciences. Indeed may be they would understand them better... for just as women's bodies are more soft than men's, so too their understanding is more sharp.... If they understand less it is because they do not go out and see so many different places and things but stay home and mind their own work. For there is nothing which teaches a reasonable creature so much as the experience of many different things.

[Rectitude personified next speaks to Christine.] Your father, who was a natural philosopher, was not of the opinion that women grow worse by becoming educated. On the contrary, as you know he took great pleasure from seeing your interest in learning. Your mother, however, who held the usual feminine ideas on the matter, wanted you to spend your time spinning, like other women, and prevented you from making more progress and going deeper into science and learning in your childhood. But as the proverb says, what nature gives may not be taken away. So you gathered what little drops of learning you could and consider them a great treasure and are right to do so. 'Madame' [Christine replied], 'what you say is as true as the Pater noster.' [Christine de Pisan, *Cyte of Ladyes*][1]

This may seem timid stuff, but it was as much as could be said convincingly in an age when Aristotle was still much quoted to the effect that 'the female state is . . . as it were a deformity.' Generally speaking, the arguments against women were a rehash of the old misogynist themes: woman is cursed by the sin of Eve, crooked because made from a rib, bestial by nature, concupiscent but crafty. Education would refine, and hence heighten, her natural depravity. Husbands must defend themselves by keeping wives on a tight rein, etc. We need not rehearse the arguments; Alberti (pp. 187-9) inadvertently parades some. But the innovative voices in the dispute called for the education of women and defended their intellectual capabilities.

ERASMUS OF ROTTERDAM (C. 1467–1536)

The leading humanist of his day, Erasmus lent his authority to the still faint call for having girls pursue study, but he limited the ideal to the daughters of the rich and nobly born. In the long run, however, education for highborn ladies was to be the thin end of the wedge.

The distaff and spindle are in truth the tools of all women and suitable for avoiding idleness. . . . Even people of wealth and birth train their daughters to weave tapestries or silken cloths . . . it would be better if they taught them to study, for study busies the whole soul. . . . It is not only a weapon against idleness but also a means of impressing the best precepts upon a girl's mind and of leading her to virtue. [Erasmus, *Christiani matrimonii institutio*][2]

In his colloquy between an abbot (Antronius) and a learned woman (Magdala), Erasmus contrasted traditional and more progressive views:

ANTRONIUS: It isn't feminine to be intellectual; women are made for pleasure.

MAGDALA: Suppose now that I take more pleasure in reading

a good author than you do in hunting, drinking or gaming. Won't you think I live pleasantly?

ANTRONIUS: I would not live that sort of life....

MAGDALA: But why does this household stuff [books] displease you?

ANTRONIUS: Because a spinning wheel is a woman's weapon.

MAGDALA: Is it not a woman's business to mind the affairs of her family and to instruct her children?

ANTRONIUS: Yes, it is.

MAGDALA: And do you think so weighty an office can be performed without wisdom?

ANTRONIUS: I believe not.

MAGDALA: This wisdom I learn from books....

ANTRONIUS: I can tolerate books—but not Latin ones.

MAGDALA: Why so?

ANTRONIUS: Because that tongue is not fit for a woman.

MAGDALA: I want to know the reason.

ANTRONIUS: Because it contributes nothing toward the defense of their chastity.... The common people think as I do, because it is such a rare and unusual thing for a woman to understand Latin....

MAGDALA: Why then is it not becoming for me to learn Latin, that I may be able daily to have conversation with so many eloquent, learned and wise authors and faithful counselors?

ANTRONIUS: Books destroy women's brains who have little enough of themselves .... Bookishness makes folk mad .... By my faith, I would not have a learned wife.... I have often heard it said that a wise woman is twice a fool....

MAGDALA: A woman that is truly wise does not think herself so; but on the contrary, one that knows nothing thinks herself to be wise, and that is being twice a fool.

ANTRONIUS: I can't well tell how it is, that as panniers don't become an ass, so neither does learning become a woman. [Erasmus, *Colloquies*][3]

AGRIPPA VON NETTESHEIM (c. 1486–1535)

The brilliant and itinerant Cornelius Heinrich Agrippa, physician, philosopher, lawyer, orator, indeed polymath, was incapable of sticking

*to the straight and narrow path of intellectual and doctrinal orthodoxy,
with the result that he provoked the vindictiveness of academics, princes,
and clerics. He won temporary favor from emperors and from cities in
Germany, Italy, and Switzerland, but afterward plummeted into dis-
favor and debt. In his exercise* On the Nobility and Excellence of
Women *(1529), he answers the clerical misogynists in their own terms :*

The only difference between man and woman is physical....
In everything else they are the same. Woman does not have a
soul of a different sex from that which animates man. Both
received a soul which is absolutely the same and of an equal
condition. Women and men were equally endowed with the
gifts of spirit, reason, and the use of words; they were created
for the same end, and the sexual difference between them will
not confer a different destiny....

Wishing to take on human nature in its lowest and most abject
state, so as the more effectively by this humiliation to expiate
the first man's pride of sinning, Jesus Christ chose the male sex
as the more despicable, not the female, who is nobler and more
regenerate than the male. Moreover, because the human species
was driven to evildoing more by the sin of man than that of
woman, God wanted the sin to be expiated in the sex that had
sinned, whereas he wanted the sex which had been taken by
surprise and tricked to bring forth Him in whom the sin was to
be revenged. [Agrippa, *De nobilitate et praecellentia foeminei sexus
declamatio*][4]

LOUISE LABE (c. 1520–66)

*She was a poet born in Lyon, gateway to Italy and the first French head-
quarters of the Renaissance. The following extracts, from a dedicatory
preface to a friend, show a sense of fresh delight in the enlargement of
experience which education had brought her. Curious stories are told of
Louise Labé, who may have been a courtesan and may have fought a battle
dressed as a man. She was a good poet.*

Since a time has come, Mademoiselle, when the severe laws of
men no longer prevent women from applying themselves to the

sciences and other disciplines, it seems to me that those of us who can should use this long-craved freedom to study and to let men see how greatly they wronged us when depriving us of its honor and advantages. And if any woman becomes so proficient as to be able to write down her thoughts, let her do so and not despise the honor but rather flaunt it instead of fine clothes, necklaces, and rings. For these may be considered ours only by use, whereas the honor of being educated is ours entirely.... If the heavens had endowed me with sufficient wit to understand all I would have liked, I would serve in this as an example rather than an admonishment. But having devoted part of my youth to musical exercises, and finding the time left too short for the crudeness of my understanding, I am unable, in my own case, to achieve what I want for our sex, which is to see it outstrip men not only in beauty but in learning and virtue. All I can do is to beg our virtuous ladies to raise their minds somewhat above their distaffs and spindles and try to prove to the world that if we were not made to command, still we should not be disdained as companions in domestic and public matters by those who govern and command obedience. Apart from the good name that our sex will acquire thereby, we shall have caused men to devote more time and effort in the public good to virtuous studies for fear of seeing themselves left behind by those over whom they have always claimed superiority in practically everything....

If there is anything to be recommended after honor and glory, anything to incite us to study, it is the pleasure which study affords. Study differs in this from other recreations, of which all one can say, after enjoying them, is that one has passed the time. But study gives a more enduring sense of satisfaction. For the past delights us and serves more than the present.... When we write down our thoughts, no matter how much our mind runs on infinities of other matters ... long afterward, on looking back at what we wrote, we return to the same point and humor as we were in before. Then our joy is doubled, for we revive the pleasure experienced in the past.... From Lyon, this 24th of July, 1555. [J. Aynard, ed., *Les poétes lyonnais précurseurs de la Pléiade*] [5]

AGRIPPA D'AUBIGNE (1552-1630)

Satirical writer and historian, Calvinist, companion at arms of King Henry IV, and grandfather of Madame de Maintenon (below, pp. 250-51), Aubigné wrote the following letter to his daughters :

My daughters, your brother has brought you my summary of Logic in French, 'Logic for girls,' as M. de Bouillon calls it. I am letting you have it on condition that you make use of it only for yourselves and not against your companions or superiors, as it is dangerous for women to use such things against their husbands. Moreover, I recommend that you conceal its art and terminology, as I myself have, whenever possible. . . . I do not blame your eagerness to learn with your brothers, but I would be loath either to discourage or encourage you. Still, if anything, I would be more inclined to the former than the latter. [Proceeds to give an account of the learned women he has known or heard of: Queen Elizabeth, Margaret of Navarre, Louise Labé, 'the Sappho of her time,' Mademoiselle de Gournay.]

I have just given you my opinion of the advantages that women may derive from a superior education. However, I have nearly always found that such preparation turned out to be useless for women of middling rank like yourselves [Aubigné was a nobleman of modest means], for the more wretched among them rather abused than used their education, while the others, finding that their labor had been useless, bore out the common saying that when the nightingale has little ones, he sings no more. There is the fact, moreover, that a disproportionate elevation of the mind is very apt to breed pride. I have seen two bad effects issue from this: (1) contempt for housekeeping, for poverty, and for a husband less clever than oneself, and (2) discord. And so I conclude that I would be most reluctant to encourage girls to pursue book learning unless they were princesses, obliged by their rank to assume the responsibilities, knowledge, competence, administration, and authority of men. Then doubtless, as in the case of Queen Elizabeth, an education can stand girls in good stead. [Aubigné, *Oeuvres Complètes*][6]

14 Girl working as a goldsmith
Detail from an anonymous 15th-century engraving

15　Prostitute
16th-century engraving, after Lucas van Leyden

2 The Merchant's Wife

Leon Battista Alberti (1404–72), in some respects the most remarkable of all Florentine humanists, had quite a range of serious interests, from Greek poetry and the study of soils to canon law and household management. Although his work On the Family, *done in dialogue form, draws generously on Xenophon's* Oeconomicus, *it expresses much that was fifteenth-century, Florentine, and upper-class. Now nothing, it seems, is more Renaissance than a Renaissance merchant, and none cleaves to the caricature (or model) more than merchants from Florence. The following selections from Alberti's dialogue offer the picture of an ideal wife as drawn by a rich old Florentine merchant, Giannozzo Alberti, one of the work's chief interlocutors. If monks took vows of poverty, chastity, and obedience, we may say of Giannozzo's wife that she took the vows of obedience, chastity, and riches .. riches through care and economy. For the material object of her whole existence, apart from childbearing, is in the efficient managing of a monied and large household. Says Giannozzo:*

After my wife had been settled in my house a few days, and after her first pangs of longing for her mother and family had begun to fade, I took her by the hand and showed her around the whole house. I explained that the loft was the place for grain and that the stores of wine and wood were kept in the cellar. I showed her where things needed for the table were kept, and so on, through the whole house. At the end there were no household goods of which my wife had not learned both the place and the purpose. Then we returned to my room, and, having locked the door, I showed her my treasures, silver, tapestry, garments, jewels, and where each thing had its place. . . .

Only my books and records and those of my ancestors did I determine to keep well sealed. . . . These my wife not only could not read, she could not even lay hands on them. I kept my records at all times . . . locked up and arranged in order in my study, almost like sacred and religious objects. I never gave my wife permission to enter that place, with me or alone. I also ordered her, if she ever came across any writing of mine, to give it over to my keeping at once. To take away any taste she might have for looking at my notes or prying into my private affairs, I often used to express my disapproval of bold and forward females who try too hard to know about things outside the house and about the concerns of their husband and of men in general. . . .

[Husbands] who take counsel with their wives . . . are madmen if they think true prudence or good counsel lies in the female brain. . . . For this very reason I have always tried carefully not to let any secret of mine be known to a woman. I did not doubt that my wife was most loving, and more discreet and modest in her ways than any, but I still considered it safer to have her unable, and not merely unwilling, to harm me. . . . Furthermore, I made it a rule never to speak with her of anything but household matters or questions of conduct, or of the children. Of these matters I spoke a good deal to her. . . .

When my wife had seen and understood the place of everything in the house, I said to her, 'My dear wife . . . you have seen our treasures now, and thanks be to God they are such that we ought to be contented with them. If we know how to preserve them, these things will serve you and me and our children. It is up to you, therefore, my dear wife, to keep no less careful watch over them than I.'

. . . She said she would be happy to do conscientiously whatever she knew how to do and had the skill to do, hoping it might please me. To this I said, 'Dear wife, listen to me. I shall be most pleased if you do just three things: first, my wife, see that you never want another man to share this bed but me. You understand.' She blushed and cast down her eyes. Still I repeated that she should never receive anyone into that room but myself. That was the first point. The second, I said, was that she should take care of the household, preside over it with modesty, serenity, tranquillity, and peace. That was the second point. The third thing, I said, was that she should see that nothing went wrong in the house.

[Addressing the other interlocutors] . . . I could not describe to you how reverently she replied to me. She said her mother had taught her only how to spin and sew, and how to be virtuous and obedient. Now she would gladly learn from me how to rule the family and whatever I might wish to teach her.

... Then she and I knelt down and prayed to God to give us the power to make good use of those possessions which he, in his mercy and kindness, had allowed us to enjoy. We also prayed ... that he might grant us the grace to live together in peace and harmony for many happy years, and with many male children, and that he might grant to me riches, friendship, and honor, and to her, integrity, purity, and the character of a perfect mistress of the household. Then, when we had stood up, I said to her: 'My dear wife, to have prayed God for these things is not enough.... I shall seek with all my powers to gain what we have asked of God. You, too, must set your whole will, all your mind, and all your modesty to work to make yourself a person whom God has heard.... You should realize that in this regard nothing is so important for yourself, so acceptable to God, so pleasing to me, and precious in the sight of your children as your chastity. The woman's character is the jewel of her family; the mother's purity has always been a part of the dowry she passes on to her daughters; her purity has always far outweighed her beauty.... Shun every sort of dishonor, my dear wife. Use every means to appear to all people as a highly respectable woman. To seem less would be to offend God, me, our children, and yourself.'

[Finally, turning to the interlocutors again] ... Never, at any moment, did I choose to show in word or action even the least bit of self-surrender in front of my wife. I did not imagine for a moment that I could hope to win obedience from one to whom I had confessed myself a slave. Always, therefore, I showed myself virile and a real man. [L. B. Alberti, *The Family in Renaissance Florence*][7]

3 The Court Lady

Baldassare Castiglione (1478–1529), North Italian nobleman, diplomat, and humanist, served at the princely courts of Milan and Mantua. His celebrated dialogue on the courtier, Il Cortegiano (1528), soon translated into the major European languages and brought out in dozens of editions, was immensely influential, notably in aristocratic and court circles. As regards the history of women, the book's true novelty is this: in it for the first time—nuns and prostitutes aside—women (i.e., court ladies) are given an explicit role outside the circle of the family and household. The author puts the recipe defining the court lady into the mouth of a leading participant in the dialogue, a real historical personage, Giuliano de' Medici (1479–1516), Duke of Nemours:

I think that in her ways, manners, words, gestures, and bearing, a woman ought to be very unlike a man; for just as he must show a certain solid and sturdy manliness, so it is seemly for a woman to have a soft and delicate tenderness, with an air of womanly sweetness in her every movement. . . .

[Again] . . . many virtues of the mind are as necessary to a woman as to a man; also, gentle birth; to avoid affectation, to be naturally graceful in all her actions, to be mannerly, clever, prudent, not arrogant, not envious, not slanderous, not vain, not contentious, not inept, to know how to gain and hold the favor of her mistress [queen or presiding lady at court] and of all others, to perform well and gracefully the exercises that are suitable for women. And I do think that beauty is more necessary to her than to the Courtier, for truly that woman lacks much who lacks beauty. . . . But since Count Ludovico [another interlocutor] has set forth in great detail the chief profession of the Courtier, and has insisted that this be arms, I think it is also fitting to state what I judge that of the Court Lady to be, and when I have done this I shall think to have discharged the greater part of my assignment.

Leaving aside, then, those virtues of the mind which she is to have in common with the Courtier (such as prudence, magna-

nimity, continence, and many others), as well as those qualities
that befit all (such as kindness, discretion, ability to manage her
husband's property and house and children, if she is married, and
all qualities that are requisite in a good mother), I say that, in my
opinion, in a Lady who lives at court a certain pleasing affa-
bility is becoming above all else, whereby she will be able to
entertain graciously every kind of man with agreeable and
comely conversation suited to the time and place and to the
station of the person with whom she speaks, joining to serene
and modest manners, and to that comeliness that ought to
inform all her actions, a quick vivacity of spirit whereby she
will show herself a stranger to all boorishness; but with such a
kind manner as to cause her to be thought no less chaste, prudent, and gentle than she is agreeable, witty, and discreet: thus,
she must observe a certain mean (difficult to achieve and, as it
were, composed of contraries) and must strictly observe certain
limits and not exceed them.

Now, in her wish to be thought good and pure, this Lady
must not be so coy, or appear so to abhor gay company or any
talk that is a little loose, as to withdraw as soon as she finds herself involved, for it might easily be thought that she was pretending to be so austere in order to hide something about herself
which she feared others might discover; for manners so unbend-
ing are always odious. Yet, on the other hand, for the sake of
appearing free and amiable she must not utter unseemly words
or enter into any immodest and unbridled familiarity or into
ways such as might cause others to believe about her what is
perhaps not true; but when she finds herself present at such
talk, she ought to listen with a light blush of shame.

. . . There is no man so profligate and so forward as not to
have reverence for those women who are esteemed to be good
and virtuous, because a certain gravity, tempered with wisdom
and goodness, is like a shield against the insolence and brutish-
ness of presumptuous men; wherefore we see that a word, a
laugh, or an act of kindness, however small, coming from a
virtuous woman is more esteemed by everyone than all the
blandishments and caresses of those who so openly show their
want of shame—and if they are not unchaste, by their wanton

laughter, loquacity, insolence, and scurrilous behavior of this sort, they appear to be so.

And since words that have no subject matter of importance are vain and puerile, the Court Lady must have not only the good judgment to recognize the kind of person with whom she is speaking, but must have knowledge of many things, in order to entertain that person graciously; and let her know how in her talk to choose those things that are suited to the kind of person with whom she is speaking. . . . In this way she will be adorned with good manners; she will perform with surpassing grace the bodily exercises that are proper to women; her discourse will be fluent and most prudent, virtuous, and pleasant; thus, she will be not only loved but revered by everyone, and perhaps worthy of being considered the equal of this great Courtier, both in qualities of mind and of body.

[A discussion follows of the bodily exercises that befit the court lady. Moreover, her manner of dressing should conform to her station and temperament.]

And to repeat briefly a part of what has already been said. I wish this Lady to have knowledge of letters, of music, of painting, and know how to dance and how to be festive, adding a discreet modesty and the giving of a good impression of herself to those other things that have been required of the Courtier. And so, in her talk, her laughter, her play, her jesting, in short in everything, she will be most graceful and will converse appropriately with every person in whose company she may happen to be, using witticisms and pleasantries that are becoming to her.

[Another interlocutor replies, Gasparo Pallavicino, Marquis of Cortemaggiore, who thinks it absurd and impossible for women to have any learning. He argues that woman is a kind of imperfect man, the birth of any woman 'a defect or mistake in nature'. Giuliano de' Medici, returning to the defense of women, then replies:]

. . . if you tell me that man is more perfect than woman, if not in essence, at least in accidental qualities, I will answer that these accidental qualities necessarily belong either to the body or to the mind; if to the body, man being more robust, more quick and agile, and more able to endure toil, I say that this little argues perfection, because among men themselves those who have these qualities more than others are not more esteemed for that; and in wars, where the operations are, for the most part, laborious and call for strength, the sturdiest are not more esteemed; if to the mind, I say that women can understand all the things men can understand and that the intellect of a woman can penetrate wherever a man's can.

... Then if you examine ancient histories (although men have always been very chary in writing praise of women) and modern histories, you will find that worth has constantly prevailed among women as among men; and that there have always been women who have undertaken wars and won glorious victories, governed kingdoms with the greatest prudence and justice, and done all that men have done. As for the sciences, do you not remember reading of many women who were learned in philosophy? Others who excelled in poetry? Others who prosecuted, accused, and defended before judges with great eloquence? As for manual works, it would be too long to tell of them, nor is there need to adduce any proof as to that. [The dispute regarding the alleged superiority of men goes on for some pages, with the advocate of women, Giuliano, always getting the upper hand. Then there is a long series of anecdotes about outstanding women; the examples are drawn from antiquity, scripture, the Middle Ages, and the contemporary period.] [Castiglione, *The Book of the Courtier*][8]

4 Protestants

The Protestant revolution against the medieval church cut so deeply that no serious moral or social question escaped its effects. Marriage, divorce, and the condition and status of women soon registered the impact. The Protestant cry against the cloister brought a revitalized emphasis upon the dignity and spirituality of marriage. Henceforth marriage was as good as celibacy and virginity, if not better. Quite obviously women stood to gain from this change. Paradoxically, moreover, owing to the reemphasis on the spiritual core of marriage, divorce swiftly came to be seen as a genuine possibility, at all events in cases in which the spiritual bond had been manifestly dissolved. Impotence and adultery immediately figured among the chief grounds for divorce, and the adultery of husbands became no less serious than that of wives.

Women achieved some prominence as workers and even agitators in the more extreme affirmations of Protestantism, the movement of Anabaptists and radical sectaries. Catherine Zell (below) was a Protestant female 'activist,' though not one of the extravagant sort. A century later (Chapter X) Protestant women were to be active in political as well as religious matters. The historical and psychological causes behind the relative prominence of women within the Protestant movement cannot, regrettably, be explored here. We must content ourselves with noting that the Protestant stress on the Word of God, on the universal reading of the Bible in the vernacular languages, greatly accentuated the importance of literacy for all members of the Reform churches. In theory at least, if not always in fact, women, the poor, and the humiliated were the true benefactors of this new turn. Martin Bucer, a leading reformer, called for the establishment of free public schools in all parishes:

As we acknowledge that all the faithful, however poor their place and low their condition, are made in the image and likeness of God and are redeemed by the blood of the Son of God, to be remade and reformed in that image, the good and loyal ministers of the people of God must work to remake and re-establish that image by means of the doctrine of salvation. And this they shall teach to the young [above all through the reading of the Holy Bible. Hence be it ordained] that all the children

of Christians, girls as well as boys, be carefully taught to read.
[Bucer, *De Regno Christi*][9]

LUTHER (1483–1546)

*Father and son of the Reformation, Martin Luther, throughout the
years of his ministry, repeatedly touched upon questions of marriage,
divorce, and the nature of women. In his famous tract* The Babylonian
Captivity of the Church (*1520*), *he rejected the traditional sacrament
of marriage and allowed three grounds for divorce—adultery, impotence,
and disbelief. The passage on impotence is revealing:*

Now let us discuss the matter of *impotence*. Consider the following case: A woman, wed to an impotent man, is unable to prove
her husband's impotence in court, or perhaps she is unwilling
to do so with the mass of evidence and all the notoriety which
the law demands; yet she is desirous of having children or is
unable to remain continent. Now suppose I had counseled her
to procure a divorce from her husband in order to marry
another, satisfied that her own and her husband's conscience and
their experience were ample testimony of his impotence; but
the husband refused his consent to this. Then I would further
counsel her, with the consent of the man (who is not really her
husband, but only a dweller under the same roof with her), to
have intercourse with another, say her husband's brother, but to
keep this marriage secret and to ascribe the children to the so-
called putative father. The question is: Is such a woman saved
and in a saved state? I answer: Certainly, because in this case
an error, ignorance of the man's impotence, impedes the
marriage; and the tyranny of the laws permits no divorce. But
the woman is free through the divine law, and cannot be compelled to remain continent. Therefore the man ought to concede
her right, and give up to somebody else the wife who is his only
in outward appearance.

Moreover, if the man will not give his consent, or agree to
this separation—rather than allow the woman to burn
[I Corinthians 7:9] or to commit adultery— I would counsel
her to contract a marriage with another and flee to a distant unknown place. What other counsel can be given to one constantly

struggling with the dangers of natural emotions? Now I know that some are troubled by the fact that the children of this secret marriage are not the rightful heirs of their putative father. But if it was done with the consent of the husband, then the children will be the rightful heirs. If, however, it was done without his knowledge or against his will, then let unbiased Christian reason, or better, charity, decide which one of the two has done the greater injury to the other. The wife alienates the inheritance, but the husband has deceived his wife and is defrauding her completely of her body and her life. Is not the sin of a man who wastes his wife's body and life a greater sin than that of the woman who merely alienates the temporal goods of her husband? Let him, therefore, agree to a divorce, or else be satisfied with heirs not his own, for by his own fault he deceived an innocent girl and defrauded her both of life and of the full use of her body, besides giving her an almost irresistible cause for committing adultery. [Luther, *Babylonian Captivity*][10]

In a letter of August 6, 1524, written to three nuns, Luther affirmed that there are two reasons for a nun's abandoning the cloister, one because of her having been forced into a convent against her will.

The other reason has to do with the flesh. Women are ashamed to admit this, but Scripture and life reveal that only one woman in thousands has been endowed with the God-given aptitude to live in chastity and virginity. A woman is not fully the master of herself. God fashioned her body so that she should be with a man, to have and to rear children. The words of Genesis, Chap. I [27–28] plainly indicate this, and parts of her body show God's purpose .... Therefore let this suffice. No woman should be ashamed of that for which God made and intended her. [*D. Martin Luthers Werke*][11]

Luther's informal conversation not seldom included observations of this sort:

Men have broad shoulders and narrow hips, and accordingly they possess intelligence. Woman have narrow shoulders and broad hips. Women ought to stay at home; the way they were created indicates this, for they have broad hips and a wide fundament to sit upon, keep house and bear and raise children [Date: 1531].

Marriage consists of these things; the natural desire of sex, the bringing to life offspring, and life together with mutual fidelity [Date: 1532].

Crotus [Rubeanus, c. 1480–c. 1539, a humanist] wrote blasphemously about the marriage of priests, declaring that the most holy bishop of Mainz was irritated by no annoyance more than by the stinking, putrid, private parts of women. That godless knave, forgetful of his mother and sister, dares to blaspheme God's creature through whom he was himself born. It would be tolerable if he were to find fault with the behavior of women, but to defile their creation and nature is most godless. As if I were to ridicule man's face on account of his nose! For the nose is the latrine of man's head and stands above his mouth [Date: 1532]. [Luther, *The Table Talk*][12]

In August 1545, Luther delivered a sermon on marriage at Merseburg, occasioned by the marriage of the dean of the cathedral in that town. He reemphasized views which he had been expressing since the early 1520s.

It is written in the first book of Moses: 'God created man in his own image, in the image of God he created him; male and female he created them. And God blessed them, and God said to them, "Be fruitful and multiply, and fill the earth and subdue it." . . .

Therefore all men should marry and be married, and since through the fall of our first parents we have been so spoiled that we are not all fit for marriage, yet those who are not fit for the married state should so live that they walk chastely and honorably and give offense to no one, though at the beginning it was not so and all were fit to become married. . . . [But those] who desire and want to be married [i.e., nuns and priests] and are also fit and competent to do so, even though they enter the marriage state contrary to human laws, do what is right, and nobody should be scandalized by what they do. . . .

The pope and his cardinals, monks, nuns, and priests have tried to improve things and ordain a holy estate in which they might live in holiness and chastity. But how holy, pure, and chaste [their] lives ... have been is so apparent that the sun, moon, and stars have cried out against it.... Why, then, did this happen? Because they tore down and despised God's holy ordinance of the estate of matrimony and they were not worthy to enter into marriage....

But here you say: Yes, but we have vowed and sworn to God that we shall be chaste and live without women; I am obliged to keep this vow; therefore I cannot be married. My answer to that is: Right, do what you have to do; be chaste and pure. Why don't you keep it, why don't you do it? Who is stopping you from being chaste and pure? Yes, you say, but I can't keep it. What a proper fool you are; why do you vow what you neither know nor can keep? ... Who commanded you to vow and swear something which is contrary to God and his ordinance, namely, to swear that you are neither a man nor a woman, when it is certain that you are either a man or a woman, created by God. Why, then, do you swear that you are not a man or a woman?

If you are able to remain chaste and be pure by your own strength, why then do you vow to be chaste? Keep it, if you can; but it is a mere nothing that you should want to boast about your vow and then plead that they have led you astray. Do you want to know to whom you have vowed to keep chastity? I'll tell you: the miserable devil in hell and his mother....

St Augustine writes in one place concerning married people, that even if one of them is somewhat weak etc., he should not be afraid of the sudden and infallible Day of the Lord; even if the Day of the Lord were to come in the hour when man and wife were having marital intercourse, they should not be afraid of it. Why is this so? Because even if the Lord comes in that hour he will find them in the ordinance and station in which they have been placed and installed by God. [Luther, *Sermons*][13]

CALVIN (1509–64)

Born in northern France and schooled in law, after an early flirtation with humanism John Calvin turned to religion, sired the hard line of Protestantism, and became the greatest reformer after Luther. His trenchant and uncompromising views on marriage are expressed in his great work of theology, Institutes of the Christian Religion (*1536*).

Then there came those times [the Middle Ages] when the esteem for abstaining from marriage grew into a crazy superstition. Virginity was so greatly prized that it became very difficult to think that there was any other virtue worthy of being compared to it. And although marriage was not condemned as something filthy, yet its dignity was so overshadowed that a man could really aspire to perfection, it was thought, only if he remained celibate. This is what inspired the church laws forbidding priests to marry. [Calvin, *Institution de la religion Chrestienne*][14]

Man was not created to live in solitude but to have a companion somewhat like himself. After the Fall, he was all the more subjected to this companionship, the society of women. The Lord, therefore, gave us a remedy for this in marriage. It follows that all companionship outside of marriage between a man and a woman is damned and that marriage has been given to us in order to bridle our lust....

I confess that virginity is not a virtue to be disdained. But as it is not given to everyone and given to some only for a time, those who are tormented by incontinence and cannot overcome it should have recourse to the remedy of marriage in order that they may preserve chastity according to the degree of their calling....

Let no man despise marriage as a thing profitless and unnecessary; and let no man desire to pass it by unless he can live without a woman.... Let him who has the gift of continence abstain from marriage for as long as he can be continent, but no longer. If the power to conquer and tame the lust of the flesh fails him, let him understand by this that God has imposed the necessity of marriage upon him.... If those who are incontinent disdain to cure their infirmity by means of the remedy of marriage, they sin. And let no man who actually refrains from fornication flatter himself, as if he were not guilty of lewdness when his heart burns inwardly with wicked lust....

Knowing that their association is blessed by God, married

couples are thereby warned and commanded not to pollute the relationship with unbridled and self-indulgent lust. For even though the dignity of marriage hides the shame of incontinence, this is not to say that marriage is an invitation to sensuality. Married couples should not think that all things are permitted to them. Let every man go soberly to his wife and every woman soberly to her husband, and let them behave in such a way as to do nothing against the sanctity of marriage. The Lord's will should be seen in the light of such modesty, in order to keep marriage from brimming over in lasciviousness. Censuring those who abuse marriage by lecherous intemperance, St Ambrose says something hard but fitting: that is, that they are adulterers with their own wives. [Calvin, *Institution*][15]

MARTIN BUCER (1491–1551)

A German Dominican monk, Bucer quickly came out for Luther (1518) and was for many years the leading reformer at Strasbourg, as well as a key figure in the organization of Protestant churches at Augsburg, Constance, and Ulm. His major work, On the Kingdom of Christ *(1550), was addressed to the young English king, Edward VI. Like Calvin, Bucer was haunted by the terrifying promise of the kingdom of the flesh. Both men gave way, accordingly, to a boundless paternalism: they laid great accent on parental authority, called for the civil power to crack down, and poured out a flood of adamantine moral strictures. So far as advances in the history of women go, their views led two steps forward and one back: 'respectable' women gained more rights, but people of 'easier' morals suffered in the ensuing climate, and later on certain cities would see the execution of alleged prostitutes (see p. 227). Nevertheless, Bucer's conception of marriage and divorce was at the vanguard of development. His attitude toward the spiritual equality of the partners in marriage issued in a view of divorce which accorded unheard-of rights to Protestant women (e.g., the right to remarry), rights soon to be claimed in parts of Germany, Holland, Scandinavia, and Scotland, but not, for example, in England until the second half of the nineteenth century.*

Having held in the previous chapter of his work that adulterers should be put to death, Bucer goes on to argue that a woman may repudiate her adulterous husband and remarry:

For the Holy Spirit says that there is neither male nor female in Christ. In all things that pertain to salvation one should have as much regard for woman as for man. For though she is bound to keep her place, to put herself under the authority of her husband, just as the church does in relation to Christ, yet her subjection does not cancel the right of an honest woman, in accordance with the laws of God, to have recourse to and demand, by legitimate means, deliverance from a husband who hates her. For the Lord has certainly not made married woman subservient to have her be polluted and tormented by the extortions and injuries of her husband but rather so that she may receive discipline from him, as if from her master and savior, like the church from Christ. A wife is not so subject to her husband that she is bound to suffer anything he may impose upon her. Being free, she is joined to him in holy marriage that she may be loved, nourished, and maintained by him, as if she were his own flesh, just as the church is maintained by Christ. . . . Again, though a wife may be something less than her husband and subject to him, in order that they be rightly joined, the Holy Spirit has declared, through its apostle, that man and woman are equal before God in things pertaining to the alliance and mutual confederation of marriage. This is the meaning of the apostle's saying that a wife has power over the body of her husband, just as a husband has power over the body of his wife (1 Corinthians 7]. . . . Hence if wives feel that their association and cohabitation with their husbands is injurious to salvation as well of one as of the other, owing to the hardening and hatred on the part of their husbands, let them have recourse to the civil authority, which is enjoined by the Lord to help the afflicted. [Bucer, *De Regno Christi*][16]

TRADITIONAL ACCENTS

In reshaping society, revolutions may tear up venerable procedures, but they carry over, too, immense legacies from the past. The Protestant Revolution retained much that was ancient and traditional. Attention has been called to its paternalistic strain. Following are two selections whose accents reveal the powerful, persisting hand of the past.

In a treatise on the freedom of the will (1527), the radical reformer

Balthasar Hübmaier (burned 1528) describes the condition of the soul and conceives of Eve as flesh:

The reason that the fall of the soul is partly reparable, however, and not fatal, even here on earth, but the fall of the flesh is to a certain extent irreparable and deadly, is that Adam, as a type of the soul (as is Eve, of the flesh), would have preferred not to eat of the forbidden tree. He was also not deceived by the serpent, but Eve was (1 Timothy 2: 14). Adam knew very well that the words of the serpent were contrary to the words of God. Yet he willed to eat the fruit against his own conscience, so as not to vex or anger his rib, his flesh, Eve. He would have preferred not to do it. But when he was more obedient to his Eve than to God, he lost his knowledge of good and evil, so that he could not wish nor choose anything good.... Neither could he reject or flee from anything evil, for he no longer knows what is good or bad in the sight of God. Everything has lost its savor for him, except what is savory and pleasing to his Eve, that is, his flesh.... [Finally man is restored through Christ:] Now the soul is free and can follow either the spirit or the flesh. If it follows Eve, that is, the flesh, it becomes an Eve and carnal. But if it is obedient to the Spirit, it becomes a spirit. [Hübmaier, *On Free Will*][17]

John Calvin loathed the idea that women might take on priestly functions. At one point in his Institutes, *he stops to deride the notion of women administering baptism, a practice then common among Anabaptists:*

The custom of the church, before St Augustine was born, may be elicited first of all from Tertullian, who held that no woman in church is allowed to speak, teach, baptize, or make offerings: this in order that she may not usurp the functions of men, let alone those of priests. [Adduces Epiphanius:] It is a mockery to allow women to baptize. Even the Virgin Mary was not allowed this.

In this connection [the plea for letting women baptize] the example of Zipporah is mistakenly cited [Exodus 4:25]. For they point out that she seized a stone and circumcised her son, thereby placating the angel of God. But they stupidly infer that

16 Woman washing ore
Woodcut from *De Re Metallica* by G. Agricola, 1556

17 Woman the man
16th-century German engraving

God approved of this act.... Nothing was farther from the aim of Moses' wife than to serve God. Seeing her child in danger of death, she complained and grumbled and angrily hurled the foreskin to the ground; and in abusing her husband, she went sour and kicked against God. In short, her performance was the result of a disorderly impetuosity, inasmuch as she became angry and spat things out against God and her husband because she was forced to shed her son's blood. [Calvin, *Institution*][18]

CATHERINE ZELL (c. 1497–c. 1562)

Born in Strasbourg to a cabinetmaker's family, Catherine was married in 1523 to Mathew Zell, Lutheran, ex-priest, and prominent reformer. In the circumstances, with the papal-Catholic backlash already started, the marriage was somewhat risky. The bishop of Strasbourg resolved to excommunicate and if need be destroy Zell and a number of other priests who had married and gone over to the Reformation. Catherine then, and many times thereafter, boldly rushed to Mathew's defence, on this occasion by writing directly to the bishop, pointing out his duties (!), and threatening to publish the letter. We know her best from her late correspondence (1556–8) with a younger Lutheran minister, Ludwig Rabus of Memmingen, whose loathing for the Protestant radical movement turned him violently against the Zells. They were too tolerant for him and virtually of the devil's party. One of his letters charged that the Zells—though Catherine was by then a widow—had injected so much anxiety and agitation into the church of Strasbourg that they would not escape God's judgment. Stung, Catherine replied and sought to vindicate herself by publishing the correspondence, consisting almost entirely of her own letters.

During the sixteenth century Germany saw a line of Protestant female activists, among them for example, Catherine, Argula von Grumbach, and Ursula von Munsterberg. The following selections, drawn from Catherine's letters to Rabus, convey something of her spirit (not always attractive) and quality:

I, Catherine Zell, wife of the late lamented Mathew Zell, who served in Strasburg, where I was born and reared and still live, wish you peace and enhancement of God's grace....

From my earliest years I turned to the Lord, who taught and guided me, and I have at all times, in accordance with my understanding and His grace, embraced the interests of His church and earnestly sought Jesus. Even in youth this brought me the regard and affection of clergymen and others much concerned with the church, which is why the pious Mathew Zell wanted me as a companion in marriage; and I, in turn, to serve the glory of Christ, gave devotion and help to my husband, both in his ministry and in keeping his house.... [There follows a passage on the couple's years of work in the cause of the church of Strasbourg.]

Ever since I was ten years old I have been a student and a sort of church mother, much given to attending sermons. I have loved and frequented the company of learned men, and I conversed much with them, not about dancing, masquerades, and worldly pleasures but about the kingdom of God ....

Yet I resisted and struggled against that kingdom. Then, as no learned man could find a way of consoling me in my sins, prayers and physical suffering, and as none could make me sure of God's love and grace, I fell gravely ill in body and spirit. I became like that poor woman of the Gospel who, having spent all she had on doctors to no avail, heard speak of Christ, went to Him, and was healed. As I foundered, devoured by care and anxiety, vainly searching for serenity in the practices of the church, God took pity on me. From among our people He drew out and sent forth Martin Luther. This man so persuaded me of the ineffable goodness of our Lord Jesus Christ that I felt myself snatched from the depths of hell and transported to the kingdom of heaven. I remembered the Lord's words to Peter: 'Follow me and I shall make you a fisher of men'. Then did I labor day and night to cleave to the path of divine truth.... [Catherine again goes into the couple's work at Strasbourg.]

While other women decorated their houses and ornamented themselves, going to dances, wedding parties, and giving themselves to pleasure, I went into the houses of poor and rich alike, in all love, faith, and compassion, to care for the sick and the confined and to bury the dead. Was that to plant anxiety and turmoil in the church of Strasbourg?..

In 1524 a hundred-and-fifty burghers had to flee from the little town of Kenzingen, in Breisgau. That night they came to Strasbourg. I took eighty into our house. For the next four weeks there were never fewer than fifty or sixty people at table. Many nobles and burgesses helped us to take care of them. And what about the disorders we started in 1525 [at the time of the great peasant uprising], I and a lot of other devoted people? In the wake of the massacre of the poor peasants, many of those who got away, wretched and terrified, came to us in Strasbourg. The almoner Master Hackfurt, myself, and two widows lodged a great crowd of them in the [old] Franciscan cloister, and I got many other honorable men and women to help. A number of surviving noblemen in the town council know this, as do certain respectable rich women who also came to our aid. They could speak up....

[Sharply criticizes Rabus for his intolerance of Anabaptists and the radical sectaries.] Consider the poor Anabaptists, who are so furiously and ferociously persecuted. Must the authorities everywhere be incited against them, as the hunter drives his dog against wild animals? Against those who acknowledge Christ the Lord in very much the same way we do and over which we broke with the papacy? Just because they cannot agree with us on lesser things, is this any reason to persecute them and in them Christ, in whom they fervently believe and have often professed in misery, in prison, and under the torments of fire and water?

Governments may punish criminals, but they should not force and govern belief, which is a matter for the heart and conscience not for temporal authorities. [Urges Rabus to consult the leading reformers on this question and provides him, ironically, with a list.] ... When the authorities pursue one, they soon bring forth tears, and towns and villages are emptied....

Strasbourg does not offer the example of an evil town but rather the contrary—charity, compassion, and hospitality for the wretched and poor. Within its walls, God be thanked, there remains more than one poor Christian whom certain people would have liked to see cast out. Old Mathew Zell would not have approved of that: he would have gathered the sheep, not destroyed them....

Whether they were Lutherans, Zwinglians, Schwenkfeldians, or poor Anabaptist brethren, rich or poor, wise or foolish, according to the word of St Paul, all came to us [to the Zells in Strasbourg]. We were not compelled to hold the same views and beliefs that they did, but we did owe to all a proof of love, service, and generosity: our teacher Christ has taught us that......

[Hans Lenglin, a man with views like Rabus, had said:] Better to be a papist than an Anabaptist or a Schwenkfeldian.... [Catherine replies, addressing Rabus:] You think that people will let themselves be pushed into prejudgments and shackles. Not at all. Freedom and intellect have been taken and won. [Johann C. Füsslin, ed., *Beiträge zur Erläuterung der Kirchen Reformations*][19]

5 Witches

The witch craze of the sixteenth and seventeenth centuries, a puzzling and complex phenomenon, produced the perfect climate for misogyny. This ancient clerical disease now developed a lethal strain: the victims were mainly women and the inquisitors, clergymen. The notion that women were 'Pythian', (like Delphic priestesses, subject to frenzied and visionary perceptions of the supernatural), perhaps as a recompense for not being 'rational', had been about for centuries. There are periods or historical moments when, owing to surrounding circumstances, the effects of such an attitude can be profound. People tend, after all, to conform to the expectations of their society. Women saints have more often inclined to extravagant mysticism than their male counterparts. And diabolic possession, the reversal of the union with Christ, struck both witch hunters and hunted as more a woman's malady than a man's.

The bloody fashion for witches and witch hunters seems to have started in the Alps, where the Waldensian heresy had survived. Those who helped to launch the fashion, the Dominicans, had originally been founded to combat this heresy and now 'discovered beneath the forms of one heresy, the rudiments (as they thought) of another,' (H. R. Trevor-Roper). The Waldensians had accepted women preachers. Not surprisingly then, when the witch hunters set about elaborating a Satan cult to father on their victims, they had no trouble turning up women celebrants. Since the whole diabolic religion was handled by simply reversing Christian orthodoxy, what could have been more appropriate? Its rituals took place by night rather than by day, were in the hands of women rather than men, aped the Mass by using such things as sliced turnips to take the place of the host, and flouted Christian ideals of purity by kissing the devil—in the form of a cat, dog, or goat—on his anus. The cult was thus heretical, erotic, and largely in the hands of women; it was evil and terrifying in that witches were alleged to use the devil's power to murder, maim, make sterile, ruin crops, and so forth.

Another element in the antifeminism of the witch hunters was quite likely connected with the beginnings of emancipation for women. Being fragmentary and partly subject to whim, this very deliverance could foster tensions and occasion backlash.

WOMEN THE MOST INFECTIOUS

The most authoritative catechism of demonology, the Malleus Maleficarum, (*Hammer of Witches*), *was brought out in 1486 by two
Dominican inquisitors, Heinrich Kramer and James Sprenger, whose
field of action was Germany and the Tyrol. By 1520 their catechism had
gone through fourteen known editions. Let us see why women had a
greater penchant for witchcraft than men:*

As for the question, why a greater number of witches is found
in the fragile feminine sex than among men ... [this] is indeed
a fact that it were idle to contradict, since it is accredited by
actual experience, apart from the verbal testimony of credible
witnesses.... And the first [reason] is, that they are more
credulous....The second reason is, that women are naturally
more impressionable, and more ready to receive the influence
of a disembodied spirit; and that when they use this quality well
they are very good, but when they use it ill they are very evil.
The third reason is that they have slippery tongues, and are unable to conceal from their fellow-women those things which by
evil arts they know; and, since they are weak, they find an easy
and secret manner of vindicating themselves by witchcraft....

There are also others who bring forward yet other reasons, of
which preachers should be very careful how they make use. For
it is true that in the Old Testament the Scriptures have much
that is evil to say about women, and this because of the first
temptress, Eve, and her imitators; yet afterwards in the New
Testament we find a change of name, as from Eva to Ave
(as St Jerome says), and the whole sin of Eve taken away by the
benediction of Mary. Therefore preachers should always say as
much praise of them as possible.

But because in these times this perfidy is more often found in
women than in men, as we learn by actual experience, if anyone
is curious as to the reason, we may add to what has already been
said the following: that since they are feebler both in mind and
body, it is not surprising that they should come more under the
spell of witchcraft.

For as regards intellect, or the understanding of spiritual
things, they seem to be of a different nature from men; a fact
which is vouched for by the logic of the authorities....

But the natural reason is that she is more carnal than a man, as is clear from her many carnal abominations. And it should be noted that there was a defect in the formation of the first woman, since she was formed from a bent rib, that is, a rib of the breast, which is bent as it were in a contrary direction to a man. And since through this defect she is an imperfect animal, she always deceives. . . .

And indeed, just as through the first defect in their intelligence they are more prone to abjure the faith; so through their second defect of inordinate affections and passions they search for, brood over, and inflict various vengeances, either by witchcraft, or by some other means. Wherefore, it is no wonder that so great a number of witches exist in this sex. . . .

To conclude. All witchcraft comes from carnal lust, which is in women insatiable [H. Kramer and J. Sprenger, *Malleus Maleficarum*][20]

Jean Bodin (1530–96)—French jurist, magistrate, political theorist, one of the most learned men of his day, and a darling of the intellectual historians—was not the least gullible of witch haters:

As I remarked before, it is clear from the books of all who have written on witches that for every male witch there are fifty female witches. . . . In my opinion this is not due to the frailty of the sex—for most of them are intractably obstinate—it is more likely that what reduced them to this extremity was bestial cupidity. . . . And it is likely that this is why Plato placed woman between man and the brute beast [reference probably to the *Timaeus*, 90–2]. For one sees that women's visceral parts are bigger than those of men whose cupidity is less violent. On the other hand, men have larger heads and therefore have more brains and sense than women. The poets expressed this metaphorically when they said that Pallas Athena, goddess of wisdom, was born from the brain of Jupiter and had no mother: they meant to show that wisdom never comes from women, whose nature is nearer to that of brute beasts. We may as well add that Satan first addressed himself to woman, who then seduced man. Furthermore, I consider that God wanted to weaken and tame Satan by giving him power ordinarily and primarily over the least worthy of creatures, such as snakes, flies, and other beasts which the law of God calls foul; next over other brute beasts rather than over men, then over woman rather than over man, and over men who live like beasts rather than over the others. Again, Satan makes use of wives to ensnare their husbands. [J. Bodin, *De la démonomanie des sorciers*][21]

The Englishman Reginald Scot, a skeptic, published his book Discoverie of Witchcraft *in 1584. King James I had it burned soon after 1603 because it was too soft on witches. Scot did not deny the reality of witchcraft, but neither did he accept all the theoretical baggage and paraphernalia. In the following passage he lists some typical notions of the time.*

The cause why women are oftener found to be witches than men: [it is said that] they have such an unbridled force of fury and concupiscence naturally that by no means is it possible for them to temper or moderate the same. So as upon every trifling occasion, they (like brute beasts) fix their furious eyes upon the party whom they bewitch. Hereby it comes to pass that women, having a marvelous fickle nature, when grief so ever happens unto them, immediately all peaceableness of mind departs; and they are so troubled with evil humors, that out go their venemous exhalations, engendered through their ill-favored diet, and increased by means of their pernicious excrements, which they expel. Women are also [it is said] monthly filled full of superfluous humors, and with them the melancholic blood boils; whereof spring vapors, and are carried up, and conveyed through the nostrils and mouth, etc., to the bewitching of whatsoever it meet. For they belch up a certain breath, wherewith they bewitch whomsoever they list. And of all other women, lean, hollow-eyed, old, beetlebrowed women are the most infectious. [R. Scot, *The Discoverie of Witchcraft*][22]

The presumption that demons could have sexual intercourse with human beings is found in early Jewish thought and was taken over by Christians. A popular book for midwives, published by an Italian doctor in 1596, offers this account:

The Demon, being of an angelic nature, can procreate only by working through human nature.... He must first assume the body of a dead woman and, pretending to be a whore, have carnal intercourse with a man so as to get his seed. He may also procure the seed from such as have nocturnal pollutions or who deliberately abuse themselves; then, keeping it in its natural temperature, which he can easily do—since spiritual substance has absolute power over corporal substance—he must assume a male body and transport that seed which he got as a succubus into the uterus of a woman by having carnal relations with her as an incubus. [Scipio Mercurio, *La Commare o Riccoglitrice*][23]

The Dominican inquisitors Heinrich Kramer and James Sprenger offered a similar account (1486):

With regard to the bewitchment of human beings by means of Incubus and Succubus devils, it is to be noted that this can happen in three ways. First, as in the case of witches themselves, when women voluntarily prostitute themselves to Incubus devils. Secondly, when men have connection with Succubus devils; yet it does not appear that men thus devilishly fornicate with the same full degree of culpability; for men, being by nature intellectually stronger than women, are more apt to abhor such practices. Thirdly, it may happen that men or women are entangled with Incubi or Succubi against their will. This chiefly happens in the case of certain virgins.... [*Malleus Maleficarum*][24]

WITCH-HUNTING METHODS AND REFUTATIONS

To disbelieve in witches is the greatest of heresies: *thus the* Malleus *and thus the prevailing moral wind. Against an enemy upheld by Satan all means were good—torture, false promises, or just plain wheedling. Friedrich von Spee, a Jesuit poet and confessor of witches, came to see the absurdity of their confessions and wrote a book, the* Cautio Criminalis (1631), *describing the methods of witch hunters. Since a defender of witches exposed himself to denunciation as a witch and death by fire, Spee's book was anonymously issued.*

If some utterance of a demoniac [i.e., crazy person] or some malign and idle rumor then current—for proof of the scandal is never asked—points especially to some poor and helpless Gaia [i.e., female culprit], she is the first to suffer.

And yet, lest it appear that she is indicted on the basis of rumor alone, without other proofs, as the phrase goes, lo a certain presumption is at once obtained against her by posing the following dilemma: Either Gaia has led a bad and improper life, or she has led a good and proper one. If a bad one, then, say they, the proof is cogent against her; for from malice to malice the presumption is strong. If, however, she has led a good one, this also is none the less a proof; for thus, they say, are witches wont to cloak themselves and try to seem especially proper.

Therefore it is ordered that Gaia be haled away to prison. And lo now a new proof is gained against her by this other dilemma: Either she then shows fear or she does not show it. If she does show it (hearing forsooth of the grievous tortures wont to be used in this matter), this is of itself a proof; for conscience, they say, accuses her. If she does not show it (trusting forsooth in her innocence), this too is a proof; for it is most characteristic of witches, they say, to pretend themselves peculiarly innocent and wear a bold front.

Lest, however, further proofs against her should be lacking, the Commissioner has his own creatures, often depraved and notorious, who question into all her past life. This, of course, cannot be done without coming upon some saying or doing of hers which evil-minded men can easily twist or distort into ground for suspicion of witchcraft. . . .

Without any scruples, therefore, after this confession she is executed. Yet she would have been executed, nevertheless, even though she had not confessed; for when once a beginning has been made with torture, the die is already cast—she cannot escape, she must die.

So, whether she confesses or does not confess, the result is the same. . . . If she does not confess, the torture is repeated—twice, thrice, four times: everything one pleases is permissible, for in an excepted crime [i.e., one in which, by reason of its enormity, all restraints upon proceedings are suspended] there is no limit of duration or severity or repetition of the tortures. . . .

If, now, any under stress of pain has once falsely declared herself guilty, her wretched plight beggars description. For not only is there in general no door for her escape, but she is also compelled to accuse others, of whom she knows no ill, and whose names are not seldom suggested to her by her examiners or by the executioner, or of whom she has heard as suspected or accused or already once arrested and released. These in their turn are forced to accuse others, and these still others, and so it goes on: who can help seeing that it must go on without end? [*The Witch Persecutions*][25]

Torture does not account for all the confessions. Women have often espoused social codes and restraints hostile to themselves. Many women spontaneously accused themselves of witchcraft.

The Belgian physician Johann Wier (1516–88)—accused by Bodin of sleeping with an alleged sorcerer (Agrippa von Nettesheim—advanced a psychological explanation in his De Praestigiis Daemonum, *(1563, and subsequent revised editions). Wier argued that the women who confessed to being witches were suffering from mental aberrations. Admitting that this might be caused by the devil, he pointed out that the cause might equally lie in melancholia, drugs, imprisonment, anxiety brought on by torture, or the sheer vapidity of women's brains. Often, too, the accusations were the work of quack doctors, mostly monks and priests:*

These people, being ignorant, are also of an unbridled impudence and wickedness.... They shamelessly boast of medical knowledge totally alien to them and are not ashamed to give lying answers in order to deceive the unfortunate common people who ask their advice about all sorts of maladies. I say then that they are not ashamed to say that the illness was caused by witchcraft and spells.... They usually even blame it on some innocent and honest matron. [Johann Wier, *De Praestigiis Daemonum*][26]

Wier systematically refutes the component beliefs of the witch cult. Virgins and nuns who confessed to copulating with incubi should, he suggests, be examined, and he gives a description of the hymen (Bk. II, ch. 37), whose existence was not yet a well-established biological fact. Elsewhere, he controverts the widely held belief that succubi could transport semen to im-

pregnate women. As he said to his patron, Duke William V of Cleves-Jülich, his object was to deny:

... that childish old hags called witches can do anything to harm men or animals.... I fight with natural reason against the deceptions which proceed from Satan and from the crazy imagination of the so-called witches. My object is also medical, in that I have to show that those illnesses, whose origins are attributed to witches, come from natural causes; and finally my object is legal. [Wier, *De Praestigiis Daemonum*][27]

Since witches are usually old women of melancholic nature and small brains (women who get easily depressed and have little trust in God), there is no doubt that the devil easily affects and deceives their minds by illusions and apparitions that so bewilder them that they confess to actions that they are very far from having committed.... Therefore, I dare not class them among heretics because none deserves to be so called until proof has been given of fanatical and obstinate persistence in error... From consideration of their age and sex, Christians should be less ready to throw these poor mindless old women into dark, black, stinking prisons unfit for humans and inhabited by evil spirits that torment the prisoners. Nor should they be delivered ... to be cruelly tortured, until these most wretched of God's creatures, already disturbed in their minds by the assiduous machinations, charms and illusions of the devil, after long imprisonment and racking by diverse tortures ... come, I say, to prefer death to their own wretched lives, freely confessing all the crimes suggested to them, rather than run the risk of being led back to those evil-smelling caverns and perpetual torture. By such means a poor old woman, already set for burning, was brought to confess that she had caused the long winter and extreme cold and persistent ice of 1575. And there were men of authority who thought this truer than truth itself, although there is nothing more absurd in all nature. [Wier, *De Praestigiis Daemonum*][28]

WITCH HUNTS

The whole sanguinary business peaked in the second half of the sixteenth century but continued for another hundred years. The fierce conflict between Catholic and Protestant worked to key people up to the passions of high dogma. Between 1587 and 1593 twenty-two villages in the region of Trier surrendered 368 witches to the bonfires. Two other villages survived the spasm with a female population of one each. Toulouse and its vicinage, in 1577 alone, reportedly saw the burning of 400 witches. Parts of western Germany were especially stricken. Here is an eyewitness account from Trier:

Inasmuch as it was popularly believed that the continued sterility of many years was caused by witches through the malice of the Devil, the whole country rose to exterminate the witches. This movement was promoted by many in office, who hoped for wealth from the persecution. And so, from court to court throughout the towns and villages of all the diocese, scurried special accusers, inquisitors, notaries, jurors, judges, constables, dragging to trial and torture human beings of both sexes and burning them in great numbers. Scarcely any of those who were accused escaped punishment. Nor were there spared even the leading men in the city of Trier. For the Judge [Dr Dietrich Flade, burned 1589] with two Burgomasters, several Councilors and Associate Judges, canons of sundry collegiate churches, parish priests, rural deans, were swept away in this ruin. So far, at length, did the madness of the furious populace and of the courts go in this thirst for blood and booty that there was scarcely anybody who was not smirched by some suspicion of this crime.

Meanwhile notaries, copyists, and innkeepers grew rich. The executioner rode a blooded horse, like a noble of the court, and went clad in gold and silver; his wife vied with noble dames in the richness of her array. The children of those convicted and punished were sent into exile; their goods were confiscated; plowman and vintner failed—hence came sterility. A direr pestilence or a more ruthless invader could hardly have ravaged the territory of Trier than this inquisition. . . . The persecution lasted for several years; and some of those who presided over the administration of justice gloried in the multitude of the stakes, at each of which a human being had been given to the flames.

At last, though the flames were still unsated, the people grew impoverished, rules were made and enforced restricting the fees and costs of examinations and examiners, and suddenly, as when in war funds fail, the zeal of the persecution died out. [*Gesta Trevirorum*] [29]

In England, under the Puritans, witches—more mercifully? —were sometimes hanged. There is a report of the witch craze at Newcastle in the dead center of the seventeenth century:

John Wheeler of London, upon his oath said, that in or about the years 1649 to 1650, being at Newcastle, he heard that the magistrates had sent two of their sergeants, namely Thomas Shevel and Cuthbert Nicholson, into Scotland to agree with a Scotch-man, who pretended knowledge to find out witches by pricking them with pins, to come to Newcastle where he should try such who should be brought to him, and to have twenty shillings a piece for all he should condemn as witches, and free passage thither and back again.

When the sergeants had brought the said witch-finder on horse-back to town, the magistrates sent their bell-man through the town, ringing his bell and crying, All people that would bring in any complaint against any woman for a witch, they should be sent for and tried by the person appointed.

Thirty women were brought into the townhall and stript, and then openly had pins thrust into their bodies, and most of them was [*sic*] found guilty, near twenty-seven of them, by him and set aside.

The said reputed witch-finder acquainted Lieutenant-Colonel Hobson that he knew women, whether they were witches or no, by their looks, and when the said person was searching of a personable and good like woman, the said Colonel replied and said, surely this woman is none and need not be tried, but the Scotch-man said she was, for the town said she was, and therefore he would try her; and presently in sight of all the people laid her body naked to the waist, with her clothes over her head, by which fright and shame all her blood contracted into one part of her body, and then he ran a pin into her thigh, and then suddenly let her coats fall, and then demanded whether she had nothing of his in her body but did not bleed, but she being amazed replied little, then he put his hand up her coats, and pulled out the pin and set her aside as a guilty person, and child of the Devil, and fell to try others whom he made guilty.

Lieutenant-Colonel Hobson perceiving the alteration of the foresaid woman, by her blood settling in her right parts, caused that woman to be brought again, and her clothes pulled up to her thigh, and required the Scot to run the pin into the same place, and then it gushed out of blood, and the said Scot cleared her, and said she was not a child of the Devil.

So soon as he had done and received his wages, he went into Northumberland to try women there, where he got of some three pound a piece. But Henry Ogle Esq., a late member of Parliament, laid hold on him and required bond of him to answer the sessions, but he got away for Scotland, and it was conceived that if he had stayed he would have made most of the women in the north witches for money....

The said witch-finder was laid hold on in Scotland, cast into prison, indicted, arraigned and condemned for such like villany exercised in Scotland. And upon the gallows he confessed he had been the death of above two hundred and twenty women in England and Scotland, for the gain of twenty shillings a piece, and beseeched forgiveness. And was executed. [Ralph Gardiner, *England's Grievance Discovered*][30]

X The Early Modern Period

1 The Law Again

Most of the disabilities under which women had suffered in the Middle Ages survived the early modern period. Women were still debarred from public office and the professions, and by and large their husbands continued to manage and enjoy their property. We turn here to another aspect of the law as it affects women: penal legislation. We shall get a more coherent image if we confine ourselves to one country, France. The most supple instrument for legal change in France was royal action. The kings, when dealing with family law, aimed at strengthening the family, preserving property for heirs, and making the law uniform in the different provinces. Parents are given very full powers when dealing with children tempted to marry beneath their social station. The pertinent laws applied equally to male and female minors. On paper the female might even appear to have the advantage, her minority being shorter. In practice, however, girls were married off earlier and a boy had more hope of resisting until he was legally old enough to make his own decision. The lax priest ready to marry runaway lovers was a thorn in the side of the royal legislator. But it should be emphasized that runaways were not always lovers. Kidnapping a rich heiress, 'dishonoring her' (an automatic outcome), and then offering to make amends by marriage, was a favorite trick of fortune hunters.

[Extract, statute, Henri II, Paris, February, 1556.] Petitions have been made to Us concerning marriages daily contracted in Our realm by children of good family under the sway of an indiscreet and carnal impulse and without their parents' knowledge or consent.... [Wherefore We decree] that such children may be excluded from all inheritances. Further, the said parents may revoke and annul all gifts and other advantages already bestowed on such children.... We do not wish this to apply to marriages contracted by sons of over thirty years of age or by daughters of over twenty-five ... nor to apply when [their] mothers have remarried, in which cases it shall be sufficient to ask their advice; but the children shall not be required to await their consent. [*Code Matrimonial*][1]

[Extract, statute, Henri III at Blois, May, 1579. Articles on Marriage. Art. XLII.] It is Our wish that all who have suborn-ed sons or daughters of less than twenty-five years of age, either with a promise of marriage or otherwise, without the wish, knowledge, desire and express consent of their fathers, mothers and guardians, be punished by the death penalty without hope of grace or pardon regardless of any consent which the said minors may allege they gave at the time of the abduction or earlier. All who participated in the abduction or lent their advice, comfort or aid in any manner whatsoever shall be punished in the same way [*Code Matrimonial*]²

[Extract, statute, Louis XIII in Paris, January, 1629. Art. V, XXXIX.] The Statute of Blois concerning marriage shall be ob-served exactly, and we add to it ... that any marriage contract-ed contrary to its terms shall be null and void. On pain of a dis-cretionary fine, We forbid parish priests or any other members of the regular or secular clergy to celebrate the marriage of persons from outside their parish without permission from [those persons'] own parish priests or the diocesan bishop or arch-bishop. ... CLXIX. It being Our desire to preserve the autho-rity of fathers over their children and the honor and freedom of marriage ... as well as to prevent, for the future, families of rank being connected with persons either unworthy or of diffe-rent morals, We hereby renew the statutes which punish abduc-tion [with the death penalty]. [*Code Matrimonial*]³

Restraints on minors did not apply to widows over twenty-five. A statute of 1560 blocked their giving any property to second husbands or second husbands' families as long as children, or the offspring of children, survived from their first marriages. Article CLXXXII of Henri III's statute of 1579 reveals the fears underlying these measures:

And since many widows, even those who have children by earli-er marriages, remarry out of foolish desire with people unworthy of their rank and, what is worse, with their men servants: We have ordained that all gifts ... which such widows who have children by their first marriages shall make to such people ... shall be null and void: and such women, from the time of con-tracting such marriages, are and shall be deprived of the control

of their estates and We forbid them to sell or alienate any part
thereof in any way whatsoever ... and declare any contracts
[they shall make] null and of no effect. (*Code Matrimonial*)[4]

*A statute of 1697 and a proclamation of 1730 reaffirmed the severity of
the earlier acts, but it is clear, from other sources, that these laws were
applied with discretion and with an eye for the details of the given case.
Girls of birth and rank, heiresses, and rich young widows aroused particular concern. But the appropriate set of laws could easily be turned
against girls of the lower classes, as in the following case, revealing the
court's sympathy for a family threatened with a* mésalliance.

Case tried before the High Court of Aix in 1689. Joseph Cabassol
... was the eldest of the seven children of a lawyer at the High
Court of Aix.... [After his parents' death he succeeded to his
inheritance. Then some years later] he fell in love with the
woman Anne Geniere, a widow [who] had been brought before
the Provost of Marseille because of her scandalous life. Convicted of prostitution and pimping, she had been sentenced
by the judge to three years' banishment.... This sentence was
confirmed, after appeal, by a decision of the High Court of
Aix in 1683.

On 19 April 1688, Joseph Cabassol and Anne Geniere appeared before the bishop of Avignon, told him they were inhabitants of that town, that they wanted to get married, and that
there was no canonical impediment. In proof of this, they
brought three witnesses ... and asked to be dispensed from
publishing banns [request granted] .... They were married the
following day ... and returned to Aix on the following
fourth of May....

On the fourteenth of that same month of May, Joseph
Cabassol's family, hearing of his marriage, his uncle, two
brothers, and a sister put in a petition to have it annulled.

In Joseph Cabassol's defense, it was said that an adult of
thirty years of age is free according to all the laws of God and
man to choose his own wife .... Joseph Cabassol said that
neither his uncle nor his brothers and sister were entitled to
attack his marriage.

Monsieur de Saint-Martin, Director of Public Prosecutions

. . . admitted that the consent of brothers and uncles is not necessary in the case of the marriage of an adult. . . .

One could not, however, conclude that such persons are
never entitled to oppose the marriage of an adult. . . . The
grounds for attacking this marriage were essentially two: that it
was celebrated without publishing the banns and that it was not
celebrated by the parties' own parish priest. . . . It was claimed
that Anne Geniere had rented two furnished rooms, paying for
three years rent in advance, in the town of Avignon. But we can
state right away that this pretended domicile is not of the sort
required by the holy decretals and the statutes . . . [which de-
mand] that one should have lived a year or the best part of a
year in a parish before one becomes really a parishioner. But the
defendants had lived neither a year nor anything like it in
Avignon when they got married there. . . . And so they did not
satisfy the first condition. . . . If it were enough to change house
for a while in order to establish domicile in order to get married,
then the forethought of the Council of Trent would be illusory
and that of the Royal Statute would be useless. One could make
a parish priest for oneself according to one's needs, and where
then could parents turn to get their authority respected? . . .
Would this not be authorizing the worst license and covering it
with a specious veil of marriage? . . . In order to determine
whether the plaintiffs are entitled to petition for the invalida-
tion of the marriage we must decide whether . . . the defendants' marriage is prejudicial to their honor. . . . If Anne
Geniere had no other faults but those of her low rank and fortune, we would find the plaintiffs too fastidious. . . . But this is a
woman who, over and above the inequality . . has led a scandalous life. She has been stigmatized by a sentence which is a perpetual monument to her infamy. . . . If a man who wastes his
patrimony can be declared incapable of managing his affairs,
does it not seem that since Cabassol is wasting his honor, and
managing his true interests so badly, we should listen to the
voice of his relatives? . . . When the vapors with which mad
passion have confused his mind withdraw . . . he will approve
what he condemns today. . . .

For these reasons we believe that the petition to invalidate
the marriage should be allowed . . and that the defendants be

condemned to give alms to the amount of ten pounds each to the hospitals of this town and forbidden to frequent each other, yet that they be allowed the recourse of taking any steps they think fit toward lodging an appeal in an ecclesiastical court.... Judgment given in conformity with these conclusions on the 14th March, 1689. [*Code Matrimonial*] [5]

Female adultery was another way whereby an inheritance might pass from the grasp of the legitimate heirs.

Adultery, according to canon law, is as reprehensible in a husband as in a wife. But it is different in the secular courts, for a woman's infidelity has graver results. She gives her husband heirs who are not his children. It is theft to foist heirs born of debauchery on an entire family: it is a usurpation of the property, nobility, and name of the family.

In France the wife's adultery is punished by the loss of her matrimonial rights; sometimes her dowry is given to her husband, who has her locked up and pays her a pension. If, however, the husband was himself living in public adultery, he could not take legal action against his wife.... When the dowry is granted to the husband, he is obliged to preserve it for the children.... The penalty for an adulterous wife is [*Novel* 134 of Justinian]... to be relegated to a convent for two years; after that, if her husband has not taken her back, she must remain there for the rest of her life, and this involves a sort of civil death and the loss of all inheritances.... If the woman, after her husband's death, were to obtain the freedom to remarry, these effects would be nullified. There is an example of a woman who got her freedom in just such a way. A sentence delivered by the Court of Paris on 21 June 1684, granted it to Marie Joisel, whose first husband, Mr Hars, had had her locked up.... A husband who kills a wife caught in adultery easily obtains grace but may not profit by her money. [François Serpillon, *Code Criminel*] [6]

A women fearful of her barrenness and eager for an heir could face harsh penalties:

When a woman fraudulently substitutes a child for another or makes a false claim to have given birth, or when someone pretends to be the father or mother of a child not his own, this is a sort of kidnapping and is severely punished, for it disturbs the order of families and foists false heirs on them.... A wet nurse who substitutes another child when the one entrusted to her died would be punished by the death penalty; so too if she put her own child in the place of the one entrusted to her. [Serpillon, *Code Criminel*][7]

Penal legislation was tough on actions that came between family and property, including marriage outside one's class, but it also struck at abortion and infanticide, and the grounds were partly religious.

[Extract, statute, Henri II, Paris, February 1556.] We have been informed of an execrable crime commonly committed in our realm, which is that women, having conceived children ... hide their pregnancy.... And, at the time of their delivery, give birth secretly, then destroy the children by suffocation ... or by other means, without having afforded them the benefit of the Holy Sacrament of Baptism. Next they throw them into shameful and secret places or bury them in unconsecrated ground, thus depriving them of Christian burial. When they are accused of this before Our judges, they ... allege that their children were stillborn ... and for lack of proofs ... Our judges ... fall into conflicting opinions: some advocating the death penalty, others torture .... The women, after enduring the torture without confessing anything, are usually sent to prison with the result that they fall into similar crimes once more and go back to their evil ways, to Our very great regret and the scandal of Our subjects.... We order that any woman duly convicted of having concealed ... her pregnancy and confinement... whose child later on turns out to have been deprived of the Holy Sacrament of Baptism and of public and customary burial shall be held and considered to have murdered her child and shall suffer the death penalty. [*Code Matrimonial*][8]

Although the above law remained in force and preachers were required to read it periodically to their congregations, there are indications that it was cautiously invoked.

Before a girl may be convicted of having destroyed the fruit of

her womb, several circumstances must be present. (1) There
must be a *corpus delicti*; this is the first and most essential condition; in its absence, there is no presumption that a crime has
been committed.... (2) The girl must not have admitted her
pregnancy to anyone capable of testifying. (3) The child must
not have been buried in any of the usual public cemeteries. In
the absence of any of these conditions required by the statute of
1556, the crime cannot be proven.... A sentence of 16 July
1716, declared concealment of pregnancy only punishable by
the terms of the statutes [of 1556 and 1708] when the child had
been deprived of baptism and Christian burial.... The statute
of Henri II does not require girls to admit their pregnancy to
officers of the law or notaries or other public officials. They
cannot be forced to do so. It is enough, by the terms of the
statute, if they admit it to people of integrity who, in case of
necessity, may testify to this.

In the absence of a *corpus delicti*, the prosecution cannot force
a girl [i.e., by torture] to state what has happened to her child;
she is not obliged to reveal her turpitude. The child might be
being reared by a father who prefers not to be known. [Serpillon,
Code Criminel][9]

If it was hard to prove infanticide, it was harder still to prove abortion.

Our jurists distinguish.... If the embryo was dislodged before
ensoulment was likely to have taken place, then the penalty is
lighter ... because one cannot call this homicide, since there
was as yet no soul; yet, since it is not lawful to prevent the hope
of a human being, the penalty would be banishment; but if it
was dislodged after the fortieth day [following conception], it is
legally homicide.... These distinctions do not affect the fact
that by the terms of the statute of 1556 the crime is punishable
by death whether the premeditated abortion was induced before
or after ensoulment ... but one must admit that these crimes,
although frequent, are rarely punished because of the difficulty
of convicting the guilty. [Serpillon, *Code Criminel*][10]

GERMANY: SOME PENALTIES

Protestant as well as reform-minded Catholic suffered from the infection

of Puritanism, making for a kind of spastic tightening up of morals,
particularly in sexual relations, with the result, for about a century or
more, that penalties were stepped up for crimes of all sorts. We draw upon
some illustrations from a German city. Franz Schmidt, public executioner
at Nuremberg from 1573 to 1617, kept the diary from which the follow-
ing selections come. The entries on infanticide speak for themselves. In
cases of bigamy, adultery, and prostitution, the laws at Nuremberg and
elsewhere in Germany normally called for flogging and expulsion from the
city; but the penalties could be more severe, as Schmidt's diary shows. The
suspicion arises that charges of compounded or aggravated adultery and
fornication were highlighted, if not trumped up, the better to justify the
harshness of some of the penalties.

March 6th [1578] Appollonia Vöglin, of Lehrberg, who
murdered a child. She gave birth to an infant at the farm of her
master, and killed it; executed by drowning at Lichtenau.

January 26th [1580] Margaret Dorfflerin (50 years old)
from Ebermannsstatt, Elizabeth Ernstin (22 years old) from
Anspach, Agnes Lengin (22 years old) of Amberg, three child
murderesses. The woman Dorfflerin, when she brought forth her
child in the garden behind the fort, left it lying alive in the snow
so that it froze to death. Ernstin, when she brought forth her
child alive in Master Beheimb's house, herself crushed its little
skull and locked the body in a trunk. But the woman Lengin,
when she brought forth her child alive in the house of a smith,
throttled it and buried it in a heap of refuse. All three beheaded
with the sword as murderesses and their heads nailed above the
great scaffold, no woman having been beheaded before this at
Nuremberg [hitherto execution had been by drowning].

January 10th [1583] Mary Kürssnerin, a young prostitute,
who was a watchman's [musketeer's?] daughter, a girl who had
thieved considerably and a handsome young creature with
whom the young Dietherr had dealings; Elizabeth Gütlerin, a
bath attendant; Katherine Aynerin *alias* die Gescheydin, a
blacksmith's wife and a handsome creature; all three children
of citizens, and prostitutes, were here pilloried and afterwards
flogged out of town. Such a dreadful crowd ran out to see this
that several people were crushed to death under the Frauenthor.
Subsequently Mary's ears were cut off and she was hanged.

[Summer?] 1584   Anna Peyelstainin of Nuremberg, *alias* Moser Annala, because she had carnal intercourse with a father and son (who themselves both had wives, she having a husband) and similarly with twenty-one men and youths, her husband conniving; was beheaded here with the sword, standing. Her husband, called Jerome Peyelstain, was whipped out of town.

September 25th [1595]   Ursala Grimin, landlady of the Rotenharz in St Lawrence Square, a prostitute, bawd, and procuress, because she had often committed adultery; had prostituted her serving maids; was skilled in enticing men to lechery .... On which account she was stood in the pillory; flogged as far as the stocks, there branded on both cheeks, and afterwards whipped out of town.

July 23rd [1605]   Barbara Zeylerin of Hohenhasslach, re-siding at Feldorff in the Palatinate, married and had borne five children, who had immoral relations with Endrass Heroldt at Herspruck twelve years ago, and, recently, also with a father and his son, a rich peasant, with the father many times in eight years, with the son thrice in one year, father and son being, however, unaware of each other's doings. Beheaded with the sword here as a favor.

November 6th [1610]   Magdalen Fischerin of Culmbach, daughter of 'Black' Merden, an unmarried servant who lost her maidenhood by a Lanzknecht five years ago, served at the ringmaker Fürheller's house in the Kreuzgasse, and had a child by father and son. Beheaded with the sword here as a favor.

February 28th [1611]   Elizabeth Mechtlin, called by her father's name, wife of Sahr, a confectioner in the wine market, who betrayed her husband three times, but was taken back again by him. Lastly, she went away with a man, then lived about as a common prostitute; also committed lewdness with two brothers, Hannssen Schneider, confectioners, among the butchers' stalls. Beheaded with a sword as a favor instead of being hanged.

June 23rd [1612]   Andrew Feuerstein, who kept a school with his father; debauched sixteen schoolgirls. Beheaded as a favor instead of being hanged. [Master Franz Schmidt, *A Hangman's Diary*][11]

ENGLAND: PROPERTY

In England, as already seen, a woman's goods and chattels became her husband's property on marriage. He enjoyed the usufruct of her freehold land for the duration of their marriage or, if she bore him a child 'heard to cry once,' for his own lifetime. The land passed then to the woman's children and, failing them, to her next of kin. This was the rule of common law. In the mercantile and capitalist society of the sixteenth and seventeenth centuries, other assets besides freehold land assumed importance, and the law of equity devised means whereby families could safeguard those too, to keep them from falling irretrievably into the hands of sons-in-law. Separate property could be assured to married women by formal transactions such as marriage settlements and wills. Lest a husband coerce his wife into alienating her property to him, a restraint came to be placed on her power to dispose of it. The aim was to keep property within the blood kinship group—including the woman's children—not to emancipate women. However, this happened too—to the daughters of the rich; the poor, having no investment property to protect, did not have recourse to equity, and their daughters continued to suffer the rigors of the common law.

The following select court cases illustrate some of the difficulties arising from women's inability to have full rights over property. The courts were leery of setting precedents that might encourage tradesmen to trust estranged wives. In the first case, a majority of judges find for the husband, arguing that the destitute wife has no remedy at common law but must apply to the ecclesiastical courts or Chancery. There was a dissenting minority of judges, however, and in the second case quoted, the Lord Chief Justice rules (thus setting a precedent) that a deserted wife can pledge her husband's credit for necessaries. It should be noted that neither of the wives concerned was divorced. A wife who obtained a divorce from the ecclesiastical courts might have got an order for alimony, while of course one who enjoyed separate property was not destitute.

Judge Hide's Argument in the Exchequer Chamber in the case of Manby versus Scott, 1663.

A *feme covert* [married woman] departs from her husband against his will and continues absent from him divers years; afterwards the wife desires to cohabit with her husband again, but the husband refuseth to admit her; and from that time the wife lives separate from him: during this separation the husband forbids a tradesman of London to trust his wife with any goods or wares; yet for divers years before and afterwards allows his wife no maintenance; the tradesman, contrary to the prohibition of the husband, sells and delivers divers wares to the wife upon credit, at a reasonable price; and the wares ... are necessary for her and suitable to the degree of the husband: The wares are not paid for; wherefore the tradesman brings an action upon the case against the husband, and declares that the husband was indebted to him in 40 pounds for divers wares and merchandises.... This case is the meanest that ever received resolution in this place, but ... it is of as great consequence to all the King's people of this Realm as any case can be; it concerns every individual person of both sexes, that is or hereafter shall be married in this kingdom.... This case toucheth the man in point of his power and dominion over his wife, and it concerns the woman in point of her substance and livelihood....

It is agreed by all ... who have argued ... that a *feme covert* generally cannot bind or charge her husband by any contract made by her, without the authority or assent of her husband precedent or subsequent, whether express or implied....

First, I hold that the husband shall not be charged by such a contract, although he do not allow any maintenance for his wife.

Secondly, admit the husband were chargeable generally by such a contract, yet I conceive that this action doth not lie for the plaintiff ... in this particular case.

... a *feme covert* cannot ... do any act without her husband, for her will and mind (as also her self) is under and subject unto the will and mind of her husband; and consequently she cannot make any bargain or contract (of herself) to bind her husband....

If the contract of the wife made without the allowance or consent of the husband shall bind him upon pretense of necessary apparel, it will be in the power of the wife (who by the Law of God, and of the Land, is put under the power of the husband ...) to rule over her husband, and undo him .... The wife shall ... judge of the fitness of her apparel, of the time when 'tis necessary for her to have new clothes, and as often as she pleaseth, without asking the advice or allowance of her husband; and is such power suitable to the judgment of Almighty God inflicted upon women, for being first in the transgression? 'Thy desire shall be to thy husband and he shall rule over thee.' Will wives depend on the kindness and favors of their husbands, or be observant towards them as they ought to be, if such a power be put into their hands?

Secondly, admit that in truth the wife wants necessary apparel, woolen and linen thereupon, she goes into Pater-Noster Row to a mercer and takes stuff, and makes a contract for necessary clothes, thence goes up into Cheapside and takes up linen there in like manner, and also goes into a third street, and fits herself with ribbons, and other necessaries.... Next morning this good woman goes abroad into some other part of London, makes her necessity and want of apparel known, and takes more wares upon trust ... after the same manner she goes to a third and fourth place ... none of these tradesmen knowing or imagining she was formerly furnished by the other, and each of them believing she hath great need of the commodities sold her; shall not the husband be chargeable and liable to pay every one of these, if the contract of the wife doth bind him? Certainly every one of these hath as just cause to sue the husband as the other ... and where this will end no man can divine or foresee.

... It is objected [by opposing judges] that the husband is bound, of common right, to provide for and maintain his wife; and the law having disabled the wife to bind herself by her own contract, therefore the burden shall rest upon the husband, who by law is bound to maintain her....

But apply this general proposition to our particular case, and then see what logic there is in the argument. I am bound to maintain and provide for my wife: therefore (my wife) departing from me against my will, shall be her own carver, and take up what apparel she pleaseth upon trust ... and I shall be bound to pay for it; this is our case.... Besides, although it is true that the husband is bound to maintain his wife, yet that is with this limitation, *viz.* so long as she keeps the station wherein the law hath placed her ... for if a woman of her own head, without the allowance or judgment of the Church, which hath united them, in the holy State of Matrimony ... depart from her husband against his will (be the pretense what it will) she doth thereby put herself out of the husband's protection.... But 'tis objected, it appears not in whose default the departure was, whether in his or her default. Thereunto I answer, that the law doth not allow a wife to depart from her husband in any case, or for any cause whatsoever of her own head. An express command is laid upon her by the law of God to the contrary, Cor. 7, 10. 'To the married I command, yet not I but the Lord; let not the wife depart from her husband.' . . . it is alleged that the wife in our case did return, and desire to cohabit with her husband again, which he refused. . . .

The wife, in our case, by departing from her husband against his will, breaks all these commands, and her own vow . . . and are all these offenses washed away with a bare desire, without submission or contrition? No, certainly, confession and promise of future obedience ought to precede her remitter or restitution to the privileges of a wife . . . the wife ought to be a penitentiary before the husband is bound to receive her, or give her any maintenance. . . .

It is said [by the opposing judges] although the wife departs . . . yet she ought not to starve. If a woman be of so haughty a stomach, that she will choose to starve rather than to submit . . . let her take her own choice. . . . So say I; if a woman who can have no goods of her own to live on, will depart from her husband against his will, and will not submit herself unto him, let her live on charity, or starve in the name of God; for in such case the law says, her evil demeanor brought it upon her, and her death ought to be imputed to her own wilfulness. . . .

Judgment was given for the Defendant [the husband]. [*Modern Reports of Select Cases Adjudged in the Courts*] [12]

Money or goods given a woman that is forlorn by her husband shall be recovered from the husband, except where she elopes.

1707   *Holt* upon evidence laid down these rules for the jury: Where a woman goes away from her husband, and a tradesman gives her credit for any goods, etc. after that he knows she left her baron [husband], then he trusts her at his peril; but if a man runs away from his wife, or turns her away, and leaves her not wherewithal to maintain herself, then he gives his wife credit for money or necessaries; but if the baron turns away his wife or leaves her, and before she takes up anything, the husband does propose to maintain her at home (tho' yet he will not lie in bed with her as a man should with his wife), yet if any money was, after such offer or proposal made and refused, disbursed for the wife, that was to be at the peril of any person so disbursing the money, unless the jury be of opinion that such offer was deceitful and fraudulent. For a wife is to be maintained by her husband where and how he thinks fit, according to his ability. [*A Report of all the Cases Determined by Sir John Holt*][13]

The system had its disadvantages for husbands. By treating women as perpetual minors, it encouraged irresponsibility. The following case also involves a husband reluctant to pay his wife's bills, although they were not estranged.

c. 1700   It was proved that she was very extravagant, and used to pawn her clothes for money, and tho' redeemed by the husband, she had pawned them again, and that she needed no clothes when she bought these goods; and further, that the defendant the last time he paid the plaintiff, warned his servant not to trust her any more.

Holt C. J. Where a husband turns away his wife, he gives her credit wherever she goes, and must pay for necessaries for her: But if she runs away from her husband, he shall not be bound by any contract she makes. And while they cohabit together, the husband shall answer all contracts of hers for necessaries; for his assent shall be presumed upon the account of cohabiting, unless the contrary appear; in which case, as by warning, etc., there is no room for such an assumption: And there is no necessity in this case, and notice to the servant was sufficient. [*Cases Determined by Sir John Holt*][14]

2 Diaries and Letters

By the seventeenth century, women of the upper classes were comfortable enough with the pen to use it for noting down their day-to-day doings. These casual diaries, as opposed to the brilliant chronicles kept by their contemporaries at court, give us a close-up picture of housekeeping and estate-running as it was then and had been for millennia. The important technological changes came later. In the year 1689, the Comtesse de Rochefort was living on her estate near Avignon, attempting to better it by thrift. Many of the activities she mentions would have been familiar to Xenophon. Wool, for instance, was still carded and spun in the home. Unlike Xenophon's ideal housewife, however, she needed to know about outdoor matters as well: farming, afforestation, the law. Her husband, as was common in his class, was away that year on a military campaign. He was in financial straits and, when called up, had taken all their money to pay his expenses. Much of the countess' time is taken up with trying to balance accounts while having no liquid cash in hand at all. It was a strain, and after his return she succumbed for a time to a nervous depression.

25 May, 1689.   I wrote to M. Carretier, my attorney at the Court of Toulouse, to ask for news. . . . I wrote to M. Penaut, my attorney at Montpellier, to proceed with our suit against the community of Beaucaire. The same day I wrote also to M. Belot, attorney at the Court of Toloze, for news of M. Brocardy's case.

M. Odoacre, the community's arbiter arrived today. He and the royal attorney began discussing things after dinner. It does not look to me as though we can hope for an amicable settlement. . . . Today I also went to Mormont to look at the woods. I found that far too much had been cut, but what is left is growing back very well. The part that is for sale is worth more than 40 écus, for the wood is thicker there. . . .

1 June.   I ordered that on all our lands prayers be offered for M. de Rochefort until he returns.

The butcher from Roche paid me 34 livres, 10 sols of what he owes me, plus 71 pounds of mutton at 2 sols and 4 deniers per pound, and 15 pounds of beef at 18 deniers. Adding it all up, he has paid off 43 livres, 10 sols of his debt. . . .

Toward evening, being at Bégude, I inspected my crops and found them very fine. However, the tenant tells me that if he had sowed earlier the wheat would be finer and more plentiful. I decided therefore to let him follow his own judgment as to when he should sow. He also told me that the ditches need scouring, and I admitted that they did.

I got the carders in today to work on a hundredweight of washed wool from which I aim to make 8 cannes [1 canne = between 2 and 3 meters] of crépon, 14 of light wool, 13 of floss serge, and 30 of caddis.

3 June. I forgot to note that on the first of the month I had work started on one of the two mill stones at the Rochefort mill. It was very urgent because the wheat was coming out unground. I am giving the mason his food while he works on it.

10 June. M. Jean Artaud came to see me to offer to lease the small farm house at Beaujeu. . . .

13 June. We began reeling the silk today. . . . Nine pounds of cocoons produced fifteen ounces of fine silk.

14 June. I got up early to supervise the storing of the casks in the cellar. I had the vats made and the small cellars got ready for the fair. I'm having a large wooden vat made for pressing the grapes. . . .

A small pewter carafe I had made has been delivered. I have also had dishes and two dozen plates remade. All my pewter has been reworked and I have had it marked as well.

I sent 4 lbs. of soap to Pernes, where I'm having thread bleached. . . .

The same day I sent to M. Patron, the trimmer, to ask how much braid would be needed for my livery. He said I would need 80 cannes [160 meters] of the wide and 30 [60 meters] of the narrow and that to make that much would take 10 lbs. of heavy silk and 8 lbs. of fine floss silk. . . . I sent 2 cannes of red caddis to T. to make the footmen's jackets. . . .

Catin came from Rochefort today where she had been supervising the carders. She brought 100 chickens which were left of those I had bought; adding the 28 I had here, that makes 128. I have over 40 hens as well, one cock and 10 turkeys. . . .

15 June.   I ordered the guard at Rochefort to sell my wine. He sold two casks to the butcher and is keeping the third one for the harvest.

I have arranged to have the Gazette sent and held for me twice a week at Tarascon.

20 June.   I got up early and heard Mass, then went to see my meadow at Maubuisson. I have had all the wines in my cellar tasted; they were pronounced to be excellent. There are 22 casks altogether. I have decided to keep three and sell the rest.

I spent the rest of the day cutting out and having under-clothes made up for my children.

21 June.   I got up early as usual to write to M. de Rochefort and to M. Sicard. After Mass, I had the attics prepared for the new wheat; what's left of the old will be ground into flour for the servants. Next I gave orders to have my old skirts cut up to make dresses for my son, the chevalier.

M. Treven de Villeneuve came to see me to tell me that ... he was obliged to ask me for money owed for two pensions, which amounts to 733 livres, 6 sols, 8 deniers. I answered that it was not too good a time to ask me for money, that M. de Rochefort had taken all I had to pay for his campaign and that I even had letters from the government dispensing me from pay-ing any money out before his return. . . .

27 June.   I got up early to prepare for the bleeding I am to have done on my ankle because of the bad headaches I have been suffering for some time . . . .

5 July   . . . the Sisters of Mercy wrote from Avignon asking for their pension and back payments. I wrote asking them to wait until the harvest, when I would pay them; otherwise I would use my *lettres d'Etat* to stop their suit.

6 July   . . . I spent the rest of the day making an inventory of the furniture, beds, chairs and so forth to make sure that nothing gets damaged during the fair.

I had good news from M. de Rochefort.

12 July.   I spent the morning having beds made up in the rooms that are to be let during the fair.

I wrote to my attorney . . . .

I went down to the cellar and tasted my wines. I had the three best casks marked; they will be kept for Monsieur, and three others for the commonalty.

27 July.   I spent the day doing my accounts. . . .

17 September. I sent M. Trevenin the rest of what I owed him. . . . The tenant at Jonquieres says . . . the owner of a neighboring farmhouse has been encroaching on our land. This will have to be looked into at once. . . .

26 September.   M. de Rochefort came home. . . .

30 May, 1690.   From November 10 until February I was so depressed with melancholy at the bad state in which I saw my business that I was neither eating nor sleeping; . . . melancholy is good for neither the body nor the soul. . . . Now I'm partly over it. . . . I am getting back to work. . . . God has remedied my affairs when I was least expecting it. With His grace, I hope to get things into shape in a few years. But the house will have to be carefully run; I must economize all I can or else in a bad year it is impossible to make ends meet. And then we must deprive ourselves of a lot so as to be able to help the poor. . . . [*Une Grande Dame dans son ménage au temps de Louis XIV, D'après le journal de la comtesse de Rochefort*][15]

Confinements were the most memorable events in this Yorkshire lady's life. Like bleak milestones they recur at periodic intervals.

30 September, 1648.   About this year, my dear and only sister, the Lady Danby, drew near her time for delivery of her sixteenth child. Ten whereof had been baptized, the other six were stillborn, when she was about half gone with them, she having miscarried of them all upon frights . . . falls and such like accidents. . . . The troubles and afflictions of these sad times [of civil war] did much afflict and grieve her . . . wanting the company of her husband [who] . . . being engaged in his king's service, was not permitted to leave it. . . . These things, added to the horrid rudeness of the soldiers and Scots quartered amongst them, which vexing and troubling her much with frights, caused her to fall into travail sooner than she expected, nor could she get her old midwife. . . . After exceeding sore travail she was delivered of a goodly son about August 3d . . . she was exceedingly troubled with pains, so that she was depriv-

ed of the benefit of sleep for fourteen days, except a few frightful slumbers; neither could she eat . . . and as she grew weaker, a month [after] . . . her delivery, said . . . in a weak voice, 'I am going to God, my God, now' . . . then, giving a little breathing sigh, delivered up her soul. . . . Although she was married to a good estate, yet did she enjoy not much comfort, and I know she received her change with much satisfaction. . . .

[6 August, 1652.] About seven weeks after I married it pleased God to give me the blessing of conception. The first quarter I was exceeding sick in breeding, till I was quick with child; after which I was strong and healthy, I bless God. . . . Mr Thornton had a desire that I should visit his friends [at Newton]. I passed down on foot a very high wall. . . . Each step did very much strain me. . . . This . . . killed my sweet infant in my womb . . . who lived not so long as we could get a minister to baptize it . . . after the miscarriage I fell into a most terrible shaking ague . . . . The hair on my head came off, my nails of my fingers and toes came off, my teeth did shake, and ready to come out and grew black. . . .

Alice Thornton, my second child was born at Hipswell near Richmond in Yorkshire the 3d day of January, 1654.

Elizabeth Thornton, my third child, was born at Hipswell the 14th of February, 1655 [died 5 September, 1656].

Katherine Thornton, my fourth child, was born at Hipswell . . . the 12th of June 1656.

. . . on the delivery of my first son and fifth child at Hipswell the 10th of December, 1657 . . . the child stayed in the birth, and came crosswise with his feet first, and in this condition continued till Thursday morning . . . at which I was upon the rack in bearing my child with such exquisite torments, as if each limb were divided from the other . . . but the child [was] almost strangled in the birth, only living about half an hour, so died before we could get a minister to baptize him. . . .

17 April, 1660.   It was the pleasure of God . . . to bring forth my sixth child . . . a very goodly son . . . after a hard labor and hazardous. [The child died two weeks later.]

19 September, 1662.   . . . I was delivered of Robert Thornton . . . it pleased the great God to lay upon me, his weak

handmaid, an exceeding great weakness, beginning, a little after my child was born, by a most violent and terrible flux of blood, with such excessive floods all that night that ... my dear husband, and children and friends had taken their last farewell. [She takes a powder which helps and] ... I was delivered and spared from that death....

23 September, 1665.   [Pregnant once more] I being terrified with my last extremity, could have little hopes to be preserved this ... if my strength were not in the Almighty.... It pleased the Lord to make me happy with a goodly strong child, a daughter, after an exceeding sharp and perilous time [the child died on January 24].

Christopher Thornton, my ninth child, was born [on Monday, 11 November, 1667] ... it pleased his Saviour ... to deliver him out of this miserable world [on] the 1st of December, 1667. [On 17 September, 1668, Mrs Thornton's husband died.] [*The Autobiography of Mrs Alice Thornton*] [16]

Madame de Sévigné's letters are famous in social and literary history, and in quoting them we may appear to depart from our policy of concentrating on more ordinary women. The following extracts deal, however, with a very ordinary fear common to all women throughout the centuries, when childbirth was a hazard and contraception was either little known or largely ineffective. Another letter writer, a Protestant doctor, Guy Patin, in a letter written about eleven years earlier, tells how he had heard that 'six hundred women have confessed [to their confessors] that they had destroyed the fruit of their wombs'. Madame de Sévigné's daughter, Madame de Grignan, married in 1669, had already had one child and one miscarriage, and was pregnant again. Her mother saw the beginnings of a pattern which she did not like.

27 April, 1671.   I don't like hearing of your listlessness; I am like scandalmongers, and I always believe the worst. This is what I was afraid of. My dear child, if this misfortune should be confirmed, take good care of yourself.

6 May.   I send a thousand kisses to Grignan in spite of his misdoings; I beg him at least, since he has caused the harm to cause the cure, that is, that he should take every care for your

health. Let him be master of that as you must be mistress of everything else.

18 May.   I accept what M. de Grignan says. Ah, my dear Count, I believe you; there is no one who would not have done what you have had they been in your place. . . . Consider, however, that the youth, the beauty, the health, the gaiety, and the life of a woman you love can all be destroyed by frequent occurrences of the pain you make [her] suffer.

12 July . . . bring your pregnancy to a happy end and after that, if M. de Grignan loves you and has not undertaken to kill you, I know well what he will do—or rather what he will not do.

18 October.   Listen, M. le Comte, I am talking to you. I shall return your charm with bluntness. You take pleasure from your labors: instead of pitying my daughter you merely laugh; it is clear enough that you don't know what it is like to give birth. But listen, I have a piece of news for you which is that if, after this son, you do not let her rest a while, I shall believe you don't love her, and that you don't love me either; I shan't come to Provence. Your swallows may summon me in vain . . . and I was forgetting this: I shall take your wife from you. Do you imagine I gave her to you so that you might kill her, so that you might destroy her health, her beauty, and her youth? This is no laughing matter. At the right time and place I shall ask you this favor on my knees . . . providing that I don't come to find a woman who is pregnant and again pregnant and all the time pregnant. . . .

21 October.   How your belly weighs on me, my poor darling.

6 January, 1672.   Your thinness kills me: Ah, where is the time when you used to eat the head of one woodcock per day and were dying with the fear of being too fat? If you get pregnant at this point, you may be sure that you will never get over it as long as you live. M. de Grignan is crowing too loud! He is hankering. If he succumbs to the temptation, don't believe he loves you. When one truly loves, one loves everything, and a beauty like yours which gives no trouble is not something to forget. If M. de Grignan destroys it, you may take it as proven that his affection is not of sterling quality.

6 January.   I want to warn you of something which I shall

uphold in your husband's presence and in yours. It is that if, after your periods start again, you as much as think of making love with M. de Grignan, you may consider yourself already pregnant and if one of your midwives tells you differently, then your husband has bribed her. After giving you this advice, I shall say no more. [Madame de Sévigné, *Lettres*][17]

The following incident reminds us that the double standard applied to male and female adultery had everything to do with preserving family property and nothing to do with Christian principle, although the latter provided camouflage. The morality to which the Countess d'Egmont was sacrificed was the prevailing one, but the extremes to which it was taken in her case were unusual. Hence the revulsion of Madame de Pompadour (1721–64), who is telling the story.

The Countess d'Egmont ... inherited an immense fortune and, being young, beautiful, and lovable, was sought in matrimony after her husband's death, by the most distinguished men at court. One day her mother's confessor came and asked the Countess if he might see her in private and thereupon revealed to her that she was the fruit of an adultery which her mother had been trying to expiate for twenty-five years. 'Your mother,' said the priest, 'was unable to prevent your first marriage although she trembled at it. God did not permit you to have children thereby, but if you remarry, Madame, you risk taking into another family an enormous fortune which does not belong to you and which has come to you as the result of a crime.' Madame d'Egmont listened to all this in terror. Her mother at that instant came in, flung herself on her knees and, through her tears, begged her daughter to preserve her from eternal damnation. Madame d'Egmont tried to reassure her mother and herself and asked, 'How?' The priest answered, 'Devote yourself entirely to God so as to efface your mother's sin.' The Countess, overwhelmed by all this, promised to do what he demanded and decided to become a Carmelite. I heard the story [Madame de Pompadour is talking] and spoke to the king of the barbarous treatment which this unfortunate woman was suffering at the hands of the duchess and her confessor. But we could not think how to help her. The king, in his generosity, persuaded the queen to offer her a place as lady-in-waiting, and got some of the duchess' friends to try to persuade her to stop her daughter's entering the Carmelite Order. It was all to no avail, and the wretched victim was sacrificed. [Madame du Hausset, *Mémoires*][18]

After her husband's death, Jeanne-Françoise Frémyot de Chantal (1572–1641), saint and aristocrat, withdrew from the world to found the order of Visitation nuns. Her daughter was still young, and the nun continued to send her letters of motherly advice from the convent. These contain what were probably fairly standard sentiments of the time. The following extract is from a letter written in 1622, when the daughter was about to meet the fiancé who had been chosen for her. Worldly and unworldly considerations mingle oddly and interestingly in the letter and seem momentarily to merge when, in an uncharacteristic lapse from clarity, St Jeanne asks her daughter to throw herself into 'his' arms and it is unclear whether the embrace meant is that of God or of the rich M. de Toulongeon.

Well, my dear daughter, here is M. de Toulongeon who, having eight or ten free days at his disposal, is going to travel to you by post in order, he says, to find out whether you will think him too swarthy, for, as regards his temper, he hopes not to displease you. For my part, I tell you truly, not only do I find no fault with this match but I find in it everything one could wish. Our Lord has afforded me thereby a satisfaction such as I do not recall ever finding before now in the things of this world. His birth and wealth are not what impress me most but rather his wit, his character, his wisdom, his probity, his reputation: in short, Françoise, let us thank God for such a find. My child, prepare yourself to love and serve God in your gratitude better than you have ever done and let nothing keep you from frequently partaking in the sacraments . . . do not be beguiled by the petty vanities of clothes and rings: you are going to be rich; but, my dear daughter, remember always that one must use the riches that God gives us without becoming attached to them . . . . Truly I am glad that it was your relatives and myself who arranged this match without you: for this is how wise people act. . . .

Your brother, whose judgment is reliable, is delighted with the match. It is true that M. de Toulongeon is some fifteen years older than you, but, my dear child, you will be far happier with him than you would with some crazy, irresponsible debauchee like the young men of today. You are going to marry a man who is not at all like that, who is not a gambler, who has spent his life honorably at court and at the wars and has been granted considerable emoluments by the king. You would be lacking in the good judgment which I know you to have if you did not receive him with warmth and simplicity. Do so, my dear, with a good grace, and be assured that God has thought for you and will continue to do so if you fling yourself into his arms; for he tenderly guides all those who trust in him. [*Lettres de la Sainte Mère Jeanne-Françoise Frémyot*] [19]

3 Education

> I am a woman, poor and old
> Ignorant too: I never read
> A book. In church I see a gold
> Bright, painted heaven where the dead
> Have lutes and harps. And there as well
> I see the wicked boil in hell.
> One frightens me; the other brings me joy.
>
> [François Villon, 1431-65][20]

The woman in Villon's poem knew her place. If she knew little else, then that, most authorities would have agreed, was all to the good.

In the early modern period the case for giving women a higher education was stated with increasing frequency. It was even argued syllogistically in Latin in a piece published in 1641 by Anna Maria von Schurman, a female prodigy who lived in Utrecht. Her prestige and that of other women scholars made it impossible for opponents of women's education to go on resting their case on women's intellectual inferiority. Forced to retrench, they fell back upon that great axiom of the age: people should keep their place and not be educated above it. Woman's place, needless to say, was the kitchen and her husband's bed. Aptitude for study was irrelevant to this argument. Society did not aspire to be a meritocracy, and neither did the family. Attainments above one's station were a threat to social and domestic order. Great ladies might be as educated as they chose. Ordinary women should learn no more than was right for their social station. These sentiments are succinctly expressed in the following speech from Molière's play Les Femmes Savantes *(1672). They are not Molière's own. He was a comic writer who dealt with explosive material. The conservative, rather ridiculous burgess making this speech has been infuriated by the extravagant pedantry of his womenfolk. Both he and they, as audiences recognized, typified prevalent attitudes of the day.*

I'm speaking to you, sister. You won't tolerate the least peculiarity in grammar, but there are plenty in your own conduct. I don't like all these useless books of yours. Apart from the big Plutarch that keeps my neckbands pressed, you should burn them all. Get rid of this fierce-looking telescope and all the rest of these gadgets.... Stop trying to find out what's happening on the moon and mind what's going on in your own house where everything is upside down. It's not decent, and there are plenty of reasons why it isn't, for a woman to study and know so much. Teaching her children good principles, running her household, keeping an eye on her servants, and managing her budget thriftily are all the study and philosophy she needs. Our fathers knew what they were talking about when they said a woman is learned enough if she can tell a doublet from a pair of breeches. Their wives didn't read ... instead of books, they had a thimble and needles and thread to sew their daughters' trousseaux. Women today ... want to write books and become authors. No learning is too deep for them ... and here, in my house, they know everything except what they need to know. In my house, they know all about the moon and the pole star and about Venus, Saturn, and Mars, which are no concern of mine and ... nobody knows how the pot is cooking.... Reasoning is the pursuit of everyone in my household, and all their reasoning has driven out reason. [Molière, *Les Femmes Savantes*][21]

Elitist attitudes to education die hard. The following texts make no secret of the considerations that underpin them:

Today, [1763] even the lower classes want to study. Laborers and artisans send their children to boarding schools in the small towns where living is cheap, and when they have received a wretched education, which has taught them merely to despise their fathers' trades, they fling themselves into the monasteries, become priests or officers of justice, and frequently turn out to be a danger to society.

The Brothers of Christian Doctrine, nicknamed the 'Ignorantines,' have made things worse. They teach reading and writing to people who should never have learned more than a little drawing or how to handle the plane or the file and who now don't want to do this.... The good of society requires that the lower classes' knowledge should go no further than their occupations. No man who can see beyond his depressing trade will ply it with patience and courage. The lower classes scarcely need to know how to read or write except for those members of it who live by these skills or are helped by them to make their living.... It is therefore in the interest of the state for there to be few boarding schools, provided that these few be good ... it is better to have few students provided they are well educated.... [L. R. Caradeuc de la Chalotais, *Essai d'education nationale*][22]

England, 1792. However desirable it may be to rescue the lower kinds of people from ignorance ... it cannot be right to train them *all* in a way which will probably raise their ideas above the very lowest occupations of life and disqualify them for those servile offices which must be filled by some members of the community, and in which they may be equally happy with the highest, if they will do their duty.... The children of the poor should not be educated in such a manner as to set them above the occupations of humble life, or so as to make them uncomfortable among their equals. [Sarah Trimmer, *Reflections upon the Education of Children in Charity Schools*][23]

The older arguments from women's inferiority continued to be aired. Sometimes they were propped up by science—as when the philosopher Malebranche dwelt on the weakness of the fibers of women's brains. Rousseauism, a new fashion, a new sensibility, which sought to return to the patriarchal roots of society and the simple ways of the noble savage, naturally casts women for a dependent role. The rich middle classes, themselves a product of the cities, were charmed by Rousseau's pastoral dream. The eighteenth-century bourgeois was pleased to keep his wife in an idleness which exhibited his status and in a dependence consonant with his traditions. We cite Rousseau's influential manual on education (1762):

Men and women are made for each other, but their mutual dependence is not equal.... We could survive without them better than they could without us. In order for them to have what they need ... we must give it to them, we must want to give it to them, we must consider them deserving of it. They are dependent on our feelings, on the price we put on their merits, on the value we set on their attractions and on their virtues.... Thus women's entire education should be planned in relation to men. To please men, to be useful to them, to win their love and respect, to raise them as children, care for them as adults, counsel and console them, make their lives sweet and pleasant: these are women's duties in all ages and these are what they should be taught from childhood on. [Jean-Jacques Rousseau, *Emile*][24]

ELEMENTS OF PRACTICE

Let us leave theory and come to practice. Supposing a family of modest means wanted to educate its daughters, how available were schools? The answer would appear to be that that depended. Primary schools had existed for girls as well as boys from the later Middle Ages: twenty-one primary-school mistresses were listed on the Paris tax rolls of 1380, and in Catholic countries convents provided private boarding and some free day schools, particularly after the seventeenth century. It was not, however, until the second half of the nineteenth century that systematic efforts were made by states to set up an elementary school for each sex in every large community. The quality of the education was affected by the preference for keeping people mentally as well as bodily in their station in life. The danger for the poor was that 'education' could boil down to spelling their way through a few Bible stories and learning how to spin. For rich girls it might mean acquiring a few accomplishments. Standards also varied from one country to another. For example, the wives of north European merchants traditionally kept their books. This astonished English travelers, since Englishwomen did not study arithmetic.

1668. The prodigious increase of the Netherlands in their domestic and foreign trade, riches and shipping is the envy of the present, and may be the wonder of all future generations: And yet the means whereby they have thus advanced themselves are sufficiently obvious ... [the writer lists several, then:] Seventhly, the education of their children, as well daughters as sons; all which, be they of never so great quality or estate, they always take care to bring up to write perfect good hands, and to have the full knowledge and use of Arithmetic and

Merchants-Accounts; the well understanding and practice whereof doth strangely infuse into most that are the owners of that quality, of either sex, not only an ability for commerce of all kinds but a strong aptitude, love and delight in it; and since the women are as knowing therein as the men, it doth encourage their husbands to hold on in their trades to their dying days, knowing the capacity of their wives to get in their estates, and carry on their trades after their deaths: whereas if a merchant in England arrive at any considerable estate, he commonly withdraws his estate from trade, before he comes near the confines of old age; reckoning that if God should call him out of the world, while the main of his estate is engaged abroad in trade, he must lose one third of it, through the unexperience and unaptness of his wife to such affairs, and so it usually falls out.

Besides, it hath been observed in the nature of Arithmetic, that like other parts of the Mathematics, it doth not only improve the rational faculties, but inclines those that are expert in it to thriftiness and good husbandry, and prevents both husbands and wives in some measure from running out of their estates, when they have it always ready in their heads what their expenses do amount to, and how soon by that course their ruin must overtake them. [Sir Josiah Child, *A New Discourse of Trade*][25]

There is no part of Europe so haunted with all sorts of foreigners as the Netherlands, which makes the inhabitants, as well women as men, so well versed in all sorts of languages so that, in exchange time, one may hear seven or eight sorts of tongues spoken upon their burses: nor are the men only expert herein; but the women and maids also in their common hostries; and in Holland the wives are so well versed in bargaining, cyphering, and writing, that in the absence of their husbands in long sea-voyages, they beat the trade at home, and their words will pass in equal credit: these women are wonderfully sober. [James Howell, *Epistolae Ho-Elianae* 1754][26]

France, 1683. Teach your daughters to read and write correctly. It is disgraceful but common to see women of wit and good manners unable to pronounce what they read. They either hesitate or read in a singsong.... Even worse is their spelling and the way they form and link letters. At least teach them to keep the lines straight and to write a clear and legible hand. A girl should know the grammar of her own language. This does not mean learning rules as boys do with Latin; it will be enough if you train them to pick the correct tense, to use the appropriate forms and to express themselves clearly.... They ought also to know the four rules of arithmetic; you may make good use of this by making them keep accounts.... It is well known that exact bookkeeping makes for good order in a household.

It would be advisable for them to know something of the law: the difference for example between a will and a gift; what a contract is, an entail and a partition between co-heirs. They should be familiar with the principal laws or customs of the province where they live, what is required to make such transactions valid and the meaning of separate property, joint estate, real property and chattels. If they get married, their affairs will turn on such matters....

Girls of great birth and fortune must be informed of the duties of lords of the manor. Teach them what may be done to prevent the abuses, infringements of rights, wranglings and fraud so prevalent in the country. Explain how small schools may be set up on their estates and charities arranged for the relief of the sick poor.... When explaining about the duties of lords of the manor, do not forget their rights. Explain what a fief is, an overlord, a vassal ... rents, tithes.... They need to know such things in order to run an estate.

After these most important matters, I think it is not a bad idea to allow girls, within the limits of their leisure and intelligence, to read such profane books as do not excite the passions; it is even a useful way to turn them against comedies and novels.

Give them stories from Greek and Roman history.... Do not leave them ignorant of the history of France which has fine passages.... All these things enlarge the mind and inspire the soul with noble feelings....

It is usually considered that a girl of rank who is well brought up should learn Italian and Spanish; but these seem to me the most useless of studies unless a girl is going to enter the household of some Spanish or Italian princess.... Moreover, these two languages scarcely serve to read any but dangerous books liable to have a bad effect on women; there is more to be lost than gained by such studies. Latin would be a far more reasonable choice.... But I would allow it only to girls of good sense and modest behavior such as could assess this study at its true merits, who would not be tempted by vain curiosity, would conceal what they had learned, and would study it only for their own edification.

I would also, after making a careful choice, allow them to read works of poetry and oratory if they seemed drawn to them and if they were sensible enough ... but I would be cautious of disturbing an overlively imagination and I would prefer very sober works. Allusions to love, the more obscure and concealed they are, the more dangerous they seem to me.

The same precautions are necessary with music and painting: all these arts are of the same style and spirit. [Fénelon, *Traité de l'éducation des filles*][27]

Fénelon – appointed tutor to King Louis XIV's grandson six years after publishing the above – was concerned primarily with educating aristocrats. So was Madame de Maintenon, who applied many of his principles in her school at St Cyr. When ex-pupils of hers became heads of ordinary convents, she wrote them advice on how to teach middle-class girls. The text below combines extracts from two very similar letters written in 1713 to Madame de la Mairie and Madame de la Viefville, who were both attempting to adapt methods used at St Cyr, but whose pupils were of humbler origin.

There are a number of matters in which I would push them less. There is little point in girls of common extraction learning to read as well as young ladies or being taught as fine a pronunciation or knowing what a period is, etc. It is the same with writing. All they need is enough to keep their accounts and memoranda; you don't need to teach them fine handwriting or talk to them of style: a little spelling will do. Arithmetic is different. They need it.

Educate your middle-class girls in the middle-class way. [Intercalation:] Don't even contemplate embellishing their minds. Teach them their domestic duties, obedience to their

18 Phyllis riding Aristotle: matter over mind
Early 16th-century engraving by Hans Baldung Grün

19 Venetian courtesans
By Carpaccio, about 1510

husbands, and how to look after their children and train their small staff, to go regularly to church on Sundays and holidays, to be modest with customers, honest in business.... [Back to first text:] Tell them that nothing is more displeasing to God and men than stepping out of one's social station—all are ordained by Providence, and God resists our endeavors to be other than He intended us to be. Teach them to be moderate and that the peasant must not try to ape the bourgeois nor the bourgeois the gentleman. Society derides [such aping] and has more respect for those who remain in their own class and live in it decently and with honor. [Mme de Maintenon, *Lettres sur l'éducation des filles*][28]

One long-term effect of the French Revolution, seen clearly in nineteenth-century reform, was the awareness that the modern state cannot be indifferent to the welfare and education of its citizens. From the time of the Gracchi, feminists had pointed to the advantages of educating women in order that they might then educate their sons. Once it became accepted that the fortunes of the modern state depend in some essential part on an educated, or at least literate, citizenry, state education for women was seen to be essential too. Only through educated mothers could progressive ideas be channeled through to the very young. Women's role was still ancillary, and it was almost fortuitous that they benefited by the new reforms. We see this in the next selection from an Italian source (1876); the extract, interestingly, also catches the nationalism and republican anticlericalism of the time, found strongly in France too.

If it is true that the final cause of a people's progress is to be found in women and in the family, then it is high time for the state to give supreme concern to the general education of women. Women must withdraw themselves from the influence of the Church and, with a new culture, make themselves fit to work at forming free citizens. Elementary education for girls must therefore be obligatory, in the hands of the laity, and identical to that of boys. But let us consider, point by point, how the need to teach girls some science arises from the duties they will have to fulfill as wives, mothers, and educators.

Women must know something of the fundamental laws which explain the cosmic system of our planet and the simpler facts of meteorology and physics. Without such information, one does not, nowadays, possess human dignity. It is only thanks to such study that women can cease peopling the heavenly spaces with imaginary entities and acquire that freedom of mind which is the first step toward educating ourselves and others. They will [then] be able to stop believing and making their children believe – thereby stunting the development of their intellects– that rain is sent to us by Jesus, that thunder is the sign of divine anger and menace, and that successful crops and a good or bad harvest are to be attributed rather to the will of Providence than to the merits of work and the course of natural events.... They must learn the basic laws of history and social life, for from these arise the ethical ideal which is the objective of all progress and education.... Only when women have truly raised themselves toward the love of freedom and of their native country shall we see them achieve political efficacy in educating free citizens. [A. Angiulli, *La Pedagogia, lo Stato e la Famiglia*][29]

4 Rural Women

What works a wife should do in general.... First ... set all things in good order within thy house, milk the kine, suckle thy calves, strain up thy milk ... get corn and malt ready for the mill to bake and to brew ... measure it before the mill and after and see that thou have thy measure again, apart from the amount due to the miller, or else the miller dealeth not truly with thee, or else thy corn is not dry as it should be. Thou must make butter and cheese when thou may, serve thy swine both morning and evening ... take heed how thy hens, ducks and geese do lay ... and when they have brought forth their birds, see that they be well kept from crows and other vermin.... In the beginning of March is time for a wife to make her garden and to get as many good seeds and herbs as she can, and specially such as be good for the pot.... March is time to sow flax and hemp ... it should be sown, weeded, pulled, watered, washed, dried, beaten, braked, hatcheled, spun, wound, wrapped and woven.... And therefore may they make sheets, tablecloths, towels, shirts, smocks and other such necessaries, and therefore let thy distaff be always ready.... And undoubted a woman cannot get her living honestly with spinning on the distaff, but it stoppeth a gap and must needs be had.... It is convenient for a husband to have sheep ... and then may his wife have part of the wool to make her husband and herself some clothes... or blankets or coverlets or both. And if she have no wool of her own she may take wool to spin of cloth makers, and by that means she may have a convenient living and meanwhile do other works. It is a wife's occupation to winnow all manner of corns, to make malt, wash and wring, to make hay, to shear corn, and in time of need to help her husband to fill the muck wain or dung cart, drive the plow, to load hay, corn and such other. Also to go or ride to the market, to sell butter, cheese, milk, eggs, chickens, capons, hens, pigs, geese and all manner of corn. And also to buy all manner of necessary things belonging to the household, and to make a true reckoning and account to her husband [of] what she hath received and what she hath paid. And if the husband go to the market to buy or sell... he [ought] then to show his wife in like manner. For if one of them should deceive the other, he deceiveth himself, and he is not like to thrive, and therefore they must be true either to other. [Sir Anthony Fitzherbert, *The boke of husbandrye*, 1555][30]

The woman whose duties are listed above carried a sturdy share of the European economy. Married to a small farmer, she worked hard but lived, by the standards of Early Modern Europe, with some comfort. The source is English, but the round of chores was much the same in all European countries down to the nineteenth century. In the south wine-making took the place of brewing, which in the north was largely done by women and in Scandinavia almost exclusively so.

Rural wages throughout the early modern period were fixed by local magistrates at Quarter Sessions. The following fairly standard tables show that women laborers invariably earned less than men and that neither earned more than the cost of two days' meager food rations. Since agricultural work was seasonal and laborers had children to feed, starvation was inevitable. According to a contemporary statistician, Gregory King (1648—1712), a million people, nearly one-fifth of the nation, were partly dependent on charity: mostly public relief paid by the parish. Here are some wages by the day assessed by the Justices of Wiltshire in 1604.

Wages by the day for laborers in harvest and at all other times of the year in husbandry.

Men laborers in haymaking... shall not take by the day with meat and drink of wages above 4*d*. and without meat and drink not above 8*d*.

Women laborers in haymaking ... shall not take by the day with meat and drink of wages above 3*d*. and without not above 6*d*.

Men reapers of wheat and rye ... with meat and drink... not above 5*d*. and without meat and drink not above 10*d*.

Women reapers of wheat and rye ... with meat and drink not above 3*d*. and without not above 9*d*. [Historical Manuscripts Commission][31]

When they have worked the wages given them is so small that it hardly sufficeth to buy the poor man and his family bread, for they pay 6s. for one bushel of mycelin grain and receive but 8d. for their day's work. It is not possible to procure maintenance for all those poor people and their families by alms nor yet by taxes. March, 1639. [Cited in Alice Clark, *Working Life of Women in the Seventeenth Century*][32]

Servants got bed and board. It was the wage laborers who starved. Alice Clark (p 62) quotes a wage table of 1600 which assesses the pay of a woman clipper of sheep at 6d. per day with food or 12d. without; of a man clipper as 7d. with food and 14d. without, and that of 'women and such impotent persons as weed corn' at 2d. if fed, 6d. if not. The impotence of the 'impotent' must have been partly a matter of diet. Many were no doubt mothers—single women would have been servants—who reduced their strength by sharing food with their children. A single man could survive on a laborer's wages. Husbands sometimes abandoned the struggle and their families, and the indigent and abandoned mother who petitions the parish for help is a recurrent figure in the seventeenth century.

1620.   Eleanor Williams charged with keeping of a young child is now unprovided with house room for herself and her poor child, her husband having left the soil where they lately dwelled and is gone to some place to her unknown. She is willing 'to relieve her child by her painful labor but wanteth a place for abode' prays to be provided with houseroom. [J. W. Willis Bund, *Worcester County Records*][33]

1683.   An Peach a poor disconsolate widow ... sheweth that [she] hath been harborless since Candlemas last ... that [she] has been a widow above nine years left with a young child that is lame ... is far remote from all relatives [although she was] brought up a considerable person ... that she hath sold and pawned all she hath ... the very clothes off her back and gloves off her hands to support her impotent child that she can get no work, hath neither money, credit nor harbor, and is in great danger to perish without your assistance. [J. C. Cox. *Three Centuries of Derbyshire Annals*][34]

1617.   Petition of Frances Horner ... spinster .... 'Your

petitioner is a poor impotent person and is placed in a house in Newland wherein two households more are who deny her the use of the fire and many times constrain her to lodge in the fields.' Prays that she may be provided of some poor house in Newland where she may have the use of fire and lodging. [Historical Manuscripts Commission][35]

Fearful of having to relieve such misery, parishes tried to get rid of anyone likely to be a charge by banishing them if they were originally natives of some other parish and by levying fines on any of their own inhabitants who harbored impoverished strangers without giving security for them.

A Note of the Grievances of the Parish of Eldersfield [1618]. There are divers poor people in the said parish which are a great charge. Giles Cooke, not of our parish, married a widow's daughter within our parish, which widow is poor and lives in a small cottage, which is like to be a charge. Joan Whitle had lived forty years and upwards in the parish with a brother, as a servant to him; and now that she has grown old and weak he has put her off to the parish; she was taken begging within the parish and was sent to Teddington, where she said she was born, but that parish has sent her back again. Elzander Man, born in Forthampton, in the county of Gloucester, married a wife within the parish, who was received by her mother until she had two children; the said wife is now dead, and he is gone into Gloucestershire and has left his children in the keeping of the parish. Thomas Jones, born at Hasfield, in the country of Gloucester, married a wife within the parish, and has two children; the said Jones being now gone, the parishioners would know if they might send the woman to her husband, or to the place where she or her husband was born. [Historical Manuscripts Commission][36]

The following budget shows the income and expenditure of a laborer's family in Banbury, Warwickshire, in the late eighteenth century. It was recorded by a contemporary in 1795. The clothing prices in the next selection were taken from accounts kept by the overseers of the poor in another Warwickshire parish about nine miles away.

Earnings

	£	s.	d.
Laborer, 50 years of age, 8s. per week	20	16	0
Wife	nil		
Girl, 15 years of age, 1s. 6d. per week by spinning	3	18	0
Boy, 13 years of age, 3s. per week at plow	7	16	0
3 girls, 11, 9, and 7, and boy of 4 years	nil		
Earnings	32	10	0
Parish allowance, girl of eleven, lame	2	12	0
Total income £	35	2	10

Expenditure

	£	s.	d.
9¼ peck loaves per week at 1s. 2d. per loaf	27	6	0
Rent	2	12	0
Fuel	2	12	0
Clothes	2	12	0
£	35	2	0

[A. W. Ashby, *One Hundred Years of Poor Law Administration in a Warwickshire Village*][37]

A Woman's Outfit, 1790–1830

	£	s.	d.
A pair of shoes		7	0
A pair of stays		6	0
A pair of stockings		1	10
A shift		5	0
Gown		9	0
Apron		1	11½
Petticoat		4	3
Hat and head laces		1	8
Bodice		2	10
A pair of pattens		1	4
£	2	0	11

A Man's Outfit, 1790–1830

	£	s.	d.
A smock frock		10	0
A pair of shoes		10	0
Coat, waistcoat and a pair of breeches	1	1	0
A pair of stockings		1	10
Shirt		4	0
Hat		1	2
A pair of gloves		3	6
	£2	11	6

[Ashby, *Poor Law Administration*][38]

FRANCE

1689.   Throughout the countryside, one sees wild male and female animals. Black, livid, and all burned by the sun, they are attached to the ground in which they obstinately burrow and dig. They make a noise like speech. When they rise to their feet they show a human face and, sure enough, they are men. At night, they withdraw into lairs where they live on black bread, water, and roots. Their toil spares other men from having to sow, plow, and reap for a living, and they deserve better than to be without that very bread which they themselves produce. [La Bruyère, *Oeuvres Complètes*][39]

1788.   The scarcity and consequent high price of firewood in the mountain districts caused great hardship among the peasants. They managed to do without fires by living among their cattle . . . the poorer ones have only a single blanket. . . . Only the rich have feather beds. . . . Thus a girl who brings a dowry will insist on a clause in the marriage contract stipulating that her husband must provide her with a feather and not a 'field' mattress [i.e., a sack stuffed with oats]. . . . All household chores are left to the women. They milk cows, make butter and cheese, go to bed later than the men, and rise before them. If snow has fallen it is up to one of them to clear a path to the fountain. Deep—sometimes up to her waist—in snow, she will go back and forth until she has flattened out a passage for the other women. A man would think himself dishonored if he went for water himself; he would be the butt of the village. These mountain rustics have the deepest contempt for women and the despotic disdain of all wild, half barbaric tribes. They look on them as slaves born to do all the chores which they, consider base and beneath themselves.   [Le Grand Aussy *Voyage d'Auvergne*][40]

1794–5. Correjou farmers are usually well off. Their prosperity is based on the seaweed they sell and on their fine horses, their barley and their flax. . . .

Here, as in the rest of the region, the master of the house is first to serve himself; next come the men in the order prescribed by age and station; the mistress of the house, her daughters, and female friends do not approach until the last farmhand has had his share.

[The following refers to a poorer part of the same department of Finistère in Brittany.] All work here is performed by hand beneath a harsh, black sky buffeted by winds and storms. . . . The poor man can only warm himself and cook his crude victuals with wheat stubble or straw from the heath. Marriage is an arrangement involving neither friendship, trust, nor love. The local food is a crude porridge made of oats and barley, rarely of wheat; on holidays all they drink is tasteless, often brackish water; you are familiar with their poverty and their smoky dwelling; enough about their daytime existence. Let us consider their night time work.

It is in storms, in deepest darkness and when the sea is high . . . that all the inhabitants of the region, men and women, girls and children, are especially busy. Without seaweed there would be no harvest; and it is at night that they collect the seaweed: they are naked, unshod on the spikes of slippery rocks, armed with poles and long rakes; stretched over the abysses they hold back the gift which the sea brings them and would take away again if they did not haul it in. [Jacques de Cambry, *Voyage dans le Finistère*][41]

The following is a description (1802) of Aveiron by Alexis Monteil, a professor of history in that department:

In this beautiful region, we are obliged to say that the female
sex is treated barbarously. Women are obliged to work the land
and toil as farm laborers. Their appearance suffers from this,
and the majority are unattractive. Sunburn, sweat, and work
ruin their figures and features. Before they are eighteen the girls
have leathery faces, drooping breasts, calloused hands, and a
stoop. This barbarous custom, though due to numerous local
causes, would not be impossible to abolish. These good farmers
could be made to see that their fathers were their mothers'
oppressors and that they should hasten to alleviate the condition
of their own wives; that only men are suited to the virile labors
of agriculture and that nature has destined women for the
peaceful occupations of housework and the gentle cares of
motherhood. [Amans-Alexis Monteil, *Déscription du départment
de l' Aveiron*] [42]

Dowries of peasant girls:

1611. Jehanne de Granchamp, a farm laborer's daughter,
receives: the sum of three pounds, four Brioude measures of
wheat, five St Ilpize-size jars of light red wine, and, for dowry
and trousseau, that she may have no further claim on any
inheritance from her father or mother, 90 pounds.

1641. Jeanne Valence, a farm laborer's daughter, provides for
her own dowry: the sum of 30 pounds earned during the years
she spent in service in the town of Brioude; plus a new dress and
a peasant-style wool tunic, a straw mattress, a white woolen
blanket, and a pinewood chest with lock and key.

1642. Catherine Aubazat, a farm laborer's daughter, provides for herself over and above the dowry given her by her
father: the sum of 30 pounds earned while she was in service, plus
two new holland sheets, a blanket of white wool, a set of bed
curtains, three curtains to hang on the wall and an awning for
the bed in white linen, six towels, a dress of new purplish-violet
wool cloth, a tunic, and a pinewood chest with lock and key
containing her small linen.

*A notary's inventory of the possessions left by a rural laborer's wife
(1665):*

A chimney hook, andirons, a gridiron, tongs, etc., 8 pounds. 2 iron pans and copper utensils, 6 pounds. A copper and 2 cauldrons, 6 pounds. A milk jug and lid, 10 pounds. Another like it, 10 pounds. 30 pounds' weight of pewter plate, 15 pounds.

An oaken bin, 6 pounds. A table with trestles and two benches, 4 pounds. A bed with curtains, valance, feather mattress, two blankets, etc., 55 pounds. An oaken coffer as is with lock and key, 4 pounds. 4 straw-bottomed chairs, 12 shillings. A medium-sized mirror with a black frame.

In the said coffer: 4 sheets of hempen cloth of about $4\frac{1}{2}$ ells, 12 pounds. A dozen shirts, 15 pounds. A dozen and a half towels of varying sizes, 9 pounds. A dozen and a half caps (women's), 12 pounds. Two dozen neckerchiefs and handkerchiefs (women's), 10 pounds. Another parcel of linen, 6 pounds. A dozen and a half collars as is (women's), 9 pounds. A bodice with sleeves, 40 shillings. 3 hempen aprons, 30 shillings. 20 pounds' weight of unbleached thread, 10 shillings. A pair of black kirtles, a tucker, petticoat and apron of Aumale serge, 18 pounds. Another pair of kirtles, tucker, petticoat and apron, the petticoat in red Aumale serge, the tucker and apron in London serge, 22 pounds. [Albert Babeau, *La Vie Rurale dans l'Ancienne France*] [43]

5 The Protestant Promotion of Women

The emergence of Protestantism released values and forces that were to further the cause of women. But there was also a Protestant current— soon the dominant one—which swiftly made its peace with established social authority and at the same time inherited many of the traditional views regarding women. A glimpse of the Protestant 'Right' will give us a more correct appreciation of the 'Left'.

CONSERVATIVES

Mary Tudor reigned in England from 1553 to 1558 and drew, as a Catholic, the polemical fire of the Calvinist John Knox. Reviving the old misogynist arguments of Tertullian, Augustine, Ambrose, Paul, Chrysostom, etc.—all cited at length—he held that it was a violation of God's law to let a woman reign, for Eve's punishment was to have been the double one of bringing forth children in pain and being subject to the male. The diatribe was first published in Geneva in 1558.

The holy ghost doth manifestly [say]: I suffer not that women usurp authority over men: he sayeth not, that woman usurp authority over her husband, but he nameth man in general, taking from her all power and authority, to speak, to reason, to interpret or to teach, but principally to rule or to judge in the assembly of men. So that woman by the law of God and the interpretation of the holy ghost is utterly forbidden to occupy the place of God in the offices aforesaid, which he hath assigned to man, whom he hath appointed and ordained his lieutenant in earth: secluding from that honor and dignity all women.... And therefore yet again I repeat that, which I have affirmed: to wit, that a woman promoted to sit in the seat of God, that is to teach, to judge or to reign above man, is a monster in nature, contumely to God, and a thing most repugnant to his will and ordinance. [John Knox, *The first Blast of the Trumpet against the Monstrous Regiment of Women*][44]

Knox was to regret this blast when Elizabeth became queen, but he could not disavow the beliefs: they were his.

We follow with a text on marital authority published by a Protestant clergyman, William Gouge, in 1622.

Allowing that the believing wife sanctified the unbelieving husband and that women should follow their consciences in religious matters raised an implicit challenge to the authority of husbands. Consequences were not immediate. Patriarchal structures and attitudes survived, but grounds had been provided for questioning them. The stock answer to any such challenge was to be that given by Gouge:

Objection   What if a man of mean place be married to a woman of eminent place, or a servant married to a mistress, or an aged woman to a youth, must such a wife acknowledge such an husband her superior?
Answer   Yea verily: for in giving herself to be his wife, and taking him to be her husband, she advanceth him above herself, and subjecteth herself to him.

Objection   But what if a man of lewd and beastly conditions, as a drunkard, a glutton, a profane swaggerer, an impious swearer and blasphemer, be married to a wise, sober, religious matron, must she account him her superior and worthy of an husband's honor?
Answer   Surely she must. For the evil quality and disposition of his heart and life doth not deprive a man of that civil honor which God hath given unto him. Though an husband in regard of evil qualities may carry the image of the devil, yet in regard of his place and office, he beareth the Image of God: so do Magistrates in the Commonwealth, Ministers in the Church, Parents and Masters in the Family. Note for our present purpose, the exhortation of St Peter to Christian wives which have infidel husbands, 'Be in subjection to them: let your conversation be in fear'. If Infidels carry not the devil's image and are not, so long as they are Infidels, vassals of Satan, who are? Yet wives must be subject to them. [William Gouge, *Of Domesticall Duties*][45]

Some women responded enthusiastically and at times extravagantly to the claims first advanced by certain of the radical Protestant sectaries of the sixteenth century and later on by the Quakers—namely, that women too might be filled with the word of God and thus be able to preach and teach. Messianic claims and delirious rantings among early converts gave grounds for the accusation that the spirit possessing them was far from being the holy one. Jane Holmes was ducked for crying her message through the streets of Malton (c. 1650). Other Quaker preachers, women as well as men, were imprisoned or publicly flogged.

Cambridge, December 1653.   Complaint was forthwith made to William Pickering, then Mayor, that two women were preaching.... He asked their names [and] their husbands' names. They told him: they had no husband but Jesus Christ and [that] he sent them. Upon this the Mayor grew angry, called them whores and issued his warrant to the constable to whip them at the Market-Cross till the blood ran down their bodies.... So they were led to the Market-Cross.... The executioner ... stripped them naked to the waist, put their arms into the whipping-post and executed the Mayor's warrant ... so that their flesh was miserably cut and torn. [Joseph Besse, *A Collection of the Sufferings of the People called Quakers*][46]

Claims by the poor, the uneducated, and females to possess the truth were seen as a clear threat to established order. It is remarkable how often the claims of women and the claims of the lower classes were linked in conservative thinking:

Is it a miracle or a wonder (indeed, I confess it may be, to see such intolerable impudence) to see young saucy boys ... bold botching taylors and other most audacious illiterate mechanics, to run rashly (and unsent for too) out of their shops into a pulpit: To see bold impudent housewives, without all womanly modesty, to take upon them (in the natural volubility of their tongues, and quick wits or strong memories only) to prate (not preach or prophesy) after a narrative or discoursing manner, an hour or more, and that most directly contrary to the Apostle's inhibitions; But where, I say, is their extraordinary spirit poured out upon them, either in the gift of tongues, which are rather the gifts of the evil Spirit, as the Apostle James testifies, in gifts of miraculous healing the sick and sore and such like? Where, I say, are any of these in our old or young tradesmen or bold Beatrices of the female sex? [John Vicars, *The Schismatick Sifted*, 1646][47]

PROGRESSIVES

In a tract published in 1651, Mary Cary quoted and commented on the prophet Joel (2:28):

And it shall come to pass that I shall pour out my spirit upon all flesh; and your sons and your daughters shall prophesy ... and upon the handmaids will I pour out my spirit,' [and announces:] ... the time is coming when this promise shall be fulfilled, and the Saints shall be abundantly filled with the spirit; and not only men, but women shall prophesy; not only aged men but young men; not only superiors but inferiors; not only those that have University learning, but those that have it not; even servants and handmaids. [M. Cary, *A New and More exact Mappe or Description of the New Jerusalem's Glory*][48]

The theory of the near spiritual equality of the sexes had been around since the time of St Paul, at any rate in one phase of his thinking. Such Protestant sects as rejected the role of a ministry and of 'University learning' in favor of direct inspiration by the Holy Spirit were logically led to allow that the recipient of such inspiration might be a woman. St Paul's prohibition was countered by reference to Joel 2:28–29. Women preachers were found among the Anabaptists in Germany and the Low Countries as early as the 1520s. More than a century later, the English Quakers, agreeing that women might be priests, organized Women's Meetings (1671) on a countrywide basis.

1672.   For Man and Woman were helps meet in the Image of God, and in Righteousness and Holiness, in the Dominion before they fell; but after the Fall, in the Transgression, the Man was to rule over his Wife; but in the Restoration by Christ, into the Image of God, and his Righteousness ... they are helps meet, Man and Woman, as they were before the Fall.... And there are Elder Women in the Truth, as well as Elder Men in the Truth; and these Women are to be teachers of good things; so they have an Office as well as the Men, for they have a Stewardship, and must give account of their Stewardship to the Lord, as well as the Men. Deborah was a judge; Miriam and Huldah were prophetesses; old Anna was a prophetess.... Mary Magdalene and the other Mary were the first preachers of Christ's Resurrection to the Disciples ... they received the

Command, and being sent, preached it: So is every Woman
and Man to do, that sees him risen, and have the Command
and Message.... And if the Unbelieving Husband is sanctified
by the Believing Wife, then who is the Speaker, and who is the
Hearer? Surely such a Woman is permitted to speak and to
work the Works of God, and to make a Member in the Church;
and then as an Elder, to oversee that they walk according to
the Order of the Gospel. [George Fox, *A Collection of many Select
and Christian Epistles*][49]

1667.   What, are Women Priests? Yes, Women Priests. And
can Men and Women offer Sacrifice without they wear the holy
Garments? No: What are the holy Garments Men and Women
must wear? ... the Priest's Surplice? Nay.... It is the
Righteousness of Christ ... this is the Royal Garment of the
Royal Priesthood, which everyone must put on, Men and
Women. [Fox, *A Collection*][50]

*Thus George Fox (1624–91), founder of the Society of Friends
(Quakers). He tackled (or side-stepped?) St Paul's prohibition of
women preachers in another work (1656):*

Paul, according to the measure given to him, in all his Epistles,
speaking in them of things which ... are hard to understand,
which they that are unlearned and unstable, wrest ... to their
own destruction.... Joel, the Lord's prophet ... spoke from
the Lord, and saith the Lord to him ... 'I will pour out my
spirit upon all flesh, and your sons and your daughters shall
prophesy ... and upon the handmaidens in those days will I
pour out my spirit,' saith the Lord.... Here the prophet Joel
was not against the daughters prophesying, nor the apostles were
not against it, but said, 'despise not prophesying' and saith
the Lord ... 'Touch not mine anointed, and do my
prophets no harm.' So you that persecute the daughters on whom
the spirit of the Lord is poured, and believe them not, you are
them that despise prophesying, and so have broken the apostles'
command.... And Paul [*Philippians*, 4] ... entreats his yoke-
fellow to help those women which labored with him in the
gospel as you may there read. The women were joined with the

20 Beggar-woman carrying three children
Italian engraving dated about 1475

21   Position for a difficult birth
From *La Commare o la Riccoglitrice* by Scipio Mercurio, 1621

other fellow-laborers.... And in *Romans* 16, there you may see Priscilla and Aquila, Paul's helpers in Jesus Christ, who for his life laid down their necks; here the wise Priscilla was an instructor.... Now you that make a scoff and wonder at a woman's declaring, you may see that it was Mary that first declared Christ after he was risen, so be ashamed and confounded forever, and let all your mouths be stopped forever ... and if Christ be in the female as well as in the male, is he not the same? and may not the spirit of Christ speak in the female as well as in the male? is he there to be limited? who is it that dare limit the Holy One of Israel? ... and so Christ is one in all and not divided, and who is it that dares stop Christ's mouth? ... and you that will not have him reign in the female as well as in the male, you are against Scripture. [Fox, *The Woman Learning in Silence*][51]

A POLITICAL PROTEST

Politics, as well as religion, engaged women during the English Civil War and Interregnum (1642–60). Numerous wives of political refugees, Puritan and Royalist, procured the escape of husbands, solicited pardons for them, and ran estates in their absence. As a friend wrote to Sir Ralph Verney, who from his exile in France was considering sending his wife to attend to his affairs in England:

August 1646.   Women were never so useful as now, and though you should be my agent and solicitor of all the men I know (and therefore much more to be preferred in your own cause) yet I am confident if you were here, you would do as our sages do, instruct your wife, and leave her to act it with committees, their sex enables them to many privileges, and we feel the comfort of them now more than ever. [F. P. Verney, *Memoirs of the Verney Family*][52]

Much more to our point than individual wives acting on their husbands' behalf are the anonymous women who petitioned parliament on behalf of the radicals, the Levellers, in 1649. The four leaders had been arrested that year and:

'When the men durst not any more petition in behalf of Lilbourne and his associates, the women took it up.' [*The Parliamentary: or Constitutional History of England*] [53]

On April 23, hundreds of them attended the House of Commons with a petition on behalf of the arrested men. The soldiers forced them down- stairs, presented ready cocked pistols, and threw squibs among them. The women returned the next day but failed to gain a hearing. On the twenty- fifth they were back again. The sergeant conveyed a message to them from the House:

'That the matter they petitioned about was of an higher con- cernment than they understood, that the House gave an answer to their husbands, and therefore desired them to go home, and look after their own business, and meddle with their husbandry.' [B. Whitelock, *Memorials of the English Affairs*] [54]

Early in the next month (*May 5*) *the following petition was presented:*

The Humble Petition of divers well-affected women of the Cities of London and Westminster, etc. Sheweth, that since we are assured of our creation in the image of God, and of an interest in Christ equal unto men, as also of a proportional share in the freedoms of this Commonwealth, we cannot but wonder and grieve that we should appear so despicable in your eyes, as to be thought unworthy to petition or represent our grievances to this honorable House.

Have we not an equal interest with the men of this Nation, in those liberties and securities contained in the Petition of Right, and the other good laws of the land? Are any of our lives, limbs, liberties or goods to be taken from us more than from men, but by due process of law and conviction of twelve sworn men of the neighborhood?

And can you imagine us to be so sottish or stupid, as not to perceive, or not to be sensible when daily those strong defenses of our peace and welfare are broken down, and trod under foot by force and arbitrary power?

Would you have us keep at home in our houses, when men of such faithfulness and integrity as the FOUR PRISONERS our friends in the Tower are fetched out of their beds, and forced from their houses by soldiers, to the affrighting and undoing of themselves. their wives, children and families? Are not our husbands, ourselves, our children and families by the same rule as liable to the like unjust cruelties as they? . . . . Doth not the Petition of Right declare that no person ought to be judged by Law Martial (except in time of war) . . . ? And are we Christians and shall we sit still and keep at home, while such men as have borne continual testimony against the unjustice of all times, and unrighteousness of men, be picked out and delivered up to the slaughter . . . ?

No. . . . Let it be accounted folly, presumption . . . or whatsoever in us . . . we will never forsake them, nor ever cease to importune you . . . for justice . . . that we, our husbands, children, friends and servants may not be liable to be thus abused, violated and butchered at men's wills and pleasures. . . .

And therefore again, we entreat you to review our last petition in behalf of our friends above mentioned, and not to slight the things therein contained because they are presented to you by the weak hand of women. . . . For we are no whit satisfied with the answer you gave unto our husbands and friends. . . . Nor shall we be . . . except you free them [the leaders] from their present extrajudicial imprisonment and . . . give them full reparation . . . and leave them to be proceeded against by due process of law. . . . Our houses being worse than prisons to us. . . until you grant our design . . . harden not your hearts against petitioners nor deny us in things so evidently just and reasonable as you would not be dishonorable to all posterity. [*The Thomason Tracts*] [55]

6 The Surplus Daughter

The problem of disposing of surplus daughters was solved in a variety of ways: the ancient Greeks exposed them, Muslims had recourse to polygamy, Christians put them in convents. By the twelfth century a parent was no longer permitted to take religious vows on a child's behalf. The Council of Trent (1545–63) ruled that such vows could not be taken by anyone under sixteen and then only after a probationary period of a year. This did not put an end to parental coercion. A moderate-sized family might easily have as many as five or six daughters, and five or six dowries depleted almost any estate. The usual solution was to put aside dowries for the eldest or prettiest girls and pack the rest off to a convent boarding-school in the hope that they would develop a taste for the monastic life. If they did not—too bad for them. Priests very often denounced the practice:

I do not want to meddle in your family affairs ... [but] I tell you that you have no right to dispose of your children by forcing a vocation on them.... It would cost money to establish this daughter: reason enough to consecrate her as a nun.... But she has no trace of a religious calling: the present state of your finances is calling enough for her.... And so the victim is led to the temple, hands and feet tied: by which I mean against her will, dumb with fear and awe of a father whom she has always honored. Such murderous fathers are far from imitating Abraham ... who was ready to sacrifice his son to God: instead they sacrifice their children to their own estate and to their own cupidity. [Louis Bourdaloue, 1632–1704, *Oeuvres Complètes*] [56]

We present the case of Sister Paula to illustrate what is meant by a 'forced vocation'. Paula's parents were not unusual, nor was their treatment of her. She was the youngest of five sisters. The two eldest were allowed to marry. After that, the parents felt they could not afford more money for dowries. The last three girls must become nuns. The following testimony was submitted by Sister Paula in 1734, seven years after her flight from the convent. She was trying to obtain the annulment of her religious vows in a case taken before the Court of the Holy Penitentiary.

I, Paula Pietra of Milan, a professed nun in the convent of St Radegonde of the Benedictine Order ... submit that in April 1716, when I was fifteen years old and had been a boarder in St Radegonde's since the age of four and a half ... I was asked by my mother in the presence of the nuns Cotta and Quinzani whether I had a vocation to be a nun, and I told her ... that my reply was the same as the one she had had [from my sisters who had chosen not to be nuns]. She flew into a rage and raised her hand to strike me. [The nuns and her mother try to bully her into changing her mind, and her mother threatens to send her to Santa Sofia, a reformatory for girls.]

I was brought home, and after a week my mother stopped threatening me with Santa Sofia but kept on abusing and slapping and punching me, and my sisters joined in, all so that I would agree to become a nun. They said clearly that I absolutely must come around to it, and other people were witnesses to this. . . . After two months, when they saw no change in me, the bullying increased and my sisters pushed me out of their bed and made me sleep with the maid, and, as the maids kept changing, I had to suffer their foulness; and they left me without the most necessary things, like shifts and stockings, and wouldn't lend me theirs, and when my mother called me or I even caught sight of her, I used to tremble from head to foot and pray to all the saints in heaven to help me.

After another two months of suffering, my mother said to me one day that I must resolve to be a nun or else pass the rest of my life in the aforesaid Santa Sofia. To this I answered (after staying silent awhile so that she said, 'Well, aren't you answering?') that of the two I would choose the lesser evil; to which she added at once, 'Good, you'll be a nun!' Thereupon she left me with my elder sister, who produced paper and ink—which up to then they had denied me—and told me to write the news to the nuns. When I started to cry, my sister said, 'Stop fussing or I'll go and tell mother'. So I wrote to Quinzani that I was going to become a nun, and my sister brought the note to my mother right away, and she sent it to the convent, and the next day I was taken to the convent and received by the Chapter, even though the nuns, especially Quinzani, knew how I had been bullied, for I had

told them myself. [Then Paula has spells at home, required by
the Church to ensure that the future nun is sure of her vocation.
She asks her brother and brother-in-law for help. They promise
it but fail to stand up to her mother. Finally, all they do is make
more trouble for Paula.] ... back in Milan my elder sister told
me that I should hurry up and decide finally to return to the
convent.... I waited another few days, and on one of these, my
mother, in the presence of Count Sormani, gave me a slap and
said, 'When are you going to get out of my sight?' Two days
later she took me herself to the interview which is required
before entering the convent.... The Abbot only asked me
whether I was entering the convent because of a disappointment
in love. I said no. He asked was it a caprice. I said no again.
He got me to read something in Latin and in the vernacular as is
usual and then let me go. During the whole interview I wasn't as
much as the length of two feet from my mother's side, and the
one at the Archbishopric was conducted in the same way by
Monsignor Grassi. [Pressed to make her final departure for
the convent, Paula comes to take leave of her mother.] She
gave me two slaps, whereupon I turned and said, 'Madame,
remember that you maltreated me up to the last,' and left without her blessing. Countess Zanati brought me to the convent.
I did not confide in her because I knew she could not help me.
As I entered the convent ... I was determined in my mind to
find some other way of leaving [i.e., other than the legal one],
since, in view of the violence that was being done me, I had no
choice and no one to whom to turn, not even a father, who kept
out of family matters for many reasons and let my mother run
things. I never saw him except in the mornings and at lunch....
The year of my novitiate was very harsh ... in the middle of
March 1718, when I was seventeen years old, came the day
when I was to make my final vows. Not wanting to burden my
conscience with them, since I knew I couldn't keep them, having
hopes still of finding some way of getting out, I resolved to make
them only in words, while with my heart—and immediately
afterward in words too—I told God that I did not really mean
them ... and so I made my vows which I have always considered invalid.... [Another year passes during which Paula is
carefully watched and treated with great austerity.] I had got

pale, melancholy, and thin.... The nun Quinzani began taking me into the parlor when foreign gentlemen came to hear the singing. The gentlemen then began asking for me directly, and I never let a chance go by but spent almost the whole day in the parlor. There were Milanese gentlemen there too, and I told them all that I was in the convent against my will.... And so the years went by and I kept hoping ... for a chance of putting my resolution into effect.... This was why I preferred to meet foreign gentlemen in the parlor than local ones.... Finally I got to know an English gentleman who was kindly disposed and sorry for me.

He offered to take me out of the convent and promised, both by word of mouth and in writing, that he would marry me. I seized this long-awaited chance, left a note for the nuns in my bedroom ... and we took off for Venice [22 August, 1727]. There, on account of the widespread searches being made for me, I had to take refuge on an English ship which brought me to London. As soon as I got there, the Protestant Archbishop of Canterbury sent messages to me with offers of every kind of help, including an income, if I would change my religion. I sent back my thanks and the reply that I had come to England [in search of] freedom for my person, not for my conscience, and that, as I did not intend changing our holy religion, I must decline his offers....

Extract from the testimony of a witness, a notary by profession:

I will say that having been summoned ... to draw up the deed of payment of the spiritual dowry of the Signora Paula Teresa Pietra ... I presented myself in the usual parlor ... and there found Count Francesco Brunorio Pietra and the Mother Abbess ... with other nuns and the aforementioned Paula Teresa dressed as a novice.... She was weeping and shouting at her father because her father wanted her to ... make a complete renunciation and she didn't want to but said clearly that she wanted to leave the convent and did not want to be a nun and went so far as to curse her father and far more so her mother who, she said, had barbarously maltreated her when she was at home so as to force her to become a nun and that she on no account wanted to be a nun. Her father meanwhile kept threatening her, saying that if she wouldn't be a nun, he would punish her so as to make her sorry and that after all he had spent he didn't want the money to go to waste and he wanted her to be a nun. To this she answered that she didn't care about what he had spent and wouldn't be a nun; and in spite of all the nuns' efforts to calm her down with the usual sweet promises, it was impossible to do anything with her and evening came without our being able to proceed, and I must say that Sister Paula's frenzy was such that she even tore her hair and tore the veil from her head. . . .

A few friends of Paula collected evidence on her behalf. Seven years after her flight the case was finally heard. The following is part of a papal directive:

The case is grave in itself and has particularly urgent claims on the paternal solicitude both of Our Holiness and of this curia. . . for this very scandalous flight has become known almost all over Europe. To grant the fugitive a favorable rescript, without evident good reason, would be to reward her enormous past misdeed and might well give rise to a still greater scandal. On the other hand, she deserves some special compassion because she firmly and publicly professed her Catholic Faith while in an enemy country . . . and also in view of her having thrown herself voluntarily into the arms of Holy Mother Church by returning to Rome, where she has once again put on the religious habit and entered a cloister, where, may God be praised, she is living with exemplary piety. Lastly [she deserves compassion] because she left London of her own free will and did not succumb to the solicitations of a marriage not displeasing to her. . . . [Proceedings] will undoubtedly be greatly hindered by . . . the opposition of her influential family, who will do all they can—rumors to this effect have already reached Rome—to prevent the return of such a close kinswoman. Their reasons are, first, that she would claim a much larger dowry [than the spiritual dowry paid for her to the convent] because of her decision to get married . . . and, second, that if the Roman Curia were to issue a definitive ruling absolving her from her vows, this would be tantamount to condemning the impudence of those same relatives in violently forcing her to take them....

[In March 1735, the Court declared Paula's vows invalid and she went back to England, where she married her rescuer, John Durant Breval. She let it be known that she would not try to recover her spiritual dowry from the convent, but applied to the Emperor Charles VI, appealing for her share of the family inheritance. A decree of 13 November 1737, directed a magistrate in Pavia to ensure that a compromise was reached between her and her married sisters. In May 1741 a contract was concluded, and they agreed to pay her certain sums of money and an income.] [C. A. Vianello, *Il Dramma e il Romanzo di Suor Paolina dei Conti Pietra*][57]

7 Salons

In Paris the Hotel de Rambouillet [the town house of the Marquise] was a sort of academy of wit, style, virtue, and learning ... the meeting place of all who were distinguished by rank or merit, a tribunal to be reckoned with and whose decision carried at least as much weight in matters affecting the reputation of people of the court or of high society as it did with regard to books. [Saint-Simon, *Mémoires*][58]

She [the Marquise de Rambouillet] was careful to keep up her Italian so that she knew that language as well as French. . . . She always loved beautiful things and was going to learn Latin just so as to be able to read Virgil when an illness prevented her. She didn't go back to the idea afterwards but contented herself with Spanish. She is clever at everything. It was she who redesigned the Hôtel de Rambouillet which had been her father's house. Dissatisfied with all the plans she was shown (. . . for at that time all they knew how to do was to put one room at each side and stairs in the middle . . .), one evening, after having thought about it for quite a while, she cried, 'Paper! Quickly. I've thought of how to do what I wanted'. There and then she drew up the plan, for of course she knows how to draw. . . . It was from her that people got the idea of putting stairs at the side so as to have a long suite of rooms, and of raising floors and making large high doors and windows opposite each other. And indeed when the Queen Mother was having the Luxembourg built she sent the architects to look at the Hôtel de Rambouillet . . . . [It] was the theater of all pleasures, the meeting place of the gayest people from the court and the most subtle wits of the century. [Gédéon Tallemant des Réaux, *Historiettes*][59]

One of the few scenes—apart from their kitchens—where women were consistently in control was the French drawing room of the seventeenth and eighteenth centuries. Salon society was one of the acknowledged triumphs of the ancien régime; *elitist and necessarily transient, its prime product was the 'art of conversation' and, more vaguely, that sweetness of life which, Talleyrand assured, no one who had not lived before the Revolution could ever know. For the historian of women, it provides an instance when a few women of birth plucked the prize which the world of social hierarchies and double standards constantly dangled and rarely delivered. 'Stay at home,' the manuals of that society had been advising for centuries. 'Be feminine. Use your charm, and men will bring you the best of themselves and leave the rest in the crude world outside your doors.' For this promise to be kept, conditions had to be right, and in Paris, for the rich and clever, for a century and a half, they were. Education for women was new enough to excite them still and general enough in the upper classes to make for discussions on a wide variety of topics. Money, leisure, and the ingenuity of satellite men of letters went into the preparation of elaborate games and* tableaux vivants. *Houses were remodeled and alcoves created which favored casual and intimate talk. This talk throbbed with sex ('Platonic love'); husbands were notably absent; the notion—first formulated by Castiglione—was thrillingly debated that perhaps a woman might, with propriety, enjoy an intellectual relationship with an admirer while keeping her body for her husband. Could she give her hand to one man, her heart to another? The question had more resonance than may appear. In asking it, young women, who had been disposed of as brood mares are brought to stud, were groping for a way of affirming their identity. The liberal scholars like Erasmus who first favored educating women had insisted that emancipation of the female mind need not lead to emancipation of the female body. Women's efforts to extend the scope of their experience yet keep the promise made on their behalf set up tensions. So did the contrast between the drawing rooms, where they queened it, and domestic life with their husbands, where they were expected to be as subservient as ever. Mademoiselle de Scudéry kept one of the more literary drawing rooms. In her novel* Le Grand Cyrus, *published between 1649 and 1653, she describes the Platonic love which flourished at the court of Paphos (readers were expected to recognize Paris).*

Among us, love is not a simple passion as it is elsewhere; it is one of the requirements for good breeding. Every man must be in love. Every lady must be loved. No one among us is indifferent. Anyone capable of such hardness of heart would be reproached as for a crime; such liberty is so shameful that those who are not in love at least pretend to be. Custom does not oblige ladies to love but merely to allow themselves to be loved, and they put their pride in making illustrious conquests and in never losing those whom they have brought under their rule; yet they are severe, for the honor of our beauties consists in keeping the slaves they have made by the sheer power of their attractions and not by according favors; so that, by this custom, to be a lover is almost necessarily to be unhappy.... Yet it is not forbidden to reward a lover's perseverance by a totally pure affection ... whatever can render them more lovable and loving is allowed, provided it does not shock that purity or modesty which, despite their gallantry, is these ladies' supreme virtue. [Mlle de Scudéry, *Artamène ou le Grand Cyrus*][60]

Pierre Daniel Huet (1630–1721), bishop of Avranches and renowned for his learning, had this to say about the superiority of French novels over those of other countries:

1670.   I believe we owe this advantage to the politeness of our gallantry which comes, in my opinion, from the freedom with which men and women mix in France. In Italy and Spain women are almost recluses, being separated from men by so many obstacles that one sees them little and hardly ever talks to them. As a result, the art of cajoling them has been neglected there. One merely tries to get around the difficulties of approaching them and, this done, makes what use one may of the time without wasting it on forms. In France, women are their own protectors; having no other defense than their virtue and their hearts, they have made these into ramparts stronger than all the locks, bars, and duennas. Men have thus been obliged to attack this rampart by courtesy and have employed such care and adroitness to this end that they have elaborated an art almost unknown to other peoples. [P. D. Huet, *Traité de l'origine des romans*][61]

The art could become cloying. Overrefined, pedantic ladies were fair game for satirists, and the word 'précieuse' (precious female) became a term of reproach. It was suggested that they lacked temperament.

Someone once said to the Queen of Sweden that the *Precieuses* were the Jansenists [puritans] of love; the definition did not displease her. Love is a god for the *Precieuses*. It does not arouse passions in their souls but forms a species of religion. To speak more clearly, the *Precieuses* consist of a body of women among whom emulation of a few genuinely fastidious individuals has flung the rest into the most ridiculous affectation of fastidiousness.

Women of this second sort have deprived love of its most natural elements in the belief that they were making it more 'precious.' They have transferred a live, palpitating passion from the heart to the brain and converted impulses into ideas. This radical purification took its source in an honest distaste for sensuality; but these women are no less far from the true nature of love than are the more sensual sort; for love is as little to be found in mental speculation as it is in brute appetites. If you wish to know the greatest claim to merit of the *Precieuses*, I shall tell you that it was in tenderly loving their lovers without sex and getting solid sexual satisfaction from their husbands while disliking them. [Saint-Evremond, *Oeuvres*][62]

Eventually, the game of gallantry was to turn out useful both to those who, like Mademoiselle de Scudéry, wanted no closer contact with the opposite sex and to seekers after the solider pleasures who could use it as camouflage. 'Précieuses' were divided into prudes and galantes. Their solutions to women's dilemma were diametrically opposed. Mademoiselle de Scudéry's solution—not open to everyone—was to reject marriage. 'Sapho' was the name under which she portrayed herself in her novel Le Grand Cyrus.

'Then,' said Tisandre [to Sapho], 'you can hardly regard marriage as desirable.' 'It is true,' replied Sapho, 'that I consider it a lengthy slavery.' 'So you think all men are tyrants?' 'I think they may all become so ... I know of course that there are some very worthy men who deserve all my esteem and could even acquire some friendship from me; but, again, as soon as I think of them as husbands, I see them as masters so likely to turn into tyrants that I cannot help hating them there and then and thank the gods for giving me an inclination totally opposed to marriage.' 'But supposing one had the merit and happiness to touch your heart? Wouldn't you change your mind?' 'I cannot tell,' she replied, 'whether I should change my mind, but I do know that unless love had driven me out of my mind, I would never give up my freedom.' [Mlle de Scudéry, *Artamène ou le Grand Cyrus*][63]

The Abbé de Pure frequented the salon of Madame de Suze, a far from frigid lady. Many of the feminist conversations reported in his novel of 1656 were probably based on those he heard there.

'My proposal ... ladies, is to discuss how marriage might be reformed so as to ease the rigors of its slavery and the harshness of its chains....' 'That subject,' answered Eulalie, 'is less fruitless than you think.... What seems to be a vain discussion in our alcove may be of use to our grandchildren and a guide in time to come. Even if the only satisfaction we can hope for is to show that we are aware of our sufferings and do not merely put up with them because of stupidity or ignorance, at least we shall have done some honor to our sex and tempered its subjection....' [Michel de Pure, *La Prétieuse ou le Mystère des Ruelles*][64]

'A husband who is present all the time is the most incommodious object in the world!' [Pure, *La Prétieuse*][65]

'I', said Aracie, when it was her turn to speak, 'would like to limit the duration of marriage and let it end with the first child. After that first bit of work...they could divide the booty; the husband would get the child, the wife her liberty, and the father would reward her with a good-sized sum of money in keeping with the merits of her labor.' [Pure, *La Prétieuse*][66]

Platonic love went out of fashion, but salons survived. There were political salons, learned salons, literary, atheistic, and epicurean salons. Women nearly always presided. Prudery abated. Ninon de Lenclos, although her lovers were countless and some paid her rent, was visited by the most brilliant and fashionable people in France. Mademoiselle de Lespinasse lived more or less openly with d'Alembert, and articles for the great encyclopedia were prepared and discussed in her salon. Madame Geoffrin, a middle-class woman, received visits from King Gustave of Sweden and the Emperor Joseph II. She went to Poland to visit King

Stanislas Augustus and to Vienna to see Maria Theresa. Hume, Walpole, Benjamin Franklin visited. The list is endless. Another foreign intellectual, the Abbé Galiani, wrote the following nostalgic letter to Madame Necker when he had returned to Italy.

Not a Friday passes but I visit you in spirit. I arrive. I find you putting the finishing touches to your clothes. I sit at your feet. Thomas suffers in silence. Morellet complains aloud; Grimm and Suard laugh light-heartedly and Creutz never even notices.... Dinner is announced. We come out. The others eat meat. I abstain. I eat a lot of that green Scotch cod which I love. I give myself an indigestion while admiring Abbé Morellet's skill at carving a young turkey. We get up from table. Coffee is served. Everyone talks at once. The Abbé Raynal agrees with me that Boston has severed its links with England forever and at the same time Creutz and Marmontel agree that Grétry is the Pergolese of France. M. Necker thinks everything is perfect, bows his head, and goes away. That is how I spend my Fridays. [Ferdinand Galiani, letter to Madame Necker][67]

XI *From the Era of Revolution to the 1850s*

1 Germany: Philosophers Speak of Women

After the awesome carnage of the Thirty Years' War (1618–48), the German cities and principalities took more than the remainder of the century to recover from economic collapse and depopulation. The more peaceful and prosperous eighteenth century could afford not only gayer courts and increased patronage for the arts, but also more quiet corners of study and more leisured circumstances for philosophy.

IMMANUEL KANT (1724–1804)

The maker of German idealism, Kant occasionally grazes the subject of women, then finally turns to a more sustained discussion in the first part of his Die Metaphysik der Sitten *(1797). Dealing here with questions of 'mine' and 'thine', with the nature of acquisition and property, he is logically led to a consideration of marriage. In a few stern paragraphs he comes about as close as any man ever had to acknowledging a perfect equality between the sexes, but in the concluding sentence, interestingly, pure reason defers to expedience.*

Domestic relations are based on marriage, and marriage is based on the natural reciprocity or intercommunity of the sexes. This natural union of the sexes accords with our mere animal nature (*fornicatio*) or with the law. The latter is marriage, which is the union of two persons of different sex for life-long reciprocal possession of their sexual faculties.... But it is not necessary for the rightfulness of marriage that those who marry should make this [procreation] the purpose of their union, otherwise the marriage would be dissolved of itself when the production of children ceased.... [Indeed] if a man and a woman decide to enter on reciprocal enjoyment [of their sexual endowments] in accordance with their nature, they must necessarily marry each other; and this necessity is in keeping with the juridical laws of pure reason.

For intercourse—the use by one of the sexual parts of the other—is an enjoyment for which the one person is given up to the other. In this relation the human individual makes himself a thing (*res*), which is contrary to human right. But this is possible only under one condition: that as the one person is acquired by the other as a thing, that same person also equally acquires the other reciprocally, and thus regains and reestablishes the rational personality. The acquisition of a part of the human organism being, on account of its unity, at the same time the acquisition of the whole person, it follows that the mutual surrender and acceptance of one sex in relation to the other is not only admissible under the condition of marriage but further is really possible only under that condition. The personal right thus acquired is real in kind and is established by the fact that if one of the married persons flees or enters into the possession of another, the other is incontestably entitled to bring him or her back to the former relation, as if that person were a thing.

For the same reason married persons are bound to each other in a relation of equality as regards the mutual possession of their persons, as well as of their goods. Consequently marriage is truly realized only in monogamy, for in polygamy the person surrendering on one side gains only part of the person on the other and therefore is downgraded to a mere thing. It therefore follows that concubinage can no more be put under a legal contract than can the hiring of a person, for any one occasion, through an agreement to fornicate. For as regards a contract of the sort implied in the latter relation, it is clear that none who entered into it could legally be held to the fulfillment of their promise if they chose to withdraw from it. In the same way, a contract of concubinage is also not binding in law, being a sort of 'compact in turpitude.' For as a contract of hire which hires a part [i.e., the sexual organs] for the use of another, on account of the inseparable unity of the members of a person, anyone entering into such a contract would be actually surrendering as a thing to the arbitrary will of another. Hence any party to such a contract may freely annul it at any time and the other party would have no ground, in the circumstances, to complain of an injury to his or her rights. The same holds true of a morganatic or 'left-hand' marriage, contracted in order to turn the inequality in the social status of the two parties to the advantage of one by establishing the social supremacy of one over the other. Such a relation is not really different from concubinage, according to the principles of natural right, and therefore does not constitute a real marriage. Hence the question may be raised as to whether it is not contrary to the equality of married persons when the law says in any way of the husband in relation to the wife, 'he shall be thy master,' so that he is represented as the one who commands and she as the one who obeys. This, however, cannot be regarded as contrary to the natural equality of the human pair, if such legal supremacy, looking to the common interest of the household, is based only upon the natural superiority of the husband's faculties compared with those of the wife, and if the right to command is based merely upon this fact. [Kant, *The Philosophy of Law*][1]

J. G. FICHTE (1762–1814)

The din and promise of the French Revolution scared Fichte, professor of philosophy at the University of Jena, as it scared many of his contemporaries. A work he published in 1795 contains a pointed reply to the new advocates of women's rights. Fichte believed that he was the true defender of women, not they.

It is the duty of the state to protect the honor of the female sex, to see to it that women are not compelled to give themselves up to a man whom they do not love; for this honor is a part, nay, the noblest part, of their personality....

The state cannot prohibit concubinage. But as the protector of women, the state must be satisfied that the woman has voluntarily entered the infamous compact. This can be achieved only by the declaration of such a woman. On account of its infamous character, however, the declaration must not involve a solemn ceremony, like marriage, but be a statement made to such police officers as may be entrusted with affairs of this low character....

Has woman the same rights in the state which man has? This question may appear ridiculous. For if the only ground of all legal rights is reason and freedom, how can a distinction exist between two sexes which possess both the same reason and freedom? Nevertheless, it seems that the distinction has been made so long as men have lived, and the female sex seems not to have been put on a par with the male sex in the exercise of its rights. Such a universal sentiment must have a ground, to discover which it has never been more pressing than in our own day.

The question whether the female sex really has a claim to all the rights of man and of male citizens could be raised only by persons who doubt whether women are complete human beings. We do not doubt it.... But the question may certainly be asked whether and how far the female sex can desire to exercise all its rights....

As a rule, woman is either a single maiden or married. If single, she is still under the care of her father.... If she is married, her whole dignity depends upon her being completely subjected, and seeming to be so subjected, to her husband.... [Repeats and emphasizes:] woman is not subjected to her husband in such a manner as to give him a right of compulsion over her; she is subjected through her own continuous necessary wish—a wish which is the condition of her morality—to be so subjected. She has the power to withdraw her freedom, if she could have the will to do so. But that is the very point; she cannot rationally will to be free. Her relation to her husband, being publicly known, she must, moreover, will to appear to all whom she knows as utterly subjected to, and utterly lost in, the man of her choice.

Hence her husband is the administrator of all her rights and she wishes those rights asserted only in so far as he wishes it. He is her natural representative in the state and in the whole society. This is her public relation to society.... So far as her private and internal relation in the house is concerned, the tenderness of the husband necessarily restores to her all and more than she has lost....

The wife has rights in public affairs, for she is a citizen. I consider it the duty of the husband—in states where the voting franchise exists—not to vote without having discussed the subject with his wife and allowed her to modify his opinion through her own. His vote will then be the result of their common will....

Women are ineligible for public office for the following simple reasons. Public officials are responsible to the state; hence they must be perfectly free and dependent always only upon their own free will, otherwise such responsibility would be unjust and

contradictory. Woman, however, is free and independent only
as long as she has no husband. Hence the exclusive condition
under which a woman might become eligible for office would be
in a promise not to marry. But no rational woman can give such
a promise, nor can the state rationally accept it. For woman is
destined to love, and love comes to women of itself, does not
depend upon her free will. But when she loves, it is her duty to
marry and the state must not create obstacles to this. Now if a
woman holding public office were to marry, two possibilities
would follow. First, she might not subject herself to her husband
in matters regarding her official duties, which would be utterly
against female dignity, for she cannot say then that she has
given herself up wholly to her husband. Where are the strict
limits that divide official from public life? Or, secondly, she
might subject herself utterly to her husband, as nature and morality require. But in that case she would cease to be the official
and he would become it. The office would become his by marriage, like the rest of his wife's property and rights. But this the
state cannot allow.

[Fichte then replies to the 'advocates of women's rights,' who
allege that the social system conspires to deny higher education
to women. Drawing the stock distinction between feeling
(represented by women) and reason (represented by men), he
introduces a natty refinement: feeling or natural sentiment in
woman 'originally unites with reason because it would cancel
reason unless it did so unite,' which 'is why woman's whole
system of feeling is rational and made to correspond with reason'. The result is that women get all the higher education they
need from 'their condition' and 'our male conversation'.]
[Fichte, *The Science of Rights*][2]

*Far from being reactionary or atypical, Fichte's views are—save for
their philosophical coating—the conventional and long-established views
of his day (men legally controlled the property of their wives). Indeed, in
one respect he was a radical: in his insistence that where men had the
right to vote they consult their wives before going to the polls. And if,
looking back, this now seems trivial and no charity at all, we have only to
remember that not for another century after Fichte did women begin to*

obtain the right to vote, in Germany not until 1918, Great Britain 1918, Spain 1931, France 1944, and Italy 1945.

G. W. H. HEGEL (1770–1831)

Surprisingly, the greatest of the German idealists, Hegel, took over the traditional attitudes regarding women. But it is fascinating to watch him pour these into the elaborate mold of his idealism.

Subjectively marriage may appear to derive from the particular inclination of the two persons who are entering into this relation, or from the foresight and arrangements of the parents. Objectively, however, the source lies in the free consent of the persons, above all in their agreement to make themselves one person and to surrender their natural and individual personality to this unity. Their union is in this sense a restriction imposed upon the self, but it is also their liberation, for in it they acquire their substantive self-consciousness. . . .

The ethical dimension of marriage is in the couple's consciously taking this unity to be their substantive purpose in marriage; hence it is in their love, faith, and in the communion of their whole existence as individuals. In this particular state, their [sexual] impulse is lowered to the modality of a natural moment, fated to perish in its very satisfaction, but the spiritual tie endures. . . .

With regard to sexual relations, we should note that in giving herself to intercourse, the [unmarried] girl renounces her honor. This is not, however, the case with men, for they have yet another sphere for their ethical activity beyond that of the family. Girls have their essential destiny in marriage and there only; thus the demand that their love take the form of marriage. . . .

The physical difference between the sexes has an intellectual and ethical significance based on rational grounds. . . .

One sex [man] is mind at odds with itself, having personal autonomy on the one side and on the other the knowledge and will of free universality; it is the self-consciousness of thought as it conceptualizes and it is the willing of the objective final end. The other [woman], holding itself in unity, is mind as knowledge and will of the substantive in the form of concrete individuality and feeling. In relations regarding externality, the former is powerful and enterprising, the latter passive and subjective. Hence man [the male] has his essential life in the state, in learning, and in the like, as well as in work and struggle with the outside world and with himself. Accordingly, only out of his divided self and by means of struggle does he achieve an autonomous unity with himself. He gets a calm sense of this within the family and there, at the level of feeling, is able to have a subjective morality. Here indeed, within the family, is where woman has her true definition; as a matter of ethical disposition, her distinctive way of thinking lies in family piety. . . . Women are certainly capable of learning, but they are not made for the higher forms of science, such as philosophy and certain types of artistic creativity; these require a universal ingredient. Women may hit on good ideas and they may, of course, have taste and elegance, but they lack the talent for the ideal. Men and women differ much as do animals and plants. Men and animals correspond, just as women and plants do, for women develop more placidly and retain the principle of an indeterminate unity of feeling or sentiment. When women stand at the head of government, the state is immediately plunged into danger because they conduct affairs not by the standard of universality but in accordance with random opinions and inclinations. Women acquire learning—we know not how—almost as if by breathing ideas, more by living really than by actually taking hold of knowledge. Man, on the other hand, achieves his distinction only by means of advancing thought and much skilled exertion.

Marriage is essentially monogamy and one of the absolute principles that makes possible the ethical life of the community. The coming of marriage is therefore represented as one of the great moments in the divine or heroic foundation of states.

The family, as person, has its external reality in property; the substantive personality of the family exists only in so far as it has material assets. [Hegel, *Grundlinien der Philosophie des Rechts*][3]

2 Prostitutes

[Prostitution] ... resembles slavery; if slavery is a disgrace then the slaveholder must bear his full portion of obloquy. If prostitution is a vice, both parties are vicious; if it be a crime, both parties are criminals. Now as a matter of history, no proposition aiming at punishment has ever involved both participants. [A. Flexner, *Prostitution in Europe*, 1914][4]

The harlot is one that is both merchant and merchandise.... She is commonly known for her whorish attire: as crisping and curling (making her hair as winding and intricate as her heart), painting, wearing naked breasts. Generally she dies very poor. The wealth she gets is like the houses some build in Gothland, made of snow, no lasting fabric ....She dieth commonly of a loathsome disease. I mean that disease [syphilis], unknown to antiquity, created within some hundred years, which took the name from Naples. [Thomas Fuller, 1608-61, *The Profane State*][5]

Rid society of prostitutes and licentiousness will run riot throughout.... Prostitutes in a city are like a sewer in a palace. If you get rid of the sewer, the whole palace becomes filthy and foul. [St Augustine, *De ordine*][6]

[Year, 1280]. Philippe III, King of France grants ... lest shameless and dissolute whores should flaunt their lust and license in the houses of the town [Villefranche du Lauragais] ... its inhabitants permission to build a brothel somewhere outside the town to which the said women may be admitted. The profits from the brothel shall belong to the said inhabitants. [*Chartes de Franchises du Lauragais*][7]

As not even the barest account of the development of prostitution in Europe can go into the space at our disposal, we shall keep mainly to a single country—France. From the time of Charlemagne legislators wavered between tolerance of prostitutes and efforts to restrict them to brothels in specified areas. Usually, as elsewhere in Europe, the sewer theory prevailed. Poverty always facilitated the recruitment of prostitutes, and if there was to be a category of women who were wholly chaste (the wives and daughters of the more comfortable classes), then a sewer was a handy thing for receiving the overflow of male sinfulness. During the Middle Ages and Renaissance, decent women were protected from contamination by laws compelling prostitutes to wear some distinguishing article of clothing, such as gloves, high-heeled shoes, or special hats. The appearance of syphilis at the end of the fifteenth century complicated the question: a sewer is one thing, an incubator for disease another. The early symptoms were virulent and not unlike leprosy in appearance.

1546   Sometimes the disease remained latent ... for as long as three months.... The first signs were a gloom of the soul ... fatigue ... pallor ... then small ulcers appeared on the genitals.... The skin broke out with incrusted pustules ... large as an acorn's cupule ... these sometimes corroded not only the flesh but the very bones.... Malignant catarrh eroded palate, pharynx, gullet, or tonsils. In some cases the lips, nose, eyes, or external genital organs were entirely eaten away. Gummatous tumors deformed the limbs, as large as an egg ... or loaf. In some cases these horny lumps became ulcerated, in others they persisted until death ... violent pains attacked the muscles ... the body grew thin.... These were the symptoms. We speak of them as being in the past since, although the disease is still rife, it seems to have changed its nature.[Girolamo Fracastoro, *De contagionibus et contagiosis morbis*][8]

Unsure how the contagion spread, governments at first treated it like any other plague.

Today, the 6th day of March [1497], since in this city of Paris there are a number of people sick with a contagious malady, the pox ... it has been decided by his grace the Archbishop of Paris, the King's officers, the Provost, etc., that all foreigners sick of the pox, both men and women, who were not resident in Paris when they fell ill, shall leave town within twenty-four hours of hearing this cry ... under penalty of the gallows.... Second, that all natives of this city, or people who were resident therein when they caught the disease, withdraw inside their own houses within twenty-four hours of hearing this cry, on pain

of the gallows.... Third, that all poor people who were resident
in this city when they caught the pox but have no house to stay
in shall, on pain of the gallows, repair to St-Germain-des-Prés,
where they will be lodged. [*Encyclopédie Méthodique*][9]

*When it was realized that the disease was communicated by sexual inter-
course, governments tightened the legislation on prostitution. The Orléans
statute of 1560 ended three centuries of tolerance.*

We forbid anyone to lodge or give houseroom to any stranger or
vagrant for more than a single night and charge them to report
all such to the authorities on pain of prison or a discretionary
fine. We also forbid all brothels, gambling dens, games of dice
and skittles, and desire the heaviest penalties to be inflicted for
such without any concealment or connivance on the part of
judges on pain of losing their office. [*Recueil Général des Anciennes
Lois Françaises*][10]

*The preceding law seems to have been put into rigorous effect. Aspects of
the whole question may be pursued in another source.*

By the terms of the royal decrees of [1254, 1319, 1561] ... 1569
and 1586, householders are forbidden to rent houses to any but
people of good reputation or to countenance loose living or
public or clandestine brothels on pain of being fined 60 Parisian
pounds for the first offense, 120 for the second, and the forfeiture
of their houses for the third.... By a sentence pronounced on
24 April 1613 Claudine Roger, accused of having seduced and
prostituted girls and women, was condemned to be whipped
and attached to the iron collar with a placard on her head
recording her crime, fined 20 pounds, and perpetually banished
from Chaumont Street in Châtillon; Etiennette Lebaille, accused of living a lubricious and scandalous life, was sentenced to
a whipping, a fine of 20 pounds, and perpetual banishment from
the same Chaumont Street.... A sentence of 25 July 1644
condemned Françoise Perrin, accused of pimping and licentious
living, to be whipped at the crossroads and in front of her own
house, to wear a placard on her head reading 'public pimp,'
to perpetual banishment from the town, a fine of 20 pounds, and

the forfeiture of her remaining property; Joseph Pelletier, her husband, accused of having connived at her pimping, was sentenced to leave the town for good and to pay costs.... A sentence of September 1691, reversed the Mayor of Dijon's decision to brand a woman pimp with a hot iron. [F. Serpillon, *Code Criminel*][11]

In the course of the seventeenth century the prescribed punishments became less harsh. The first prison for prostitutes, La Salpêtrière, was built in 1656 by Louis XIV. A royal proclamation of 20 April 1684 laid down the following:

Women living publicly in a state of debauchery or prostitution, or who prostitute others, shall be imprisoned in ... La Salpêtrière either by order of His Majesty or a sentence pronounced at the Court of Justice by the lieutenant of police.... The said women shall hear Mass on Sundays and holy days and shall be treated for any diseases they may contract.... They shall assemble to pray for a quarter of an hour every morning and evening and, during the day, the catechism and other pious books shall be read to them while they work. They shall be dressed in coarse wool and clogs; shall have a diet of bread, soup, and water, and shall be provided with a straw pallet, sheets, and a bedcover. They shall be made, at the discretion of the directors, to do the hardest work for as long as their strength allows.... Swearing, laziness, bad temper, and other faults shall be punished by making the offenders go without soup, by [putting them in] the iron collar, or by confinement in the *malaises* [a hole or cubicle in which the occupant could not sit, stand, or lie] or by other means which the directors shall judge necessary. [*Recueil Général*][12]

In 1713 the Crown endowed local police authority with wide powers over prostitution. A nineteenth-century historian, drawing heavily on the files of the Paris police, studied all the sentences against prostitutes for the period 1724–88 and reached the following conclusions:

(1)   Tolerance of prostitutes and houses of prostitution was complete. The police cracked down only in flagrant cases. They

issued authorizations similar to the later prostitute's police card. (2) They searched houses only when neighbors complained. (3) Penalties were only applied for second offenses. (4) Murders were committed in the brothels from time to time; girls and men were thrown from windows; noise and danger to neighbors and passers-by was a commonplace. (5) Arrests were quite arbitrary. (6) Girls always claimed that they had been driven to prostitution by need. (7) The penalties inflicted grew progressively milder during that period. (8) Prostitutes hired stalls at the St Laurent Fair. (9) The entire rue St Denis was given over to prostitutes. (10) Police sometimes protected girls from brothel owners. [A.-J.-B. Parent-Duchâtelet, *De la Prostitution dans la Ville de Paris*][13]

Here is a more sinister picture of the 1730s by another writer:

A police inspector ... had discretionary power over them which brought him 30,000 pounds a year.... When he needed money, he warned the brothel mistresses and the independent girls that girls against whom complaints had been lodged were to be arrested: this meant those who had sent him nothing in the preceding month.... Every month 300 or 400 women were picked up. Any who had money were released. The diseased were put in hospital, the rest in prison for three or six months.... Innocent girls were thrown in with the rest. In court the accused women had no defense counsel and received sentence on their knees. [M. Sabatier, *Histoire de la législation sur les femmes publiques*][14]

The police obviously wielded very wide discretionary powers when dealing with prostitutes. A decree of 1778 strengthened these powers and suspended investigative procedures that had been previously required.

No debauched women and girls to solicit in the streets, on the quays, squares and public walks, and boulevards of this city of Paris, even from windows....

No person, of whatever calling or condition, to sublet by the day, week, fortnight, month, or other term, any chamber to debauched women or girls ... under penalty of 400 francs.

All persons letting hotels, furnished houses, and lodgings, by the month, fortnight, week, day, etc., to inscribe forthwith, day by day, and without blanks, the name, surname, quality, birthplace, and ordinary domicile of each lodger, upon a police register which they shall keep for the purpose, to be checked by the commissaries of the respective quarters; not to harbor in such hotels, houses, or lodgings, any persons without ostensible description, or women or girls who have recourse to prostitution; to keep separate apartments for men and women; not to permit men to occupy private rooms with women calling themselves married, except after exhibition by them of their marriage certificate, or their written identification by known and respectable persons, under penalty of 200 francs. Signed by the Lieutenant of Police, Lenoir. 16 November, 1778. [W. Acton, *Prostitution considered in its Moral, Social and Sanitary Aspects*][15]

NINETEENTH-CENTURY CONTROLS AND CAUSES

If applied, the decree of 1778 would have brought about the abolition of prostitution. In deference to the sewer theory, it was not applied. Instead, the police used it to authorize punitive action against girls who defied them. They were thus able to set up their own system, a system which tolerated but controlled prostitutes. Early efforts to introduce a compulsory registration of prostitutes went back to 1765, but a system was not effectively established until 1816. Under the Restoration, the Morals Police were to become increasingly organized and authoritarian. Registered 'public women' were issued with a card and permitted to ply their trade in exchange for their compliance with the conditions printed on the back of it. These were the conditions in 1857:

Card-carrying women must come to the dispensary once in a fortnight for a medical examination. They must present their card when required to do so by police agents. They are forbidden to practice their profession by day.... They must be simply and decently dressed.... They may not go about bareheaded. They are expressly forbidden to address men who are in the company of women or children. They must never, at any hour, show themselves at their windows but must keep these shut and curtained at all times. They may not take up a station on the public pavement.... Areas within a radius of twenty meters from a church or temple are forbidden to them. They may not share lodgings with a male companion or with another prostitute or live in furnished rooms without permission. They must, when at their domicile, abstain from conduct likely to provoke complaints from neighbors or passers-by. Those who break the rules ... will incur penalties proportional to the gravity of the case. [Parent-Duchâtelet, *De la Prostitution*][16]

In addition to the isolated card-carrying girls there were the registered prostitutes in tolerated brothels. These were given a weekly medical examination on the premises, twice as often as the others owing to the higher incidence of syphilis among them. A girl found with a venereal infection was sent to the hospital. From 1835 on, this meant the hospital of St-Lazare, where the average length of treatment was forty-five days. At Lourcine—the hospital for female VD patients who were not prostitutes—the treatment took three months, the disease usually being in a more advanced stage. Many Lourcine patients were suspected of being clandestine prostitutes.

The case for regulating prostitution was that regulation would check syphilis. By 1857, Belgium, Prussia, Holland, Norway, and parts of Denmark and Italy had adopted the system of compulsory registration and medical supervision of prostitutes. England, Spain, and the Papal States preferred to ignore the problem.

The case against regulation was variously argued. When efforts were made to bring in control of prostitutes in British naval and military stations—via the Contagious Diseases Acts of 1864, 1866, and 1869— the campaign for repeal was supported both by feminists, who felt that such measures discriminated against and humiliated women, and by clergymen who felt that the disease was a useful check to sin. Subsequent arguments, based upon hindsight, held that only a small fraction of prostitutes could ever be got to register anyway, and that associating the police with medical care of the disease frightened off many infected people, thus doing more harm than good. The most sensible suggestion was made by the venerologist Ricord [1875].

People familiar with the wretched conditions and wages available to women in our society have long understood ... that this is one of the main reasons for prostitution and hence for the spread of syphilis. Consequently, to improve the condition of working women would be in the interests of humanity, morals, and public hygiene. [Philippe Ricord][17]

The following table on the causes of prostitution was assembled by Parent-Duchâtelet. He combined the intensive study of Paris police dossiers for the years 1828–32 with other checks and sustained research.

| | | Birthplace | | | | |
Determining Causes	Paris	large town	small town	country	abroad	Total
Poverty	570	405	182	222	62	1,441
Loss of parents, expulsion from home, or being abandoned	647	201	157	211	39	1,255
To support old or sick relatives	37	0	0	0	0	37
Orphaned eldest daughters left with small brothers, sisters, and sometimes nieces and nephews to care for	29	0	0	0	0	29
Widowed or abandoned women faced with bringing up large family	23	0	0	0	0	23
Emigrated from provinces to hide in Paris and find means of livelihood	0	187	29	64	0	280
Brought to Paris and abandoned by soldiers, shop-assistants, students		185	75	97	47	404
Servant girls seduced and then discharged by their employers	123	97	29	40	0	289
Kept women who eventually lost their lovers and did not know what else to do	559	314	180	302	70	1,425
Total..	1,988	1,389	652	936	218	5,183

[Parent-Duchâtelet, *De la Prostitution*][18]

22   How to punish a 'scold'

From *England's Grievance Discovered* by R. Gardiner

MATERNAL LOVE

The Fashionable Mamma, — or — The Convenience of Modern Dress · Vide The Pocket Holola.

23   The Fashionable Mamma
By James Gillray, 1796

Engels, writing of England in 1844, listed other reasons that caused girls to turn professional.

The moral consequences of the employment of women in factories are even worse. The collecting of persons of both sexes and all ages in a single work-room, the inevitable contact, the crowding into a small space of people, to whom neither mental nor moral education has been given, is not calculated for the favorable development of the female character.... A witness in Leicester said that most of the prostitutes of the town had their employment in the mills to thank for their present situation....

It is, besides, a matter of course that factory servitude, like any other, and to an even greater degree, confers the 'jus primae noctis' [right of first night, deflowering] upon the master. In this respect also the employer is sovereign over the persons and charms of his employees. The threat of discharge suffices to overcome all resistance in nine cases out of ten, if not in ninety-nine out of a hundred, in girls who, in any case, have no strong inducements to chastity. If the master is mean enough, and the official report mentions several such cases, his mill is also his harem; and the fact that not all manufacturers use their power does not in the least change the position of the girls. In the beginning of manufacturing industry, when most of the employers were upstarts without education or consideration for the hypocrisy of society, they let nothing interfere with the exercise of their vested rights. [F. Engels, *Condition of the Working Classes in England*][19]

Parent-Duchâtelet also found that the vast majority of the registered girls in Paris were of working-class origin, that a fourth of them were illegitimate—working-class couples rarely bothered to legalize their union —and that of 3,517 prostitutes registered in 1831:

2 had been registered at the age of 10; 3 at age 11; 3 at age 12; 6 at age 13; 20 at age 14; and 51 at age 15.

Birth certificates of 718 girls born in Paris showed that 173 of the girls' fathers could not sign their name. Registered prostitutes were required to sign an agreement to abide by the police rules, and study of those endorsements revealed that of 4,470 girls:

2,332 could not sign their name; 1,780 signed in a poor hand; 110 signed in a good hand; 248 no information.

[Parent-Duchâtelet, *De la Prostitution*]

Registered prostitutes formed the professional core of a hierarchy whose top tiers faded into 'good' society, while its wretched members at the bottom were working women who did the occasional whoring so as to supplement their earnings. How many were there altogether? Estimates by alleged authorities diverged widely. The only sure numbers are those for the registered women. Of these Paris had an average—since their numbers continually fluctuated—of 1,293 in 1812, 3,028 in 1830, 3,927 in 1840, and 4,232 in 1854. The total population of the city in 1854 was 1,500,000. Estimates as to the number of clandestine prostitutes ranged from 20,000 to 60,000. For London in the same period the figure of 80,000 was often bandied, although the Home Authorities put their number at 9,409 in 1841.

What rewards were there for the registered 'public woman' in return for braving so much opprobrium? There is a report on women in brothels.

It is generally believed that these women are paid by the brothel keepers and that these wages are in proportion to the amount they earn for the brothel. This is a mistake: they never receive anything. All they get in exchange for risking the gravest maladies and putting up with the most barbarous treatment is their food and clothing. . . . All the brothel keepers (*dames de maison*) insist imperiously on respect and deference. . . . In the first-class houses, the mistress has her own private apartment distinct from the room where the girls stay. Someone comes to call her, like a duchess, when the meal is served, and when she appears they must all rise and stay on their feet until she sits down. . . . The habit is for those individuals who spend a little time with a girl in a place of public prostitution to leave her a token of gratitude and generosity. This is the unfortunate creature's only payment and the great fear of the brothel mistresses, who know from experience that their authority over a girl ceases the moment she finds herself in possession of something. Consequently, they are careful to get the girls into debt in order to keep them dependent. . . . The girls are not paid, but the police insist that the brothel keepers feed, dress, board, and furnish them with whatever they need. They also insist that a girl who has been in a house more than three months should be given a decent outfit when she leaves. Otherwise the police refuse to interfere.... An arrangement, however, which girls often make (although the police do not recognize it) consists in dividing their earnings with the brothel keeper. The girls are then expected to keep themselves with their own half. It is a fool's bargain in which the girl is forced to spend her half feeding and keeping herself miserably. In the provinces there seems to be no other arrangement. The girls are entirely at the mercy of the brothel keepers, who claim the sole right to provide necessities at usurious prices and refuse to let the girls go unless another brothel keeper is prepared to pay their debts. [Parent-Duchâtelet, *De la Prostitution*][21]

The card-carrying girls were not all, of course, in the same category. Some were pretty and could make from two to five francs per encounter. The most wretched were the girls who went with soldiers for fifty centimes an hour. Those who frequented artisans were slightly better off: they got a franc. [Acton, *Prostitution*][22]

Prostitution does not seem to have held women for very long. Parent-Duchâtelet found that most of them left in their first year. To be struck off the police register they had to convince the police that they had other means of subsistence and were not going to practice clandestinely. In 1845, women were struck from the Paris police registers for the following reasons: 70 died (of whom 6 were minors), 26 married, 9 proved they had other means of subsistence, 135 found other work, 615 simply disappeared. Of 1,680 women struck from the lists between 1817 and 1827, the record shows that 972 got jobs in the following trades.

392 dressmakers, embroiderers, etc.	28 hat and shoemakers
108 brothel keepers	19 metal polishers
86 laundresses	17 mattress teaslers
83 hawkers	17 actresses
48 rag-and-bone women	13 midwives
47 milliners and flower girls	11 hospital nurses
47 oyster sellers	8 janitors
33 wardrobe dealers	1 music mistress in a boarding-school

247 set up shops of various sorts (haberdashery, scent, etc.)
461 became servants

[Parent-Duchâtelet, *De la Prostitution*][23]

*Some of these might be back in prostitution the following year. They
were a shifting population, partly because wages for women were designed
to ensure death by starvation or exposure. Doctors held conflicting opinions
on the question of how many prostitutes actually died of syphilis or other
diseases related to venery. Those who worked in prisons and prison
hospitals generalized on their experience and believed that most prostitutes ended badly. With the exception of the few who made it into the
ranks of the courtesans and kept women, a prostitute's life was in-
escapably wretched. She had no civic rights; police officers got bonuses for
zeal in keeping order; and sadism tended to relieve itself at the expense of
the vulnerable.*

There is nothing a card-carrying girl can do which ... cannot
be shown to be against the rules. If she does her shopping in the
morning or afternoon and runs into a policeman, he may and
often does arrest her for being in the street at an hour
forbidden by regulations.... No need to describe a police
roundup. Almost all of us have seen one on the boulevards. It is
a mass arrest, a hunt. The police form a kind of chain and
charge. The women flee, scream, fall, get bruised and, panic-
stricken, cling to trees or to the nearest pedestrian.... Hair
disheveled, filthy with dust or mud, their skirts or blouses in
ribbons, they are kicked, punched, and dragged by the hair.
These savage scenes are unforgettable. We ourselves saw a
roundup like this on 8 January 1882. [L. Fiaux, *La Police des
Moeurs en France*][24]

*We end with a close-up of one English case history. Henry Mayhew, the
author of* London Labour and the London Poor *(1851), conducted a number of collective and individual interviews with skilled
needlewomen, with the aim of establishing whether or not they could live
on their earnings.*

They were unanimous in declaring that a large number in the
trade—probably one-fourth of the whole, or one-half of those
who had no husband or parent to support them—resorted to the

streets to eke out a living. [Here is the report given by one of the girls interviewed:] I make moleskin trousers. I get 7*d.* and 8*d.* per pair. I can do two pairs in a day and twelve, when there is full employment, in a week. But some weeks I have no work at all. I work from six in the morning to ten at night.... When I am fully employed, I get from 7*s.* to 8*s.* a week. My expenses out of that for twist, thread, and candles are about 1*s.* 6*d.* a week, leaving me about 6*s.* a week clear. But there's coals to pay for out of this, and that's at the least 6*d.* more, so 5*s.* 6*d.* is the very outside of what I earn when I'm in full work. Taking one week with another, all the year round, I don't make above 3*s.* clear money each week. I don't work at any other kind of slop work [turning out cheap ready-made garments]. The trousers work is held to be the best paid of all. I give 1*s.* a week rent.... My mother is a widow.... and seldom has a day's work. Generally once in the week she is employed pot-scouring— that is, cleaning publicans' pots. She is paid 1*s.* 6*d.* in the day.... For the rest she is dependent upon me. I am 20 years of age.... We earn together, to keep the two of us, from 4*s.* 6*d.* to 5*s.* each week. Out of this we have ... 3*s.* 6*d.* to 4*s.* to find us both in food and clothing. It is of course impossible for us to live upon it, and the consequence is, I am obligated to go a bad way.... I am now pregnant.... I am satisfied there is not one young girl that works at slop work that is virtuous and there are some thousands in the trade.... If I had been born a lady, it would not have been very hard to have acted like one. [Mayhew, cit. in Acton, *Prostitution*][25]

3 Feminists and Socialism in France

1790. Habit can so accustom men to the violation of their natural rights that among those who have lost them none thinks of claiming them or is even sensible of having suffered an injustice. Is there any stronger proof of the power of habit, even over enlightened men, than to see the principle of equal rights being invoked in favor of three or four hundred men who have been deprived of them ... while being forgotten in the case of twelve thousand women? [Condorcet, *Essai sur l'admission des femmes au droit de cité*][26]

Feminism in the eighteenth century was a hot potato which no major polemicist—Diderot, Laclos, Helvetius, Condorcet, etc.—could resist juggling. It remained a live issue when polemics spilled from salon to street in 1788–9, and a number of pamphlets handled it either seriously or as comic relief. The idea of extending equality to women struck the average man (and probably woman) as side-splitting. A number of feminist tracts circulating in the early years of the Revolution were spurious. They mingle genuine demands with double entendres *and dead-pan treatment of such old conservative favorites as the question, 'Who'll wear the pants?' Yet many tracts were genuine. Women, especially working women, had grievances. They were, as one pamphlet puts it, 'The Third Estate of the Third Estate'. Arthur Young (1787) estimated that the average daily wage of a woman working in a French manufactory was 15 sous, while a man earned 30. The cost of a day's food in Paris during the same period was from 14 to 15 sous. Rural wage scales were equally discriminatory. A woman could hardly subsist without a male protector. Moreover, women were excluded from several traditionally feminine crafts. The 'Petition of the Women of the Third Estate to the King' raises these points. It is a moderate plea—less revolutionary and eloquent than Condorcet's feminist writings—but, having reached the time when women finally found their voice, we shall listen to it.*

1 January 1789. Almost all women of the Third Estate are born poor. Their education is either neglected or misconceived, for it

consists in sending them to learn from teachers who do not themselves know the first word of the language they are supposed to be teaching.... At the age of fifteen or sixteen, girls can earn five or six sous a day. If nature has not granted them good looks, they get married, without a dowry, to unfortunate artisans and drag out a grueling existence in the depths of the provinces, producing children whom they are unable to bring up. If, on the other hand, they are born pretty, being without culture, principles, or any notion of morality, they fall prey to the first seducer, make one slip, come to Paris to conceal it, go totally to the bad here, and end up dying as victims of debauchery.

Today, when the difficulty of earning a living forces thousands of women to offer themselves to the highest bidder and men prefer buying them for a spell to winning them for good, any woman drawn to virtue, eager to educate herself, and with natural taste ... is faced with the choice either of casting herself into a cloister which will accept a modest dowry or of going into domestic service....

If old age overtakes unmarried women, they spend it in tears and as objects of contempt for their nearest relatives.

To counter such misfortunes, Sire, we ask that men be excluded from practicing those crafts that are women's prerogative, such as dressmaking, embroidery, millinery, etc. Let them leave us the needle and the spindle and we pledge our word never to handle the compass or the set-square.

We ask, Sire ... to be instructed and given jobs, not that we may usurp men's authority but so that we may have a means of livelihood, and so that the weaker among us who are dazzled by luxury and led astray by example should not be forced to join the ranks of the wretched who encumber the streets and whose lewd audacity disgraces both our sex and the men who frequent them. [A. Le Faure, *Le Socialisme pendant la Révolution Française*][27]

The petition then meanders off into pious sentiments. These women were not quite revolutionaries. They did, however, pose their problem in economic terms, as Parisian women were to do with increasing vigor in the course of 1789. In May, the only workers' deputations to go and remind the Third Estate to lower prices and think of the poor were two groups of women, representing the fruitsellers and fishwives. The women's October expedition to Versailles to bring back the King and Queen ('the baker and the baker's wife'), in the hope that the royal couple would provide bread, has entered history in the simple colors of parable. Madame Campan, the Queen's secretary, describes the ambiguous mood of the following day:

On October 7th, the very same women who had mounted cannons the day before and pressed around the august prisoner's carriage to abuse her came to the palace terraces beneath the Queen's windows asking to see her. Her Majesty appeared. In this sort of crowd there are always some speakers: that is to say, some who are bolder than the rest. One woman, taking it upon herself to give advice, told the Queen that she must send away all those courtiers who cause the downfall of kings and must love the people of her good city. The Queen replied that she had loved them while at Versailles and would do so equally in Paris. 'Oh, yes,' spoke up another woman, 'but on the fourteenth of July you wanted to have the town besieged and bombarded, and on October the sixth you were going to flee to the frontiers!' The Queen answered gently that they had been told this and so had believed it and that this was the source of the misfortunes of the people and of the best kings. A third woman addressed her in German. The Queen answered that she no longer understood it and had become so thoroughly French that she had forgotten her native tongue. This provoked applause and cheers. Next they asked her to make a pact with them. 'How,' asked the Queen, 'can I make one with you, when you don't believe in the one which my duty and my own happiness require me to keep?' They asked her for the flowers and ribbons from her hat. Her Majesty took them off and handed them over herself. They were shared among the crowd, which for the next half-hour kept shouting, 'Long live Marie Antoinette! Long live Marie Antoinette!' [Mme Campan, *Mémoires sur la vie privée de Marie-Antoinette*][28]

Economic grievances were not the only ones. The subsequent history of feminism was to show that all women's disabilities were linked: low wages forced them into marriage or onto the streets; lack of education gave men grounds for refusing them political rights; and lack of political rights multiplied their difficulties in the campaign to promote reforms in wage scales, marriage laws, and education. Logically enough, therefore, some feminists demanded everything at once: juridical equality, the vote, and the right to stand for parliament. On 4 August 1789, the Constituent Assembly had proclaimed the Rights of Man. In September 1791, Olympe des Gouges published her Declaration of the Rights of Woman:

Man, are you capable of justice? It is a woman putting the question....

DECLARATION OF THE RIGHTS OF WOMAN

Woman is born free and her rights are the same as those of man. Social distinctions can be based only on the common good....
The law must be an expression of the general will; all citizens, men and women alike, must participate in making it, either directly or by means of representatives: it must be the same for all. All citizens, be they men or women, being equal in its eyes, must be equally eligible for all public offices, positions, and jobs, according to their capacity and without any other criteria than those of their virtues and talents....
[Women] ... have the right to go to the scaffold; they must also have the right to go to parliament....
Freedom of speech and opinion is one of women's most precious rights, as the legitimacy of children is thereby assured. Every woman can therefore freely say, 'I am the mother of a child belonging to you,' without being forced by barbaric prejudice to conceal the truth. If she abuses this freedom, she must answer before the law....

PERORATION

Women, wake up ... recognize your rights. Man, the slave, has multiplied his strength. To break his manacles he had to have recourse to yours. Once free, he became unjust towards his companion.... What advantages have you got from the Revolution? A more open contempt! ... What then remains to you? The claiming of your natural heritage .... Oppose the force of reason to his empty pretense of superiority.... National education is under discussion. Let us see whether our wise legislators will think soundly about educating women.

[Olympe next turns to sexual relations proper. 'The trade in women' which flourished under the old regime must disappear. Women must no longer be bought or hired 'like slaves on the African coast'. Marriage, 'tomb of trust and love,' must be reformed. Olympe sees these questions in terms of the exploitation of one class by another].

MODEL FOR A SOCIAL CONTRACT BETWEEN MAN AND WIFE

We, x and y, of our own free will, marry for the duration of our mutual affection. We wish and intend to put our fortunes in a common fund, but reserve the right to separate them again for the benefit of any children we may have either in common or separately. We recognize that our property belongs to our children by whomsoever we may have had them and that all of them have the right to the name of whichever parent acknowledges them. [Olympe des Gouges, *Les Droits de la Femme*][29]

Olympe des Gouges—her real name was Marie Gouze—wrote a number of pamphlets on other questions, attacked Robespierre and Marat among others, and was guillotined in November 1793. That same year universal male suffrage was introduced and the most active women's club, the Revolutionary Republican Women, addressed a petition to the Convention, demanding that suffrage be extended to women. Nothing came of it. An antifeminist reaction had set in. Robespierre and his party opposed the participation of women in politics, and the women's clubs were suppressed that same November. The only offices open to French women during the nineteenth century were to be those of school mistresses and post mistresses. In the realm of private law, the Napoleonic Code firmly upheld the double standard: leaving management of the conjugal fund in the husband's hands, distinguishing between male and female adultery, forbidding a married woman to go to law without her husband's permission, and prohibiting actions to establish paternity. Divorce, brought in by the Legislative Assembly in 1792, was dropped by the Chambre des Introuvables in 1814. The law's relative equity with regard to single woman meant little in reality, for the workingwoman's low wages forced her into the arms and under the rod of a male protector. It is true that things improved for the few : henceforth the daughter of rich parents had equal rights with her brothers to succeed to an intestacy. But it was arguable that this was a trivial legacy from a Revolution which had promised so much. In 1840 the statistician Villermé published the following findings, showing that female earnings had not improved since the time of Arthur Young(1780s).

[Speaking of an average working day, 15 hours.] The average salary of the workers among whom I have conducted my research comes to about 2 francs for a man and 1 franc for a woman, 45 centimes for a child between eight and twelve, and 75 centimes for one between thirteen and sixteen... Moreover, after the age of thirty-five or forty, salaries invariably decrease. Up to the age of fifteen or sixteen there is little difference between men's and women's wages; after that, women generally earn only half the wages of a man.... Generally speaking, a man can earn enough to save, but a woman scarcely makes enough to subsist on and a child of less than twelve years hardly earns the price of his food. [L. R. Villermé, *Tableau de l'état physique et moral des ouvriers*][30]

FLORA TRISTAN (1803–44)

In view of the above figures and what they signified for single women, not to speak of lone mothers, the feminist cause in nineteenth-century France was often associated, unsurprisingly, with socialism. Certain socialists were also male supremacists—Proudhon was content to let women choose between housewifery and whoredom—but Fourierists and Saint-Simonians favored female emancipation, and it was in their newspapers that the first militant socialist women began to write. There were also moderate feminists who accepted the existing social order; they hoped to bring in marriage reforms and suffrage for women on the same basis as for men (i.e., payment of 200 francs in taxes). Socialist approaches varied: some looked for sexual freedom in individual experiments; a lunatic Saint-Simonian fringe set off for Egypt (1833) to seek the female Messiah; but a few perceived that the emancipation of women was linked to the processes of fundamental social change. One of these was Flora

Tristan, who published in 1843 a program of action in the form of an appeal to the workers of France. In her view these were the objectives to pursue:

(1)   To constitute the working class by setting up a compact, solid, and indissoluble union.

(2)   The workers' union to choose and pay a defender who shall represent the working class before the nation [workers were without the voting franchise because of the 200-franc tax requirement], so as to establish universal acceptance of this class' right to exist [as an organization].

(3)   To proclaim the legitimacy of hands (*bras*) as property, 25 million French workers having no property other than their hands.

(4)   To secure the recognition of every man and woman's right to work.

(5)   To secure the recognition of every man and woman's right to moral, intellectual, and vocational training.

(6)   To examine the possibilities of organizing the labor force in present social conditions.

(7)   To construct workers' union buildings in every department of France which shall provide intellectual and vocational training for working-class children and admit working men and women who have been disabled on the job or are sick or old.

(8)   To proclaim the urgent necessity of giving working-class women moral, intellectual, and vocational training so that they may improve the morals of the men.

(9)   To proclaim the fact that juridical equality between men and women is the only means of achieving the unity of humanity. [Flora Tristan, *L'Union Ouvriere*][31]

The proponent of this program herself admitted that her feminism often discredited her with workers, her socialism with the bourgeoisie (a reaction still encountered by feminist socialists). But in her mind the two ideals were intertwined: the workingwoman's lot could not be severed from the condition of the working class as a whole. Flora Tristan had personally familiarized herself with working-class conditions in different countries. An earlier book of hers described workers in England as 'more ignorant and wretched than those in France'. She had read working-class writers, visited workers in their homes, and romanticized neither them nor their wives (who sometimes resented her).

The woman in a workingman's life is all-important. She is his only providence. Without her, everything goes to pieces ... yet what education, what moral or physical training does the working-class woman get? None. As a child, she is left to the care of a grandmother or mother who themselves were never educated. .. She, rather than her brothers, will be kept home from school to help. . . . At the age of twelve she is apprenticed to a mistress who will exploit and brutalize her just as was done at home. . . . Nothing ruins the temper, hardens the heart, and makes for ill nature like the continual suffering of a child subjected to unfair and brutal treatment. . . . In turn, she will be incapable of bringing up her sons and daughters. . . . Working-class women, I beg you to note that I am not blaming you. No, it is society I blame. . . .

Working-class women are generally brutal, ill natured, sometimes hard. True, but what brings this about? . . . They have so many things to put up with, their husbands first of all. One must admit that there are few happy couples among workers. The husband, being better educated, being head of the family by law, and bringing in more money, believes himself, and is, superior to his wife, who contributes only her small wage and is no better than a very humble servant in the house. Consequently, the husband treats his wife, at best, with contempt. The unfortunate woman, humiliated by every word and glance from her husband, rebels. . . . Thence the violent scenes, so unbearable that the husband goes to the tavern to drink rotgut wine with other husbands as wretched as himself in the hope of stunning himself. [Flora Tristan adds a note:] In all jobs open to men and women, the woman makes half what a man does. Unable to credit such flagrant injustice, one's first thought is: the man must do double the work. In fact, the opposite is true. . . . In all crafts requiring skilful fingers, women excel. As a printer said to me one day with characteristic naiveté, 'We pay them less and that's very fair because they are quicker than men. They would earn too much if we paid them at the same rate'. [End of note.]. . . I repeat, women are all-important in a workingman's life.... Remember that the worker's situation is quite different from that of the man of leisure. If the mother of a rich man's son is incapable of bringing him up, he is sent to a boarding school or given a governess. If a rich young man has no mistress, he can occupy his heart and mind with studying the arts or sciences... Lacking all these pleasures, the worker's only joy and consolation are the society of the women of his family, his companions in misfortune.... Are you beginning to understand, you men who cry 'scandal' before even examining the question, why I demand 'rights for women'? Why I want them to be man's absolute equal in society? ... I demand rights for women because I am convinced that all misfortunes come from the complete neglect and disdain hitherto shown for the natural and indefeasible rights of women. I demand them because only thus will anything be done about the education of women, which underlies that of man in general and of the workingman in particular.... The whole plight of the working class can be summed up in two words: poverty and ignorance, ignorance and poverty. There is only one way out of this trap, to begin by educating women, for it is they who are responsible for bringing up both male and female children.... Workingmen, try to grasp this: the law which enslaves women and deprives them of education oppresses you yourselves, the men of the proletariat. [Tristan, *L'Union Ouvrière*]³²

In 1844 Flora Tristan set off on a tour of working-class France to try to propagate her ideas. Harried by lack of funds, police surveillance, and exhaustion, she fell ill and died before the end of her journey.

1848

The Revolution of 1848 brought back universal male suffrage. Militant women demanded that it be extended to them and proposed to run the novelist George Sand for parliament. It was to have been a symbolic gesture intended to publicize their demands. But George Sand, brilliantly successful in her own right, did not care to brave the expected ridicule. She dissociated herself publicly and contemptuously from the obscure women who were, she felt, trying to make use of her name. The next year Jeanne Deroin, a journalist, did brave the ridicule. Her candidacy was declared unconstitutional, but she managed, nonetheless, to address a number of groups and to publicize feminist demands.

Deroin's next project, put forward in an article of August 1849, echoed Flora Tristan: it was a proposal that the workers' associations, legalized by the provisional government of the year before, band together in a union, a workers' union. But this ran counter to governmental legislation banning political associations and secret societies. To slip around this the organizers who determined to set up a union registered it as a commercial enterprise. The police kept a close watch and then in May 1850, pounced; they interrupted a meeting and arrested all participants. Twenty-nine of these, five of them women, were remanded for trial. The Union was charged with being a secret political society. The defense retorted that it was a commercial enterprise. Police searches of defendants' lodgings provided a haul of exhibits: a bullet mold, a recipe for gunpowder, and some red rosettes. These comic-opera props were important because the prosecution's aim, as newspaper accounts reveal, was to show that these were the very sort of people likely to hold political meetings. In the absence of hard evidence, their characters went on trial, not their actions. Feminism was as good a brush as any with which to tar them, and the prosecution made capital of the defendants' private lives.

[From the findings of the preliminary investigation in July:] The court, considering ... the past history of most of the accused, the inflamed opinions they hold, the documents found at the meeting, the emblems, the possession of firearms by some and the means of making them by others ... [finds] that all circumstances concur to establish the fact that the nature of these meetings was political.... Along with these defendants are several women whose role in the Union was too important not to merit particular attention. First: Jeanne Deroin, a schoolteacher. Founder of the newspaper *L'Opinion des Femmes*, Mme Desroches, as a sort of protest against marriage, has dropped her married name and uses her maiden name; she pursues what she calls the regeneration of woman both in the press and by the route of socialism. For her, existing laws do not count; she vigorously protests against them; as a woman, she cannot submit to laws made without women's participation; she has stood for parliament, and the clubs have seen her hold forth on her regenerating systems. Denying the right to possess ... she regards socialism as a religion and has devoted a dangerous talent for organization to its service. The idea for the working-class Union was hers. She assumes complete responsibility for it. She does not deny that this association was meant to help ... in procuring the future happiness of humanity. Next comes Mlle Pauline Roland. She has for many years professed communist-socialist opinions; she has promoted these by her writings in a number of newspapers.... An unmarried mother, she is an enemy of marriage because [in her view] subjecting the wife to a husband's authority institutionalizes an unacceptable inequality.... Her religion is based entirely on socialism. Next come other women arrested at the Union meeting: Mlle Laventure, a midwife who professes the same principles as Pauline Roland and has protested against marriage by having had three children; the girl Vray, delegate of an association which has only two members; the woman Nicaud, representing the laundresses' association, and possessor of a manufactory of bullets and gunpowder ... in her own lodgings. Most of these women seem to be deeply influenced by Jeanne Deroin. Some feel they should protest, but they fall back on saying, 'the same as Jeanne Deroin said,' whenever they are summoned to formulate their protests.

[November 13   The presiding judge questions Jeanne Deroin regarding the technicalities of the Union's planned credit and voucher systems.]

[November 14   The male defendants reassert the legality of their Union and gently dissociate themselves from Deroin and Roland:] In this general statement we shall not refute those accusations, whether true or false, which the prosecution has brought against individual defendants.... Even if every one of them were true, we could still say: this does not affect the Union.... We shall make only passing reference to the prosecution's association of all Union members with the individual opinions on marriage held by one or two defendants. We can reply to this with facts: twenty defendants out of the twenty-nine are married men and fathers of families....

[November 14   Jeanne Deroin's individual speech was an act of defiance rather than a defence:] Gentlemen of the jury, I

24 Women working in coal mines, 1860s. From *Les merveilles du monde souterrain* by L. Simonin

25 My daughter, Sir
By Felicien Rops

want to protest against the words of the Advocate General, who reproached me for not using my husband's name. If I do not use it, it is, first, because I do not want to involve my husband in my actions and, second, because I protest against marriage, which is a condition of slavery for women. For my part, I demand absolute equality between the sexes. It has been said that I was dreaming of promiscuity. Heavens, nothing has ever been farther from my thoughts. On the contrary, what I dream of and want is the achieving of a social state in which marriage will be purified, made moral and egalitarian, according to the precepts laid down by God himself. What I want is to transform the institution of marriage which is so full of imperfections. . . .

[Judge:] I cannot let you go on. You are attacking one of the most respectable of all institutions. You are attacking a part of the Civil Code. Keep to the question of secret societies.

[Jeanne Deroin:] Sir, I was merely defending my own morals against attack. I repeat, what I want is to make marriage moral, not to destroy it. I want to free part of humanity. That is all I had to say. [*Gazette des Tribunaux*][33]

Jeanne Deroin and Pauline Roland were condemned to six months' imprisonment for their fanatical opinions. Their male colleagues – taken more seriously – received heavier sentences, although the Union had been Deroin's idea.

POSTSCRIPT

After Louis Napoleon's coup d'etat of 1851, Jeanne Deroin fled to England; Pauline Roland, deported to Algeria, was reprieved but died of the effects of maltreatment on her way back home. A long period of reaction followed. The next revolution, the work of the Paris Commune of 1871, falls outside our period. Many women took an active part in it but with no benefit to themselves. During the last quarter of the century, the battle for entry into the French universities was won. The first French woman doctor qualified in 1875. The right of women to practice law was granted in 1900. Divorce came in 1884. A law of 1907 allowed women to dispose of their own earnings, and two subsequent laws (1938, 1942) abolished the married woman's legal incapacity. But the feminist crusades of 1790 and 1848 were not rewarded until 1944, when the right to vote was finally granted.

4 Feme v. Baron:
Marriage Reform in England

1792   The education of women has, of late, been more attended
to than formerly; yet they are still reckoned a frivolous sex. . . .
Strength of body or mind [is] . . . sacrificed to libertine notions
of beauty, to the desire of establishing themselves—the only way
women can rise in the world—by marriage. And this desire
makes mere animals of them. . . . If it can be fairly deduced
from the present conduct of the sex . . . that the instruction
which women have received has only tended to render them
insignificant objects of desire . . . and made [them] ridiculous
and useless when their short-lived bloom of beauty is over, I
presume that *rational* man will excuse me for endeavoring to
persuade them to become more masculine and respectable.
[Mary Wollstonecraft, *A Vindication of the Rights of Women*][34]

Let woman share the rights and she will emulate the virtues
of man; for she must grow more perfect when emancipated, or
justify the authority that chains such a being to her duty—if
the latter, it will be expedient to open a fresh trade with Russia
for whips. [Wollstonecraft, *A Vindication*][35]

Do you not act a similar part [to all tyrants] when you *force*
all women, by denying them civil and political rights, to
remain immured in their families, groping in the dark?
[Wollstonecraft, *A Vindication*][36]

*Mary Wollstonecraft's lone and scandalous voice aroused little response
in English women of her day. It would be seventy years before an English
feminist campaign for civil and political rights got under way. Marriage,
meanwhile, remained a girl's most likely career. And so long as she
remained completely dependent on her husband, the argument that his
interests subsumed hers rebutted any claim on her part to a vote.
The nineteenth century, however, saw this dependency eroded. When
the century opened, the married woman's rights were minimal. The
following case illustrates the limits put on her personal freedom as
late as 1840.*

THE WIFE'S DUTY TO COHABIT

Date: 1840   In this case a writ of habeas corpus was obtained, at the instance of Cecilia Maria Cochrane, directed to Alexander Cochrane, her husband, commanding him to have the body of the said Cecilia ... in the Court of Queen's Bench [together with his reasons for having forcibly taken her captive. The husband's reply to the writ was that his wife had run away from him four years before and gone to live with her mother in Paris. He had got her back by stratagem and was keeping her locked up lest she flee again].

[The judge ruled:] The question raised in this case is, simply, whether by the common law the husband, in order to prevent his wife from eloping, has a right to confine her in his own dwelling house, and restrain her from her liberty, for an indefinite time, using no cruelty.... There can be no doubt of the general dominion which the law of England attributes to the husband over the wife; in Bacon, Abridgement, title 'Baron and Feme', it is stated thus: 'the husband hath by law power and dominion over his wife, and may keep her by force, within the bounds of duty, and may beat her, but not in a violent or cruel manner'. On the other hand ... the courts will interpose their protection whenever the husband attempts to abuse the marital power.... [But] the happiness and honor of both parties places the wife under the guardianship of the husband and entitles him ... to protect her from the danger of unrestrained intercourse with the world, by enforcing cohabitation and a common residence. Mrs Cochrane has lived apart from her husband for nearly four years, without loss of character, but she must allow me to say that her husband, with the highest opinion of her virtue, might yet be excused even by her, if he felt uneasy when he learned, as stated in the return, that she had gone to masked balls in Paris with people whom he did not know ... he has a right to restrain her from the power to frequent such amusements, unprotected by his presence and without his permission.... She has not the right to bring his honor or her own into possible or even imagined jeopardy. It is urged that by refusing to discharge her I am sentencing her to perpetual imprisonment. Cases of hardship will arise under any general rule … and I cannot doubt that a greater amount of human happiness is produced in the married state, from the mutual concession and forbearance, which a sense that the union is indissoluble tends to produce, than could be enjoyed in the carelessness and want of self-government which would arise when the tie was held less firm. [A. Dowling, *Reports of Cases Argued and Determined in the Queen's Bench Practise Courts*][37]

In 1852 a different judgment was given in a similar case (Rex v. Leggat). A husband sent a writ to his son-in-law with whom his wife had taken refuge, demanding that she be surrendered. The judge upheld the fugitive wife and ruled—thus setting a precedent—that she could not be forced to cohabit. A wife henceforth might run away. But what would she live on? A divorced wife got maintenance, although the husband kept any property of hers not separately secured in her name. How available was divorce?

DIVORCE BEFORE 1857

The way to dissolve a marriage before the Reformation was by annulment obtained from the Papal Curia in Rome. Thereafter, divorce was obtainable in England only by passage of a private bill through Parliament.

Three distinct tribunals had to be resorted to—a court of law for damages against the adulterer; a court ecclesiastical for divorce à mensâ et thoro [which did not permit remarriage]; and the imperial parliament for a dissolving statute. This last gave the divorce a vinculo [permitting remarriage]. Each of these procedures was costly and all were humiliating. [J. F. Macqueen, *A Practical Treatise on the Law of Marriage, Divorce and Legitimacy*][38]

It has been suggested that the chief reason why the first Divorce Bills were granted was to continue the succession to peerages in the male line…. Lord Macclesfield [1697], petitioning the House of Lords … put forward the same ground, alleging that he would suffer unreasonable hardship if, for his wife's fault, he was deprived of the common privilege 'to have an heir of his own body to inherit what he possessed, either of honor or of estate, or that his only brother should lose his claim to both, and his birthright be sacrificed to Lady Maccles-field's irregular life'. [F. Clifford, *A History of Private Bill Legislation*][39]

In Scotland divorce was granted to both men and women on pleas of adultery or desertion, but divorce in England was normally granted only at the husband's suit. There were four exceptions in two hundred years. In the first, the case of a Mrs Addison (1801), it was established that her husband had been her sister's lover. A debate took place in the House of Lords:

20 May 1801   The Duke of Clarence said ... Mrs Addison had made out so strong a case, that if any criminal conduct of a husband toward his wife could amount to a justification of her obtaining a divorce from him ... Mrs Addison's was that very case; but when he considered the novelty of the legislature granting a divorce to a wife on a complaint of adultery on the part of the husband, the infinite mischiefs it might lead to by encouraging the foulest collusions between married couples ... and the effect the practice would have on the morals of society, he must resist the present application....

[Lord Thurlow said:] On all occasions their lordships ... governed their conduct by the peculiar circumstances of each particular case.... What is the nature of the great objection to granting the petitioner ... the divorce she prayed for ? A principle of mistrust of themselves, and a doubt lest they should, on any future application by a wife for a divorce, not conduct themselves with sound discretion. Was such a mistrust to be gravely argued as a sufficient reason to justify ... refusing justice to a petitioner? [Lord Thurlow then argued that if Mr Addison had slept with Mrs Addison's sister before the marriage, the marriage would have been void because tainted with incest.].. Did they see nothing immoral in compelling Mrs Addison after what had passed, to remain connected and under the power of her husband ? [The case was in every point] ... so widely distinct in its nature and circumstance from those that might hereafter form the ground of any future application for a divorce by a wife ... that it appeared ... irreconcilable to

every principle of justice for their lordships to refuse divorce. . . .
The Lord Chancellor (Eldon) said that his mind and
opinion had been greatly affected by the new light in which his
learned friend had placed it. He was now satisfied . . . that the
bill might pass without operating as a dangerous precedent. At
the same time, however, he must retain his opinion that . . .
adultery committed by a wife and adultery committed by a
husband were widely different in their consequences. The
adultery of a wife might impose a spurious issue upon the
husband, which he might be called upon to dedicate a part of
his fortunes to educate and provide for; whereas no such
injustice could result to his wife, from the adultery of a married
man. [*The Parliamentary History of England from the Earliest Period
to the year 1803*][40]

*The other three women who managed to secure parliamentary divorces
won them on grounds of incest and bigamy. A Mrs Dawson, whose
husband had committed flagrant adultery and flogged her with horsewhip
and hairbrush, was refused (1848) despite six petitions, and a Mrs
Teush was also refused (1805) 'on grounds of public morality,' although
the Lord Chancellor 'never recollected to hear a more favorable account of
any woman'.*

THE CRIM. CON. OF CAROLINE NORTON

*Adultery was called 'criminal conversation' and abbreviated 'crim. con'.
A wife formally accused of it had to expect a slimy passage through the
three forums where she would be tried. The first was the civil court in
which her husband would sue her alleged lover for damages. These suits
were expensive, available only to the very rich, and a favorite entertain-
ment of the public press. That overprotected flower, the upper-middle-
class wife, on finding her private life exposed to the blast of popular
ribaldry, would in effect be punished before being convicted. This
happened to Caroline Norton.*

*Mrs Norton (1808–77) was just such a flower. One of the three
beautiful granddaughters of Richard Brinsley Sheridan, she was brought
up in Hampton Court, was a well-known popular novelist, a poet, and
the mother of three sons. Her encounter with the law turned her into a
pamphleteer, and she successfully attacked some of its worst abuses. She*

*learned of these by suffering them, as many women had before her. But
unlike them, she had the skills and connections to fight back. Caroline
Norton's troubles originated with a question of preferment. She had
married a man who was a younger son.*

I believe that foreigners—and our own mercantile classes—
have little idea of the very narrow provision which the usual
'Right of the Eldest Son' leaves for the younger members of
noble English houses. . [From] the day we were married, he never
ceased impressing upon me, that as I brought him no present
fortune (my portion being only payable on my mother's death),
I was bound to use every effort with the political friends of my
grandfather to get him lucrative promotion in his profession
. . . . I did what my husband requested, I procured . . . for
[him] a place worth a thousand [pounds] a year. [C. Norton,
English Laws for Women in the Nineteenth Century] [41]

*What she had done was to write to the Home Secretary, Lord Melbourne,
who granted her husband a police magistracy and subsequently became a
close friend. In 1836 Norton, who had been quarreling with his wife,
took a suit against Melbourne for criminal conversation. Based on the
evidence of servants who had almost certainly been bribed, the case was
dismissed. The public cheered, and the general assumption was that
there had been a political plot to discredit Melbourne with the young
Queen Victoria and that Norton had lent himself to it in the hope of raising some cash (he had demanded £10,000 in damages).*

If [an English wife's] husband takes proceedings for a divorce,
she is not, in the first instance, allowed to defend herself. She has
no means of proving the falsehood of his allegations. She is not
represented by attorney, nor permitted to be considered a party
to the suit between him and her supposed lover, for 'damages'
. . . . though the result may be to ruin her. [C. Norton, *A Letter
to the Queen on Lord Chancellor Cranworth's Marriage and Divorce
Bill*] [42]

*Caroline Norton was not socially ruined; her family rallied around her,
and some years later she was again received at the royal court. But some
of the mud must have stuck. The following selection comes from a*

sixpenny pamphlet of the time, giving an account of the trial 'by an eminent reporter'.

[22 June 1836] This case which has excited such an extraordinary degree of interest came to trial this morning. Long before the time appointed for the opening of the court to the public, the galleries were crowded, it being generally understood that as much as five guineas had been given for seats.... Sir William Follet then rose to address the jury and spoke as follows.... I am sure you will feel bound to dismiss from your minds, as far as you can, idle rumors ... and if you are satisfied of the guilt of the party, you will fearlessly pronounce your verdict.... [You will return a verdict of guilty] if you find that the defendant in this case has taken advantage of his high position ... to introduce himself into the family of the plaintiff as a benefactor, a patron, and a friend—if he has taken advantage of that position to inflict upon the plaintiff the deepest injury one man can inflict upon another—if you find that this illicit intercourse has long been continued—that children have been born, and that it is impossible to ascertain the extent of the injury; and if you find that he has poisoned the source which is the purest of all feelings—the affection of a father for his dear and lovely children....

One of the servants had seen kisses pass between the parties. She had seen Mrs Norton's arm around Lord Melbourne's neck —had seen her hand upon his knee, and herself kneeling in a posture. In that room [her bedroom] Mrs Norton has been seen lying on the floor, her clothes in a position to expose her person.—(Great sensation.) There are other things too which it is my faithful duty to disclose. I allude to the marks from the consequences of the intercourse between the two parties. I will show you that these marks were seen upon the linen of Mrs Norton. [At this point the 'eminent reporter' broke into a series of asterisks.] [*Extraordinary Trial, Norton v. Viscount Melbourne for Crim. Con.*][43]

DIVORCE FROM BED AND BOARD

The Nortons could not live together again, but neither could they divorce.

He had lost the case. She could charge him with neither incest nor bigamy and was therefore in no position to divorce him, quite apart from the fact, in any case, of not having the money for such proceedings. There remained the half measure granted by the ecclesiastical courts: divorce a mensa et thoro, or separation from bed and board. This granted alimony but did not permit remarriage. The grounds were adultery or cruelty. It was, however, difficult both to prove and to define cruelty. One of the precedents often cited in nineteenth-century cruelty cases was the judgment given in the case of Evans v. Evans (1790):

That the duty of cohabitation is released by the cruelty of one of the parties is admitted, but the question occurs, *What is cruelty?* ... It is the duty of courts ... to keep the rule extremely strict. The causes must be grave and weighty, and such as show an absolute impossibility that the duties of the married life can be discharged. In a state of personal danger no duties can be discharged; for the duty of self-preservation must take place before the duties of marriage ... but what falls short of this is with great caution to be admitted.... What merely wounds the mental feelings is in few cases to be admitted, where not accompanied with bodily injury, either actual or menaced. Mere austerity of temperament, petulance of manners, rudeness of language, a want of civil attention and accommodation, even occasional sallies of passion, if they do not threaten bodily harm, do not amount to legal cruelty.... And if it be complained that by this inactivity of the courts much injustice may be suffered, and much misery produced, the answer is, that the courts of justice do not pretend to furnish cures for all the miseries of human life. They redress or punish gross violations of duty, but they go no farther.... Still less is it cruelty where it wounds not the natural feelings but the acquired feelings arising from particular rank and station; for the court has no scale of sensibilities by which it can gauge the quantum of injury done and felt.... In the older cases of this sort, which I have had an opportunity of looking into, I have observed that the danger of life, limb, or health is usually inserted as the ground upon which the court has proceeded to separation.... The court has never been driven off this ground. [J. Haggard,

*Reports of Cases Argued and Determined in the Consistory Court of
London]* [44]

*Though much cited, the Evans case was gradually followed by more
practical definitions of cruelty. In the case of Holden v. Holden (1810),
Sir William Scott ruled:*

Whenever there is a tendency only to bodily mischief, it is a peril
from which the wife must be protected; because it is unsafe for
her to continue in the discharge of her conjugal duties; and to
enforce that obligation upon her might endanger her security,
and perhaps her life.... Secondly, the law does not require that
there should be many acts.... Thirdly, it is not necessary that
the conduct of the wife should be entirely without blame ... the
imputation of blame to the wife will not justify the ferocity of
the husband. (Haggard, *Reports of Cases*) [45]

*Later in the century it came to be accepted that a threat of cruelty might
be as bad as cruelty itself. But at the time of Caroline Norton's predica-
ment the most authoritative pronouncement was Dr Lushington's, in the
case of Lockwood v. Lockwood (1839):*

There must be either actual violence committed attended
with danger to life, limb or health; or there must be a reasonable
apprehension of such violence. (W. C. Curteis, *Reports of
Cases Argued and Defended in the Ecclesiastical Courts at Doctors'
Commons*) [46]

*Before the breakup of the Norton marriage, he had committed various
acts of violence against his wife and she had been driven to take refuge
with her relatives. But the fact that she had subsequently returned to him
made it difficult to allege that cruelty in court.*

If the wife sue for separation for cruelty, it must be 'cruelty that
endangers life or limb,' and if she has once forgiven, or, in legal
phrase 'condoned' his offenses, she cannot plead them. (Norton,
Letter to the Queen) [47]

*Caroline Norton was to remain that hybrid creature: a separated married
woman. She did not enjoy the rights of a feme sole, nor had she all the*

advantages of a married woman. In a number of pamphlets she drew attention to the plight of women like herself.

A married woman in English law has no legal existence: her being is absorbed in that of her husband. Years of separation or desertion cannot alter this position. Unless divorced by special enactment of the House of Lords, the legal fiction holds her to be 'one' with her husband, even though she may never hear of him. (*Norton, Letter to the Queen*) [48]

A wife deserted by or separated from her husband, or divorced from him by the Ecclesiastical Court may by her industry and the exercise of her talents, support herself and her family, furnish her home, and accumulate a sum of money:—

Her husband, having been absent for many years, may return, take possession of her money, receive all debts owing to her, sell off her furniture, and again leave her. . . .

If she be robbed, she cannot prosecute.

If she be libeled or slandered, she cannot prosecute.

If she earn money, she cannot sue for it.

If she enter into a contract, she cannot enforce it.

She can make neither deed nor will.

But, if she be guilty of crime obnoxious to the law, she will be punished. (Unsigned but almost certainly by C. Norton, *A Review of the Divorce Bill of 1856*) [49]

Equity mitigated several of these restrictions for the wife who had separate property. Such a wife could sue and be sued and contract out of such property. In Mrs Norton's case, her husband successfully claimed a legacy left her by her father (it had not been secured to her separately), but was unable to get his hands on one settled on her by her mother.

THE CUSTODY OF INFANTS ACT (1839)

I have learned the law respecting women, piecemeal, by suffering from every one of its defects of protection. (Norton, *Letter to the Queen*) [50]

Indeed, for Norton, a trained lawyer and magistrate, had called upon every legal device to harry his wife throughout their years of separation.

It was when she learned that the law gave full rights to a father over his children, and none to the mother, that Caroline Norton first began to lobby for reform. She found that she had no right to see her children, unless Norton chose to let her. Looking into recent custody disputes, she discovered that courts had no authority to remove guardianship from a father except in very extreme cases, and that conservative opinion considered this very proper. Fear of losing their children was held to be a useful check to restless wives.

Before the passing of Serjent Talfourd's Act cases constantly occurred where, by a tyrannical use of the paternal power, the mother was excluded not only from the custody of the children, but also from access to them. Thus the apprehensions of the mother paralysed the wife who, dreading the father's power was obliged to submit to the husband's misconduct. [Macqueen, 1860, *A Practical Treatise on the Law of Marriage*] [51]

In the year 1824, there is recorded a case of disputed custody ... in which (the parties being separated, from the cruelty and brutality of the husband) the wife's child was actually taken from her, and given into the custody of the woman with whom the husband cohabited: the husband being then imprisoned for debt.... [The mother appealed, but] in spite of the gross circumstances of the case, the courts decided against her. [Pearce Stevenson, Esq. (pseudonym for C. Norton), *A Plain Letter to the Lord Chancellor on the Infant Custody Bill,* 1839] [52]

The question deserved legislative reform. Caroline Norton and others held that the courts should be given authority to assign custody to the deserving parent. A letter to Mary Wollstonecraft's daughter provides a glimpse of her activity and her family's alarm.

[February 1837.]   Dear Mrs Shelley, I have been expecting to write to you every day to send my pamphlet.... There was such a division in my family as to what I might and might not do, and such an outcry at the indelicacy of public appeal, that I delayed the press, hoping to be able to win over my people to my view. Tonight Talfourd ... has given notice of a motion in the House of Commons to alter this law.... I do not know

Mr Talfourd personally, but I asked Mr Hayward (who seems a great friend of his) to request him to undertake the task. I hardly hoped for such prompt acquiescence; but if I had to choose from the whole House of Commons, I could not choose a man whose talent and good feeling and weight with the House would give a better ... chance of success.... He has the printed proof of my pamphlet. [C. Norton, letter in J. G. Perkins, *The Life of Mrs Norton*][53]

About this time Mrs Norton was abusively attacked in a magazine and described as a feminist. She would have taken a libel action but could not:

[An English wife] cannot prosecute for libel. Her husband must prosecute; and in cases of enmity and separation, of course, she is without a remedy. [Norton, *Letter to the Queen*][54]

In August 1839, the Custody of Infants Act was passed. It granted less than she had hoped for but allowed the courts to give a mother access to her children and custody of those under the age of seven. A first breach had been made in the total hegemony of paternal authority:

Provided always ... that no order shall be made whereby any mother against whom adultery shall be established, by judgment in an action for criminal conversation at the suit of her husband, or by the sentence of an ecclesiastical court, shall have the custody of any infant or access to any infant, anything herein contained to the contrary notwithstanding. [*Statutes of the United Kingdom of Great Britain and Ireland*, 1839][55]

THE MATRIMONIAL CAUSES ACT OF 1857

This divorce act was the next major reform in family law. Its main purpose was to transfer jurisdiction on divorce from Parliament and the ecclesiastical courts to a new tribunal. This simplified proceedings and radically lowered divorce costs, thereby making it available to a larger sector of the population. Actions for 'crim. con.' were abolished. But there had been much heated controversy. Reformers had hoped to mitigate the double standard applied to male and female adultery, and the occasion seemed ripe for remedying a number of grievances. Caroline Norton had entered the debate with some compelling pamphlets.

I pray your Majesty's attention to the effect of [the married woman's] non-existence in law.... From the day of my mother's death, he [Norton] has withheld entirely and with perfect impunity my income as a wife. I do not receive, and have not received for the last three years, a single farthing from him. [She could, however, pledge his credit: run up bills in his name.] He retains, and always has retained, property that was left in my home—gifts made to me by my own family on my marriage, and to my mother by your Majesty's aunt ... articles bought from my literary earnings, books.... He receives from my trustees the interest of the portion bequeathed me by my father. I have also (as Mr Norton impressed on me, by subpoenaing my publishers), the power of earning by literature—which fund is no more legally mine than my family property.... I cannot divorce my husband for adultery, desertion, or cruelty; I *must* remain married to his name; he has ... a right to everything I have in the world—and I have no claim on him....

The natural position of woman is inferiority to man. Amen! That is a thing of God's appointing, not of man's devising. I believe it sincerely, as a part of my religion: and I accept it as a matter proved to my reason. I never pretended to the wild and ridiculous doctrine of equality. I will even hold that (as one coming under the general rule that the wife must be inferior to the husband) ... I am Mr Norton's inferior. I am the clouded moon of that sun. Put me then—(my ambition extends no further)—in the same position as all his other inferiors! In that of his housekeeper, whom he could not libel with impunity ... of an apprentice whom he could not maltreat lawlessly, even if the boy 'condoned' original ill-usage; of a scullion, whose wages he could not refuse.... Put me under some law of protection.

From time immemorial, changes in the laws of nations have been brought about by individual examples of oppression. Such examples *cannot* be unimportant, for they are, and ever will be, the little hinges on which the great doors of justice are made to turn. [Norton, *Letter to the Queen*] [56]

The Bill, as first introduced in 1854, would have granted divorce to a wife on grounds of incest only. After debate, the grounds were finally laid down as follows :

XXVII   It shall be lawful for any husband to present a petition to the said Court, praying that his marriage may be dissolved, on the ground that his wife has since the celebration thereof been guilty of adultery; and it shall be lawful for any wife to present a petition to the said Court, praying that her marriage may be dissolved, on the ground that since the celebration thereof her husband has been guilty of incestuous adultery, or of bigamy with adultery, or of rape, or of sodomy or bestiality, or of adultery coupled with such cruelty as without adultery would have entitled her to a divorce á mensâ et thoro, or of adultery coupled with desertion, without reasonable excuse, for two years or upwards. [*Statutes of the United Kingdom of Great Britain and Ireland, 1857*][57]

Although the above passage accepted the double standard, the Act incorporated a number of reforms favorable to women. For one thing, it replaced the old ecclesiastical divorce by a decree for judicial separation, and this granted to the woman separated the status of a feme sole for purposes of suing, contracting, and managing all property acquired after the date of the sentence. Section XXI of the Act, the Wife's Protection Order, reads like a direct response to Caroline Norton's canvassing :

A wife deserted by her husband may at any time after such desertion, if resident within the metropolitan district, apply to a police magistrate, or if resident in the county to justices in petty sessions, or in either case to the Court [the Divorce Court] for an order to protect any money or property she may acquire by her own lawful industry, and property which she may become possessed of, after such desertion, against her husband or his creditors, or any person claiming under him; and such magistrate, or Justices, or Court ... may make and give to the wife an order protecting her earnings and property ... and such earnings and property shall belong to the wife as if she were a feme sole ... ; if the husband or any creditor of ... the husband shall seize or continue to hold any property of the wife after notice of any such order, he shall be liable ... to restore the specific property, and also to a sum equal to double the value of the property. [*Statutes of the United Kingdom, 1857*] [58]

From here on, reforms followed at an accelerated rhythm. The era of organized feminism had begun. Already in 1856 a petition signed by 26,000 women had been submitted to Parliament, demanding a review of the rights of married women with regard to their own earnings and property. A bill to extend these rights was rejected, but a step in this direction was taken when the Act of 1857 allowed divorced women to revert to the status of feme sole. This benefit was extended to all married women by the Married Women's Property Acts of 1870, 1882, and 1893. The movement for reform had quickened. Founded in 1857, The Englishwoman's Review *began to coordinate feminist activities, and these were soon turned to bring help to women without property too.*

Notes

1 GREECE

1 Plutarch (c. A.D. 46–c. 120), 'Theseus,' *Lives*, trans. by Dryden, rev. by A.H. Clough (Boston, 1864), I, p. 16.

2 Homer, *The Odyssey*, trans. by E.V. Rieu (Penguin Classics, 1946), Bk. 7, pp. 113–14.

3 Herodotus (c. 480–c. 425 B.C.), *The Histories*, trans. by Aubrey de Sélincourt (Penguin Classics, 1954), p. 83.

4 Homer, *The Odyssey*, Bk. 22, pp. 338–39.

5 Hesiod, *Works and Days*, lines 57, 70, 77, 90, 373, 405ff., from French trans. of E. Bergougnon in *Hésiode et les Poétes élégiaques et moralistes de la Grèce* (Garnier Frères, 1940), pp. 59ff.

6 Xenophon, *La République des Lacédémoniens*, I, pp. 3–8, from French trans. of Fr. Ollier, fasc. 47, A. Rey, Imprimeur-éditeur (Lyon, Annales de l'Université de Lyon, Nouvelle série, II, Droit, Lettres, 1934) pp. 2ff.

7 Plato, *The Laws*, trans. by A.E. Taylor (Dent, 1934), Bk. 6, p. 164.

8 Aristotle, *Politics*, trans. by Benjamin Jowett (Modern Library, New York, 1943), Bk. 2, ch. 9, pp. 108f.

9 Demosthenes, 'Against Neaera,' *The Orations*, trans. by C.R. Kennedy, 5 vols , (London, 1852–63), V, p. 272.

10 Plutarch, *Lives*, I, p. 190–91.

11 Demosthenes, 'Against Aristogiton,' *Orations*, IV, p. 71.

12 Demosthenes, 'Against Aphobus I,' *Orations*, IV, pp. 93ff.

13 Demosthenes, 'For Phormio,' *Orations*, IV, pp. 211ff.

14 Diogenes Laertius, *The Lives, Opinions and Remarkable Sayings of the Most Famous Ancient Philosophers*, trans. by several hands (London, 1696), Bk. 5, pp. 331ff.

15 Isaeus (4th cent. B.C.), 'Against the Estate of Aristarchus,' *Isaeus*, trans. by E.S. Forster (Loeb Classical Library, Heinemann, 1927), p. 327.

16 Demosthenes, 'Against Leochares,' *Orations*, V, p. 30.

17 Demosthenes, 'Against Macartatus,' *Orations*, V, pp. 16–17.

18 Isaeus, 'On the Estate of Pyrrhus,' *Isaeus*, pp. 113–15.

19 Demosthenes, 'Against Stephanos II,' *Orations*, V, p. 73.

20 *The Gortyna Law Tables*, VII: 43, 47, 50, 53, ed. and trans. by R. Dareste, B. Haussoullier, Th. Reinach, *Recueil des Inscriptions Juridiques Grecques* (Paris, 1894), fasc. III, pp. 377–78.

21 ibid., V: 26, 27, 28, 29, 30, pp. 367ff.; VI: 36, p. 371.

22 Euripides (c. 480–406 B.C.), *Medea*, trans. by Philip Vellacott (Penguin Classics, 1971), lines 230–48, p. 24.

23   Aristotle, *Politics*, Bk. 2, ch. 9, p. 106.

24   Demosthenes, 'Against Neaera,' *Orations*, V, p. 272.

25   Demosthenes, 'Against Onetor,' *Orations*, IV, p. 140.

26   Cornelius Nepos (c. 100–c. 25 B.C.), *Vitae* ed. by. C. Halm (Leipzig, 1881), praef. 6, p. 2.

27   Xenophon, *The Economist*, VII: 22, adapted from trans. by A.D.O. Wedderburn and W. Collingwood (London, 1876), p. 47.

28   Lysias (c. 458–c. 380 B.C.), 'The Murder of Eratosthanes,' *Lysias*, trans. by W.R. Lamb (Loeb Classical Library, Heinemann, 1930), pp. 7ff.

29   Lysias, 'Against Simon,' *Lysias*, p. 75.

30   Demosthenes, 'Against Pantaenetus,' *Orations*, IV, p. 240.

31   Demosthenes, 'Against Aristogiton I,' *Orations*, IV, p. 70.

32   Hesiod, *Works and Days*, p. 69.

33   Posidippus, cited in G. Glotz, *L'Exposition des Enfants, Études Sociales et Juridiques sur l'antiquité grecque* (Paris, 1906), p. 199.

34   *Gortyna Law Tables*, IV: 21, 23, p. 365.

35   Cited in G. Glotz, *L'Exposition des Enfants*, p. 217.

36   Soranus of Ephesus (2nd cent. A.D.), *Gynecology*, trans. by Owsie Temkin (Johns Hopkins Press, 1956), Bk. 2, 10 [79], pp. 79–80.

37   Xenophon, *The Economist*, adapted from several translations; cf. A.D.O. Wedderburn and W. Collingwood (London, 1876), I, pp. 42ff.

38   Aeschines (c. 390–c. 314 B.C.), 'Against Timarchus,' *The Speeches of Aeschines*, trans. by Charles Darwin Adams (Loeb Classical Library, Heinemann, 1919), p. 147.

39   Demosthenes, 'Against Neaera,' *Orations*, V, p. 263.

40   Lysias, 'Against Alcibiades I,' *Lysias*, p. 353.

41   Isaeus, 'On the Estate of Menecles,' *Isaeus*, p. 45.

42   Andocides (born c. 440 B.C.), 'Against Alcibiades,' *Minor Attic Orators*, trans. by K.J. Maidment (Harvard University Press, 1941), I, p. 553.

43   *Gortyna Law Tables*, III: 14, 15, pp. 361ff.

44   Demosthenes, 'Against Eubolides,' *Orations*, V, pp. 206ff.

45   Strabo (c. 64 B.C.–A.D. 19), *The Geography*, adapted from trans. of W. Falconer (London, 1856), Bk. 8, ch. 6, p. 20.

46   Athenaeus (fl. c. A.D. 200), *The Deipnosophists, or Banquet of the Learned*, adapted from the trans. of C.D. Yonge (London, 1854), Vol. III, Bk. 13, ch. 25, pp. 910–11.

47   Lucian (c. A.D. 115–c. 200), *Le Manuel des Boudoirs*, anon. French trans. (Paris, 1888), 1st conversation (6th in some editions).

48   Claire Préaux, 'Le Statut de la femme a l'époque hellénistique, principalement en Egypte,' *Recueils de la Société Jean Bodin*, Vol. X, Part 1, pp. 148–49.

49 Plutarch, *Dialogue on Love*, from French trans. by Robert Flacelière (Société d'Edition Les Belles Lettres, Paris, 1952), pp. 44ff.

2 ROME

1 Dionysius of Halicarnassus (fl. c. 25 B.C.), *The Roman Antiquities*, trans. E. Cary (Harvard University Press, 1937), I, pp. 381ff.
2 Aulus Gellius (2nd cent. A.D.), *The Attic Nights*, (3 vols.) trans. by John C. Rolfe (Loeb Classics, New York, 1927), I, p. 323.
3 ibid., II, pp. 278–79.
4 Plutarch, 'Romulus,' *Lives*, trans. by Dryden, rev. by A.H. Clough (Boston, 1864), I, p. 67.
5 Valerius Maximus, *Facta et Dicta Memorabilia*, Bk. 6, ch. 3, paras 9, 10, from French trans. of T.C.E. Baudement (Paris, 1850).
6 Livy, *The History of Rome*, Lat. ed., C. Weissenborn and M. Müller (Leipzig, 1900), Bk. 34, chs. 2, 7, 8, pp. 139ff., 147ff.
7 From c. A.D. 161, Gaius, *The Institutes of Gaius*, I, trans. in S.P. Scott, *The Civil Law* (The Central Trust Company, Cincinnati, 1932), I, pp. 97ff.
8 Cicero (106–43 B.C.), 'For Murena,' *Orationes*, ed. by C.F.W. Mueller, 3 vols. (Leipzig, 1885), pt. 2, III, p. 310.
9 *The Digest*, XXIII, ii, 1; S.P. Scott, V, p. 245.
10 Dio Cassius (c. A.D. 150–235), *Dio's Roman History*, trans. E. Cary (Loeb Classical Library, New York, 1924), Bk. 56, VII, pp. 5ff.
11 Plutarch, 'Comparison of Numa with Lycurgus,' *Lives*, I, p. 165.
12 *Digest*, XXIII, i, 14; Scott, V, p. 242.
13 ibid., XXIII, ii, 4; Scott, V, p. 245.
14 ibid., XXIII, i, 11, 12; Scott, V, p. 242.
15 *Code of Justinian*, V, iv, 18, 20; Scott, XII, p. 149.
16 *The Theodosian Code* (A.D. 438), 9, 24, 1, trans. by Clyde Pharr (Princeton University Press, 1952), pp. 244ff.
17 *Collatio Legum Mosaicarum et Romanarum*, Berlin Codex, trans. by M. Hyamson, IV, 2, 1 (Henry Frowde, London, 1913), p. 75.
18 *Opinions of Julius Paulus*, XXVI, 14; Scott, I, p. 282.
19 *Code of Justinian*, IX, ix, 1, 2; Scott, XV, p. 8.
20 *Theodosian Code*, 9, 7, 2; Pharr, p. 231.
21 *Code of Justinian*, IX, ix, 30; Scott, XV, p. 16.
22 *Theodosian Code*, 3, 16, 1; Pharr, pp. 76ff.
23 *Code*, V, xvii, 8–11; Scott, XIII, p. 203–07.
24 *The Novels of Justinian*, 8th collection, ch. 14; Scott, XVII, p. 59.
25 *Theodosian Code*, 3, 8, 1; Pharr, p. 71.
26 'For M. Coelius,' *The Orations of Marcus Tullius Cicero*, trans. by C.D. Yonge, 4 vols. (London, 1852), III, p. 269.
27 Suetonius, *The Twelve Caesars*, trans. by Robert Graves (Penguin Classics, 1957), pp. 127–28.

28 Tacitus, *The Annals of Imperial Rome*, trans. by Michael Grant (Penguin Classics, 1956), pp. 115–16.

29 Marcel Durry, (ed.), *Eloge funèbre d'une matrone romaine: Eloge dit de Turia* (Collection des Universités de France, 1950), pp. 8ff.

30 Juvenal, *The Sixteen Satires*, trans. by Peter Green (Penguin Classics, 1967), Sat. VI, lines 269–84, pp. 136–37.

31 Ulpian (A.D. 170–228), *Rules of Ulpian*, VI; Scott, I, p. 229.

32 Gaius, *The Institutes*, II; Scott, I, p. 118.

33 *Digest*, XXIII, iii, 1, 2; Scott, V, p. 261.

34 *Code*, V, xvii, 11; Scott, XIII, p. 206.

35 ibid., V, xiv, 8; Scott, XIII, p. 190.

36 Ulpian, *Rules*, XV, XVI; Scott, I, p. 236.

37 *Digest*, XXII, v, 18; Scott, V, p. 236.

38 ibid., XVIII, i, 20 (6); Scott, VI, p. 183.

39 Gaius, *Institutes*, II, 112, 113; Scott, I, p. 125.

40 *Theodosian Code*, 3, 17, 4; Pharr, pp. 78–79.

41 Valerius Maximus, *Facta et Dicta Memorabilia*, Bk. 2, ch. 1, para 5.

42 Ulpian, *Rules*, XIII, 1, 2; Scott, I, p. 235.

43 *Opinions of Julius Paulus*, II, 26, 11, 16; Scott, I, p. 282.

44 *Code*, IX, ix, 22, 23, 25; Scott, XV, p. 19ff.

45 *Theodosian Code*, 9, 7, 1; Pharr, p. 231.

46 *Digest*, XXVI, vii, 1 (1); Scott, VI, p. 50.

47 ibid., XXIII, ii, 24; Scott, V, p. 249.

48 *Novels*, 3d collection, XI: Scott, XVI, p. 103.

49 Tacitus, *Annals of Imperial Rome*, p. 266.

50 *Theodosian Code*, 9, 9, 1; Pharr, p. 233.

51 ibid., 15, 8, 1; Pharr, p. 435.

52 *Novels*, 5th collection, VI; Scott, XVI, pp. 222–23.

53 Petronius (d. A.D. 65), *The Satyricon*, trans. by William Arrowsmith (Mentor Books, New York, 1960), p. 63.

54 Quintilian, *Institutes of Oratory*, trans. by J.S. Watson (London, 1856), Bk. 1, ch. 1, p. 6.

55 Sallust, *The Conspiracy of Catiline*, 25, trans. by S.A. Handford (Penguin Classics, 1970), p. 193.

56 Ovid, *The Art of Love*, trans. by Rolfe Humphries (Indiana University Press, 1957), III, lines 327ff., p. 163.

3 BYZANTIUM

1 St John Chrysostom (A.D. 347–407), *Homilies on Colossians*, XII, Oxford trans., rev. by J. A. Broadus, A Select Library of the Nicene and Post-Nicene Fathers of the Christian Church, ed. by P. Schaff (New York, 1889), XIII, p. 318ff.

2 Chrysostom, *Instructions to Catechumens*, trans. by W.R.W.Stephens

and T. P. Brandram, Library of Nicene and Post-Nicene Fathers, IX, p. 169.

3   *The Novels of Leo*, Novel 48, from the French of P. Noailles and A. Dain, *Les Nouvelles de Léon VI, Le Sage* (Paris, 1944), pp. 64ff.

4   *A Manual of Later Roman Law, The Ecloga ad Procheiron Mutata*, ch. 23, 4, trans. by E.H.Freshfield (Cambridge University Press, 1927), p. 145.

5   *A Manual of Roman Law, The Ecloga*, trans. by E.H. Freshfield (Cambridge University Press, 1926), ch. 2, 6, pp 74ff.

6   ibid., ch. 2, 9, p. 76.

7   *A Manual of Eastern Roman Law, The Procheiros Nomos*, ch. 4, 17, 26, trans. by E. H. Freshfield (Cambridge University Press, 1928), pp. 61ff.

8   *Novels of Leo*, Novel 89, p. 296.

9   *Ecloga ad Procheiron Mutata*, ch. 18, 14, 17, pp. 132ff.

10 *Ecloga*, ch. 2, 4, pp. 73ff.

11 ibid., ch. 3, 2, pp. 80ff.

12 *Procheiros Nomos*, IX, 13, 18, 1, pp. 75ff.

13 ibid., ch. VI, 4, pp. 67ff.

14 *A Revised Manual of Roman Law, Ecloga Privata Aucta*, XVIII 25, 26, 28, trans. by E. H. Freshfield (Cambridge University Press, 1927), pp. 79ff.

15 *Novels of Leo*, Novel 32, pp. 126ff.

16 *Ecloga*, II, 13, p. 78.

17 *Procheiros Nomos*, XI, 5, pp. 83ff.

18 Procopius (died c. 562), *The Secret History*, trans. by G.A. Williamson (Penguin Classics, 1966), p. 124.

19 Michael Psellus, *Fourteen Byzantine Rulers*, trans. by E.R.A. Sewter (Penguin Classics, 1966), p. 108.

5   THE EARLY MIDDLE AGES

1   *Leges Burgundionum*, ed. by L.R. von Salis, in *Monumenta Germaniae Historica*, Legum Sect. I, II, 1 (Hanover, 1892), p. 113, cap. C.

2   ibid., p. 107, LXXXV, 1.

3   *Leges Visigothorum*, ed. by K. Zeumer, in *Monumenta Germaniae Historica*, Legum Sect. I, I (Hanover and Leipzig, 1902), p. 190, IV, 3, 3.

4   *Leges Saxonum und Lex Thuringorum*, ed. by C.F. von Schwerin (Hanover and Leipzig, 1918), pp. 28–29, c. XLII,XLIV, XLV.

5   ibid., p. 64, c. XLV.

6   *Lex Frisionum*, ed. by C. von Richthofen, in *Monumenta Germaniae Historica*, Leges, Tom. III (Hanover, 1963), p. 665, IX, 11–12.

7   *Leges Saxonum*, pp. 28–29, c. XLI, XLVI.

8   *Lex Thuringorum*, pp. 60–61, c. XXVI-XXX.

9   *Pactus Legis Salicae*, ed. by K.A. Eckhardt, 4 vols., (Gottingen, 1953–56), III (II, 1), p. 340.

10   ibid., IV (II, 2), pp. 424–26.

11   *Textes relatifs aux institutions privées et publiques aux époques mérovingienne et carolingienne*, ed. by M. Thévenin (Paris, 1887), doc. 14.

12   *The Burgundian Code*, trans. by Katherine Fischer Drew (University of Pennsylvania Press, 1949), pp. 32, 59.

13   *Leges Visigothorum*, p. 174, IV, 2, 1.

14   *Leges Saxonum*, pp. 27–28, 29, c. XL, XLIII.

15   *Leges Burgundionum*, pp. 94–95, LXVI, 1–3.

16   *The Laws of the Earliest English Kings*, ed. and trans. by F.L. Attenborough (Cambridge University Press, 1922), p. 47, c. 31.

17   *The Burgundian Code*, pp. 45–46.

18   Gregory of Tours (c. 538–594), *Historia francorum libri decem* (many editions), Bk. 6, ch. 36.

19   *The Burgundian Code*, pp. 68, 46, 66.

20   *Fuero Jusgo* (Madrid, 1815), III, iv, 9.

21   *The Burgundian Code*, p. 31.

22   *Leges Alamannorum* (redacted c. 720), ed. by K. Lehmann and K.A. Eckhardt, in *Monumenta Germaniae Historica*, Legum Sect. I, V, 1 (Hanover, 1966), p. 115, LVI, 1.

23   *The Burgundian Code*, p. 54.

24   *Laws of the Earliest English Kings*, pp. 4ff.

6   ISLAM

1   *Majmu 'al-Fiqh*, French trans. by G.H. Bousquet, *Précis de Droit Musulman*, 2 vols. (Algiers, 1947), II, pp. 31ff.

2   *Sahih* of 'al-Bukhari, *Les Traditions Islamiques*, French trans. by O. Houdas (Paris, 1908), III, p. 569.

3   Aljoxani (13th-cent. Arab chronicler), *Historia de los Jueces de Córdoba*, Spanish trans. by J. Ribera (Madrid, 1914), pp. 134–36.

4   *Mukhtasar* of Khalil Ben Ishak (d. 1365), French trans. by G.H. Bousquet, *Précis de Droit Musulman*, 2 vols. (Algiers, 1947), II, pp. 75ff.

5   *Sahih* of al-Bukhari, *Les Traditions Islamiques*, III, p. 583.

6   ibid., III, p. 593.

7   ibid., IV, p. 395.

7   BIOLOGICAL AND MEDICAL VIEWS

1   Hippocrates, *Oeuvres Complètes*, ed. and trans. by E. Littré, 10 vols. (Paris, 1839–61), VII, p. 479.

2   Aristotle, *Generation of Animals*, trans. by A.L. Peck (Loeb Classics, Harvard University Press, 1943), Bk. 1, pp. 101, 103, 109, 113.

3   ibid., Bk. IV, vi, pp. 459 f.

4   Galen, *De Uteri Dissectione*, (Basel, 1536), Bk. 1, p. 110.

5 *Oeuvres de Galen*, ed. and trans. by Dr. Ch. Daremberg, 2 vols. (Paris, 1854–56), II, pp. 99, 101, 103, 108.

6 P. Borgarucci, *Della contemplatione anatomica sopra tutte le parti del corpo umano* (Venice, 1564), ch. 23.

7 I. de Valverde, *Historia de la composicion del cuerpo humano* (Rome, 1556), Bk. 3, xv, p. 68.

8 William Harvey, 'On Conception,' in *The Works of William Harvey*, trans. by R. Willis, M.D. (London, 1847), pp. 575, 577–78.

9 Hippocrates, *Oeuvres*, VII, pp. 476ff.

10 Albertus Magnus, *De Secretis Mulierum* (Lyons, 1615), pp. 163, 146–48.

11 Hippocrates, *Oeuvres*, VIII, p. 127.

12 Soranus of Ephesus (2nd cent. A.D.), *Gynecology*, trans. by Owsie Temkin (Johns Hopkins Press, 1956), pp. 62–67.

8 THE LATER MIDDLE AGES

1 *Works of Chrysostom*, Homilies on Timothy, IX, in Select Library of Nicene Fathers, ed. by P. Schaff, Oxford trans. (New York, 1889), Vol. XIII, p. 436 f.

2 St Augustine, *Of the Work of Monks*, trans. by H. Browne, in Select Library of Nicene Fathers (Buffalo, 1887), III, p. 524.

3 St Augustine, *On the Holy Trinity*, trans. by A. W. Haddan and W. G. T. Shedd, in Select Library of Nicene Fathers (Buffalo, 1887), III, p. 159.

4 *Corpus Iuris Canonici*, ed. by A. Friedberg, 2 vols. (Leipzig, 1879–81), Vol. I, Pt. II, C. 33, q. 5, c. 12, 13, 17, 18.

5 St Thomas Aquinas, *Summa Theologica*, trans. by Fathers of the English Dominican Province, 22 vols. (London, 1921–32), Vol. IV, Pt. I, Quest. XCII, art. 1, 2; XCIII, 4.

6 Tertullian, *De Virginibus Velandis*, in J. P. Migne, *Patrologia Latina* (Paris, 1844), Vol. II, cols. 899–900.

7 Tertullian, *De Cultu Feminarum*, I, 1, in Migne, *Patrologia Latina* (Paris, 1844), Vol. I, cols. 304–05.

8 *The Writings of Clement of Alexandria*, trans. by W. Wilson, in Ante-Nicene Christian Library, ed. by A. Roberts and J. Donaldson (Edinburgh, 1867), IV: 209.

9 *Papal Decretals Relating to the Diocese of Lincoln in the Twelfth Century*, ed. and trans. by W. Holtzmann and E. W. Kemp, Lincoln Record Society, 47 (Hereford, 1954), pp. 45–47.

10 ibid., p. 61.

11 St Cyprian (c. 200–258), *De Habitu Virginum*, in Migne, *Patrologia Latina* (Paris, 1844), Vol. IV, cols. 443, 463.

12 St John Chrysostom, *Della Verginità* (Venice, 1565), p. 15.

13 Fortunatus, *Opera Poetica*, ed. by C. Nisard (Paris, 1887), Bk. 8, 3.

14   Aquinas, *Summa Theologica*, XIII, pp. 118, 115.

15   *Corpus Iuris Canonici*, Pt. I, C. 27, q. 1, c. 10.

16   Philip the Carthusian, *Marienleben*, in *Erzählende Dichtungen des späteren Mittelalters*, ed. by F. Bobertag (Berlin and Stuttgart, 1886), p. 46.

17   Jacques de Vitry, *Vita B. Mariae Ogniacensis*, in *Acta Sanctorum* (Antwerp, June 1707), IV, pp. 636–38.

18   Philippe de Navarre (d. 1261?), *Les Quatre Âges de l'Homme*, ed. by M. Fréville (Paris, 1888), p. 20.

19   *Le Ménagier de Paris*, anonymous moral treatise (1393), ed. by J. F. Pichon, 2 vols. (Paris, 1846), I, pp. 62, 75.

20   Brunetto Latini (1210?–1295?), *Li Livres dou Tresor*, ed. by P. Chabaille (Paris, 1863), I, 5, ch. cci.

21   Bartholomaeus Anglicus, *Les Propriétés des Choses* (Lyons, 1498?), Bk. 16, item 49.

22   Michael Scot (c. 1175–c. 1234), *Physonomia* (Venice? 1508), p. 44.

23   Zuane Saraceno, *Recetario de Galeno Optimo* (Venice, 1508), unpag.

24   *Collectio Salernitana*, ed. by Salvatore de Renzi, 5 vols. (Naples, 1852–59, IV, p. 23.

25   Johann Wier, *De Praestigiis Daemonum* (Basel, 1566), Bk. 2, p. 299.

26   *Les Établissements de Saint Louis*, ed. by P. Viollet, 4 vols. (Paris 1881), II, pp. 287–88.

27   *The Lawes Resolutions of Womens Rights*, late 16th-century compilation of the anonymous T. E. (London, 1632), pp. 141, 204.

28   Cited in E. Rodocanachi, *La Femme italienne à l'époque de la Renaissance* (Paris, 1907), p. 374.

29   *Statuta Florentiae*, 3 vols. (Freiburg, 1778–83), Bk. 2, rub. 129.

30   Rodocanachi, *La Femme italienne*, p. 374.

31   *Der Sachsenspiegel*, I: 31, par. 2, cited in O. Stobbe, *Handbuch des Deutschen Privatrechts*, 5 vols. (Berlin, 1882–85), IV, p. 76.

32   *Year Book 21, Henry VII* (London, c. 1530), fol. xliii.

33   Cited in Alice Clark, *Working Life of Women in the Seventeenth Century* (London, 1919), p. 152.

34   *Coutumes de Beauvaisis*, ed. by A. Salmon (Paris, 1899), pars. 465, 466, 475.

35   *The Lawes Resolutions of Womens Rights*, p. 9.

36   Cited in A. Pertile, *Storia del diritto italiano* 8 vols. (Torino, 1896–1903), IV, pp. 58–59.

37   *Fuero Jusgo*, post-1241 codification (Madrid, 1815), IV, ii, 9.

38   *Die Kölner Schreinsbücher des 13. and 14. Jahrhunderts*, ed. by H. Planitz and T. Buyken (Weimar, 1937), in Gesellschaft für Rheinische Geschichtskunde, XLVI, pp. 197, 594.

39 *Grand Coutumier de France*, 13th-century code, II, par. 32.

40 *Coutumes de Beauvaisis*, pars. 433, 622.

41 *Très Ancienne Coutume de Bretagne*, 13th-century code, para. 82, cited in *La Femme* (Brussels, 1962), p. 250 n., Vol. XII, 2, of *Rec. de la Soc. Jean Bodin*.

42 *The Lawes Resolutions of Womens Rights*, pp. 129ff.

43 Thomas Smith, *De Republica Anglorum* (London, 1584), p. 105.

44 *The Lawes Resolutions of Womens Rights*, pp. 179–80.

45 *Coutumes de Beauvaisis*, par. 445.

46 A. Loisel, *Institutes Coustumiers* (Paris, 1936), III, i, p. 122.

47 *Les Établissements de Saint Louis*, II, pp. 25–26.

48 *Fuero Jusgo*, V, ii, 5.

49 *Las Siete Partidas*, VI, xiii, 7.

50 Jean Boutillier (14th-cent. jurist), *Somme Rurale* (Paris, 1538), II, fol. 29.

51 *Coutumes de Beauvaisis*, par. 1629.

52 *Las Siete Partidas*, IV, viii, 5.

53 *Statuti di Perugia*, ed. by G. degli Azzi 2 vols. (Rome, 1913), I, pp. 295, 115-116.

54 *Le Livre de la Bourgeoisie de la Ville de Strasbourg: 1440-1530*, ed. by C. Wittmer and J.C. Meyer, 3 vols. (Strasbourg and Zurich, 1948–61), I, docs. 443, 499, 504, 822, 857, 862, 1071.

55 *Statuti senesi scritti in volgare ne' secoli xiii e xiv*, ed. by F.L. Polidori 3 vols. (Bologna, 1863–77), I, pp. 274, 279, 306, 329.

56 Etienne Boileau, *Livre des Métiers*, ed. by G.B. Depping (Paris, 1837), pp. 80–82.

57 ibid., pp. 68–69, 73, 79.

58 *The Little Red Book of Bristol*, ed. by F.B. Bickley (Bristol, 1900), II, pp. 127-28.

59 Albrecht Dürer, *Tagebuch der Reise in die Niederlands* (Leipzig, 1884), p. 55.

60 G. Fagniez, *Documents relatifs à l'histoire de l'industrie et du commerce en France*, 2 vols. (Paris, 1899–1900), I, pp. 172–73, 204–05.

61 *Rotuli Parliamentorum*, V : 325.

62 *English Economic History*, ed. by A.E. Bland, P.A. Brown and R.H. Tawney (London, 1930), p. 7.

63 G. Duby, *Rural Economy and Country Life in the Medieval West*, trans. by C. Posten (E. Arnold, 1968), pp. 485–86.

64 *English Economic History*, pp. 71, 72.

65 *Les Edits et Ordonnances des Roys de France depuis l'an 1226* (Lyons, 1575), p. 1114.

66 *The Statutes of the Realm*, II (1816) p. 57.

67 *Les Edits et Ordonnances des Roys de France*, pp. 1103, 1116.

68 Bartholomaeus Anglicus, *Les Propriétés des Choses*, Bk. VI, item 11.

69 *Le Ménagier de Paris*, II, pp. 59ff.

70   *English Economic History*, p. 325.
71   *Collectio Salernitana*, III, p. 338.
72   Boileau, *Livre des Métiers*, pp. 419–20.
73   Cited in S. Young, *Annals of the Barber Surgeons of London* (London, 1890), p. 38.
74   Cited in The Victoria History of the Counties of England: *A History of Yorkshire* ed. by W. Page, 3 vols. (London, 1913), III, p. 453.
75   Christine de Pisan, cited in M. Laigle, *Le Livre des Trois Vertus de Christine de Pisan* (Paris, 1912), p. 146.
76   *Le Ménagier de Paris*, I, p. 15.
77   Philippe de Navarre, *Les Quatre Âges de l'Homme*, pp. 16, 49–50.
78   *Le Livre du Chevalier de la Tour Landry*, ed. by Montaiglon (Paris, 1854), from chs. 5, 7, 127.
79   *Le Ménagier de Paris*, I, p. 168–75.
80   *Libro di buoni costumi*, ed. by A. Schiaffini (Florence, 1945), pp. 105–06, 126–28.
81   G. Morelli, *Ricordi*, ed. by V. Branca (Florence, 1956), pp. 187–88.
82   G. Brucker (ed.), *Two Memoirs of Renaissance Florence*, trans. by J. Martines (Harper & Row, 1968), pp. 112ff.
83   *Original Letters*, ed. by J. Fenn (London, 1789), IV, pp. 345–65.
84   C. Du Cange, *Glossarium Novum ad Scriptores Medii Aevi* (Paris, 1766) Vol. I, 'asinus.'
85   *Coutumes de Beauvaisis*, p. 335.
86   *The Lawes Resolutions of Womens Rights*, pp. 128–29, 208.
87   Text and trans. in L. Finkelstein, *Jewish Self-Government in the Middle Ages* (New York, 1924), pp. 216–17.
88   Cherubino da Siena, *Regole della vita matrimoniale* (Bologna, 1888), pp. 12–14.
89   *Fuero Jusgo*, III, iv, 4.
90   *Statuti di Perugia*, II, p. 116.

9   THE RENAISSANCE AND REFORMATION

1   Christine de Pisan, *Cyte of Ladyes*, trans. by B. Anslay (London, 1521), Bk. 1, ch. 11; Bk. 2, ch. 36.
2   Erasmus, *Christiani matrimonii institutio* (Basel, 1526), ch. 17, unpag.
3   Erasmus, *Colloquies*, adapted from trans. by N. Bailey, 3 vols. (London, 1900), II, pp. 114–19.
4   Agrippa, *De nobilitate et praecellentia foeminei sexus declamatio* (Paris, 1713), pp. 17, 18, 57.
5   J. Aynard (ed.), *Les poètes lyonnais précurseurs de la Pléiade* (Paris, 1924), pp. 157–59.
6   Aubigné, *Oeuvres Complètes*, ed. by E. Reaume and F. de Caussade (Paris, 1873), I, pp. 445ff.

7   L.B. Alberti, *The Family in Renaissance Florence*, trans. and introd. by Rénée N. Watkins (University of South Carolina Press, 1969), pp. 208, 209, 210–11, 212–13, 217.

8   B. Castiglione, *The Book of the Courtier*, trans. by C.S. Singleton (Anchor Books, 1959), pp. 206–07, 208–09, 211, 214–15.

9   Martin Bucer, *De Regno Christi* (Lausanne, 1558), Bk. 2, ch. 48.

10 Martin Luther, 'The Babylonian Captivity of the Church,' in *Primary Works*, trans. and ed. by H. Wace and C.A. Buchheim (London, 1896), pp. 103–04.

11 *D. Martin Luthers Werke. Kritische Gesamtausgabe*, Vol. III of the *Briefwechsel* (Weimar, 1933), pp. 327–28.

12 Luther, *The Table Talk*, trans. and ed. by T.G. Tappert, in *Luther's Works*, Vol. LIV (Philadelphia, 1967), pp. 8, 25, 171.

13 Luther, *Sermons*, trans. and ed. by J. W. Doberstein in *Luther's Works*, Vol LI (Philadelphia, 1959), pp. 358–59, 361–62.

14 John Calvin, *Institution de la religion Chrestienne* (Geneva, 1560), Bk. 4, ch. xii, para. 27.

15 ibid., Bk. 2, ch. viii, paras. 41, 42, 43, 44.

16 Bucer, *De Regno Christi*, Bk. 2, ch. xxxiv.

17 Balthasar Hubmaier, 'On Free Will,' in *Spiritual and Anabaptist Writers*, ed. by G.H. Williams, in Library of Christian Classics, Vol. XXV (Philadelphia, 1957), pp. 121, 125.

18 Calvin, *Institution de la religion Chrestienne*, Bk. 4, ch. xv, paras. 21–22.

19 Johann C. Füsslin (ed.), *Beiträge zur Erlauterung der Kirchen Reformations*, Vol. V (Zurich, 1753), compilation from pp. 193–95, 196–98, 301–04, 273–75, 315–16, 210, 213.

20 H. Kramer and J. Sprenger, *Malleus Maleficarum*, trans. by Montague Summers (Arrow Books Ltd, 1971), pp. 112, 116–17, 119, 122.

21 Jean Bodin, *De la démonomanie des sorciers* (Paris, 1580), p. 225.

22 R. Scot, *The Discoverie of Witchcraft*, ed. by B. Nicholson (London, 1886), p. 227.

23 Scipio Mercurio, *La Commare o Riccoglitrice* (Venice, ed. 1621), pp. 231–32.

24 Kramer and Sprenger, *Malleus Maleficarum*, p. 351.

25 Selections from Friedrich von Spee's book in *The Witch Persecutions*, ed. by G.L. Burr, *Translations and Reprints from the Original Sources of European History*, Vol. III, 4 (Philadelphia, 1897), pp. 31, 33, 35.

26 Johann Wier, *De Praestigiis Daemonum* (Basel, 1566), Bk. 2, ch. 14, pp. 187–88.

27 ibid., pp. 4ff.

28 ibid., Bk. V, ch. 5, pp. 630ff. (the 1575 item from a later edition).

29   From the canon of Linden, *Gesta Trevirorum*, in Burr, *The Witch Persecutions*, pp. 13–14.

30   Ralph Gardiner, *England's Grievance Discovered* (London, 1655), pp. 107–09.

10   THE EARLY MODERN PERIOD

1   *Code Matrimonial*, ed. by M. le Ridant, 2 vols. (Paris, 1766,) I, p. 1ff.

2   ibid., I, pp. 18ff

3   ibid., I, pp. 26ff.

4   ibid., I, p. 21.

5   ibid., II, pp. 198ff.

6   François Serpillon, *Code Criminel; ou commentaire sur l'Ordonnance de 1670*, 2 vols. (Lyons, 1784), I, pp. 108ff.

7   ibid., I, pp. 109.

8   *Code Matrimonial*, I, p. 9ff.

9   Serpillon, *Code Criminel*, I, pp. 119ff.

10   ibid., I, pp. 114ff.

11   Master Franz Schmidt, *A Hangman's Diary*, ed. by A. Keller, trans. by C. Calvert and A.W. Gruner (P. Allan, 1928).

12   *Modern Reports; or Select Cases Adjudged in the Courts of King's Bench, Chancery, Common-Pleas, and Exchequer, since the Restauration of HisMajesty King Charles II*, 2nd ed. (London, 1700), I, pp. 124ff.

13   *A Report of all the Cases Determined by Sir John Holt, Knt. from 1688 to 1710, during which time he was Lord Chief Justice of England* (London, 1738), p. 104, Case of James v. Warren.

14   ibid., p. 103, Case of Etherington v. Parrot.

15   *Une Grande Dame dans son ménage au temps de Louis XIV, D'après le journal de la comtesse de Rochefort* (1689), ed. by Charles de Ribbe (Paris, 1889), pp. 337ff.

16   *The Autobiography of Mrs Alice Thornton of East Newton, Co. York* (Surtees Society, Durham, London and Edinburgh, 1875), Vol. 62, pp. 49ff., 84ff.

17   Madame de Sévigné, *Lettres de Marie de Rabutin-Chantal Marquise de Sévigné à sa fille et à ses amis* (Paris, 1861), I, pp. 417ff.; II, pp. 17ff.

18   Madame du Hausset, *Mémoires de Madame du Hausset, femme de chambre de Madame du Pompadour* (Bruxelles, 1825), p. 221.

19   *Lettres de la Sainte Mère Jeanne-Françoise Frémyot, baronne de Rabutin-Chantal*, ed. by E. de Barthélemy (Paris, 1860), pp. 46ff.

20   François Villon (1431–c. 1465), 'Ballade pour prier Nostre Dame.'

21   Molière, *Les Femmes Savantes* (1672), Act II, Scene 7.

22   L.R. Caradeuc de la Chalotais (the king's attorney), *Essai d'éducation nationale ou plan d'études pour la jeunesse* (1763, no place of pub.), pp. 25ff.

23 Sarah Trimmer, *Reflections upon the Education of Children in Charity Schools* (London, 1792), p. 7.

24 Jean-Jacques Rousseau, *Émile ou de l'Education*, ed. by F. and P. Richard (Paris, 1939), p. 455.

25 Sir Josiah Child, *A New Discourse of Trade* (London, 1694), pp. 1, 4ff.

26 James Howell, *Epistolae Ho-Elianae: Familiar Letters Domestic and Foreign* (London, 1754), Bk. 1, sec. 2, pp. 103ff.

27 Fénelon, *Traité de l'éducation des filles*, ed. by E. Faguet (Paris, 1913), pp. 111ff.

28 Mme de Maintenon, *Lettres sur l'éducation des filles* (Paris, 1854), pp. 322, 314.

29 A. Angiulli, *La Pedagogia, lo Stato e la Famiglia* (Naples, 1876), pp. 84ff.

30 Sir Anthony Fitzherbert, *The boke of husbandrye* (London, 1555), fols. 45–47.

31 Historical Manuscripts Commission, *Report on Manuscripts in Various Collections*, I (London, 1901) pp. 163ff.

32 Report made by the Justices of the Peace for the half hundred of Hitching concerning the poor in their district, State Papers, Domestic Series, 385, 43; cited in Alice Clark, *Working Life of Women in the Seventeenth Century* (London, 1919), p. 80.

33 J. W. Willis Bund, *Worcester County Records* (Worcester, 1900), I, p. 337.

34 J.C. Cox, *Three Centuries of Derbyshire Annals*, 2 vols. (London, 1890), II, p. 175.

35 Historical Manuscripts Commission, *Report*, I, p. 295.

36 ibid., I, pp. 298f.

37 A.W. Ashby, *One Hundred Years of Poor Law Administration in a Warwickshire Village*, in P. Vinogradoff, *Oxford Studies in Social and Legal History* (Oxford, 1912), p. 177.

38 ibid., pp. 180ff.

39 La Bruyère, *Oeuvres Complètes*, ed. by J. Benda (Gallimard, 1951), p. 333.

40 Le Grand d'Aussy, *Voyage d'Auvergne* (Paris, 1788), pp. 281ff.

41 Jacques de Cambry, *Voyage dans le Finistère ou état de ce département en 1794 et 1795*, 3 vols. (Paris, 1799), II, pp. 57, 47ff.

42 Amans-Alexis Monteil, *Déscription du département de l'Aveiron* (Paris, 1802), pp. 43ff.

43 Albert Babeau, *La Vie Rurale dans l'Ancienne France* (Paris, 1883), pp. 334ff., 323ff.

44 John Knox, *The First Blast of the Trumpet against the Monstrous Regiment of Women* (London, 1878), pp. 17ff.

45 William Gouge, *Of Domesticall Duties* (London, 1634), pp. 274ff.

46 Joseph Besse, *A Collection of the Sufferings of the People called Quakers*, 2 vols. (London, 1753), I, pp. 84ff.

47   John Vicars, *The Schismatick Sifted* (London, 1646), p. 34.
48   M. Cary, *A New and More exact Mappe or Description of the New Jerusalem's Glory* (London, 1651), pp. 236ff.
49   George Fox, *A Collection of many Select and Christian Epistles*, 2 vols. (London, 1698), II, pp. 323ff.
50   ibid., II, p. 244.
51   George Fox, *The Woman Learning in Silence* (London, 1656), pp. 2ff.
52   F.P. Verney, *Memoirs of the Verney Family during the Civil War*, 2 vols. (London, 1892), II, p. 240.
53   *The Parliamentary: or Constitutional History of England* (London, 1757), XIX, p. 106.
54   B. Whitelock, *Memorials of the English Affairs* (London, 1732), p. 398.
55   Petition of 5 May 1649, in *The Thomason Tracts*, British Museum, 669, f. 14 (27).
56   Louis Bourdaloue (1632–1704), *Oeuvres Complètes*, in *Collection intégrale et universelle des orateurs sacrés*, Vol. XV (Paris, 1845), cols. 374ff.
57   C.A. Vianello, 'Il Dramma e il Romanzo di Suor Paolina dei Conti Pietra,' in *Archivio Storico Lombardo*, LX (Milan, 1933), pp. 160ff.
58   Saint-Simon, *Mémoires*, cited in R. Picard, *Les Salons Littéraires et la Société française* (New York, 1943), p. 62.
59   Gédéon Tallemant des Réaux, *Historiettes* (Paris, 1853), II, pp. 442ff.
60   Mlle de Scudéry, *Artamène ou le Grand Cyrus* (Paris 1651), Vol. VI, Bk. 1, pp.113ff.
61   P.D. Huet, *Traité de l'origine des Romans*, 8th ed. (Paris, 1711), pp. 208ff.
62   Saint-Evremond (c. 1610–1703), *Oeuvres*, 3 vols. (Paris, 1927), I, p. 44.
63   Scudéry, *Artamène ou le Grand Cyrus*, Vol. X, Bk. II, pp. 577ff.
64   Michel de Pure, *La Prétieuse ou le Mystère des Ruelles*, ed. by Emile Magne, 2 vols. (Paris, 1938), II: 17f.
65   ibid., I, p. 285.
66   ibid., II, p. 39.
67   Ferdinand Galiani (1728–1787), letter to Madame Necker, cited in Picard, *Les Salons Littéraires*, p. 343.

11   FROM THE ERA OF REVOLUTION TO THE 1850s

1   Immanuel Kant, *The Philosophy of Law*, trans. by W. Hastie (Edinburgh, 1887), I, i, pars. 24–26 (translation here slightly revised and updated).
2   J.G. Fichte, *The Science of Rights*, trans. by A.E. Kroeger (London, 1889), pp. 424–26, 438–39, 440–42, 446.

3 G.W.H. Hegel, *Grundlinien der Philosophie des Rechts*, ed. by H. Glockner, *Sämtliche Werke*, VII (Stuttgart, 1928), pp. 240–49.

4 A. Flexner, *Prostitution in Europe* (New York, 1914), p. 107.

5 Thomas Fuller, *The Profane State* (Cambridge, 1648), pp. 343ff.

6 St Augustine, *De ordine*, Bk. 2, ch. 4.

7 *Chartes de franchises du Lauragais*, ed. by J. Ramière de Fortanier (Paris, 1939), p. 709.

8 Girolamo Fracastoro (1483–1553), *De contagionibus et contagiosis morbis*, in *Opera Omnia* (Venice, 1574), pp. 91ff.

9 *Encyclopédie Méthodique*, 192 vols. (Paris, 1787–1832), VIII: 208, 'Jurisprudence.'

10 *Recueil Général des Anciennes Lois Françaises*, ed. by F.A. Isambert (Paris, 1829), XIV, 88.

11 François Serpillon, *Code Criminel; ou commentaire sur l'Ordonnance de 1670* 2 vols. (Lyons, 1784), II, pp. 342ff.

12 *Recueil Général*, XIX, pp. 444ff.

13 A.-J.-B. Parent-Duchâtelet, *De la Prostitution dans la Ville de Paris* (3d ed., 2 vols. (Paris, 1857), II, pp. 294ff.

14 M. Sabatier, *Histoire de la législation sur les femmes publiques* (Paris, 1828), p. 172.

15 W. Acton, *Prostitution considered in its Moral, Social and Sanitary, Aspects* (London, 1857), p. 101.

16 Parent-Duchâtelet, *De la Prostitution*, I, p. 686.

17 Philippe Ricord, under entry 'Syphilis,' in the Larousse *Grand Dictionnaire Universel du XIXᵉ Siècle* (Paris, 1875), XIV, p. 1340.

18 Parent-Duchâtelet, *De la Prostitution*, I, p. 107.

19 F. Engels, *Condition of the Working Classes in England* (London 1892), pp. 148ff.

20 Parent-Duchâtelet, *De la Prostitution*, I, pp. 72ff.

21 ibid., I, pp. 436ff.

22 Acton, *Prostitution*, p. 83.

23 Parent-Duchâtelet, *De la Prostitution*, I, pp. 400, 584.

24 L. Fiaux, *La Police des Moeurs en France* (Paris, 1888), pp. 117, 129.

25 Mayhew, cited in Acton, *Prostitution*, pp. 21ff.

26 Condorcet (1743–1794), *Essai sur l'admission des femmes au droit de cité* (Paris, 1790).

27 A. Le Faure, *Le Socialisme pendant la Révolution Française* (Paris, 1863), pp. 120ff.

28 Mme Campan, *Mémoires sur la vie privée de Marie-Antoinette*, 3 vols. (Paris, 1822), II, ch. xv, pp. 85–86.

29 Olympe des Gouges, *Les Droits de la Femme* (Paris, 1791).

30 L.R. Villermé, *Tableau de l'état physique et moral des ouvriers*, 2 vols. (Paris, 1840), II, pp. 11ff.

31 Flora Tristan, *L'Union Ouvrière*, 2nd ed. (Paris, 1844), p. 108.

32   ibid., pp. 51ff.
33   *Gazette des Tribunaux* (Paris, 1850), November 13, 14, 15.
34   Mary Wollstonecraft, *A Vindication of the Rights of Women* (Dublin, 1793), p. 4.
35   ibid., p. 256.
36   ibid., p. viii.
37   A. Dowling, *Reports of Cases Argued and Determined in the Queen's Bench Practice Courts* (London, 1841), VIII, pp. 630ff.
38   J.F. Macqueen, *A Practical Treatise on the Law of Marriage, Divorce and Legitimacy* (London, 1860), p. 32.
39   F. Clifford, *A History of Private Bill Legislation* (London, 1885), I, p. 411.
40   *The Parliamentary History of England from the Earliest Period to the Year 1803* (printed by T.C. Hansard, London, 1800ff.), Vol. 35, col. 1429.
41   C. Norton, *English Laws for Women in the Nineteenth Century* (London, 1854), pp. 24ff.
42   C. Norton, *A Letter to the Queen on Lord Chancellor Cranworth's Marriage and Divorce Bill* (London, 1855), pp. 10, 16.
43   *Extraordinary Trial, Norton v. Viscount Melbourne for Crim. Con.* (London, 1836), pp. 9ff.
44   J. Haggard, *Reports of Cases Argued and Determined in the Consistory Court of London*, 2 vols. (London, 1822), I, pp. 37ff.
45   ibid., I, pp. 458ff.
46   W.C. Curteis, *Reports of Cases Argued and Defended in the Ecclesiastical Courts at Doctors Commons* (London, 1842), II, p. 283.
47   Norton, *Letter to the Queen*, p. 10.
48   ibid., p. 8.
49   Unsigned but almost certainly by C. Norton, *A Review of the Divorce Bill of 1856* (London, 1857).
50   Norton, *Letter to the Queen*, p. 62.
51   Macqueen, *A Practical Treatise on the Law of Marriage*, p. 154.
52   Pearce Stevenson, Esq. (pseudonym for C. Norton), *A Plain Letter to the Lord Chancellor on the Infant Custody Bill* (London, 1839), p. 69.
53   C. Norton, letter in J.G. Perkins, *The Life of Mrs Norton* (London, 1909), pp. 137ff.
54   Norton, *Letter to the Queen*, p. 11.
55   *Statutes of the United Kingdom of Great Britain and Ireland* (London, 1839), p. 344.
56   Norton, *Letter to the Queen*, pp. 84ff.
57   *Statutes of the United Kingdom of Great Britain and Ireland* (London, 1857), pp. 573.
58   ibid., p. 434.

Select Bibliography

Abensour, Leon *Histoire générale du feminisme*. Paris, 1921.

Balsdon, J. P. V. D. *Roman Women Their History and Habits*. London, 1962.

Baumal, Francis *Le féminisme au temps de Molière*. Paris, 1923.

Beauchet, Ludovic *Histoire du droit privé de la république athénienne*, I. Maresq, 1897.

Benton, John F. 'Clio and Venus An Historical View of Courtly Love,' in F. X. Newman, ed., *The Meaning of Courtly Love*. Albany, 1968.

Bomli, W. *La femme dans El'spagne du siècle d'or*. The Hague, 1950.

Bousquet. G. H. *La morale de l'Islam et son éthique sexuelle* Algiers, 1952.

Brissaud, Jean *A History of French Private Law*, Eng. trans. by R. Howell. Boston, 1912.

Buckler, Georgina 'Women in Byzantine Law about 1100 A. D.,' *Byzantion*, 11, 1936.

Camden, Carroll *The Elizabethan Woman: a Panorama of English Womanhood, 1540 to 1640*. London, 1952.

Cérez, Jeanne *La condition sociale de la femme de 1804 à nos jours*. Paris, 1940.

Clark, Alice *Working Life of Women in the Seventeenth Century*. London, 1919.

Corbett, P. E. *The Roman Law of Marriage*. Oxford, 1930.

Cuq, Edouard *Manuel des institutions juridiques des Romains*. Paris, 1917.

Daubié, Julie *La femme pauvre au XIXe siècle*. Paris, 1866.

Del Lungo, Isidoro *Women of Florence*, English translation by M. C. Steegmann. London, 1907.

Donaldson, James *Woman, Her Position and Influence in Ancient Greece and Rome*. New York, 1907.

Ducros, Louis *La société française au XVIIIe siècle d'après les mémoires et la correspondance du temps*. Paris, 1922.

Engels, Friedrich *The Condition of the Working Class in England in 1844*. Oxford, 1958.

Fagniez, Gustave *La femme et la société française dans la première moitié du XVIIe siècle*. Paris, 1929.

Femme, La, vols. 11–13 of the Recueils de la Société Jean Bodin. Brussels, 1959, 1962.

Figes, Eva *Patriarchal Attitudes.* London, 1970.

Finke, H. *Die Frau im Mittelalter.* Munich, 1913.

Gide, Paul *Etudes sur la condition privée de la femme.* Paris, 1885.

Glotz, Gustave *Etudes sociales et juridiques sur l'antiquité grecque.* Paris, 1906.

Grimal, Pierre, ed. *Histoire mondiale de la femme,* 4 vols. Paris, 1965–68.

Guyot, Yves *La Prostitution.* Paris, 1882.

Heusler, Andreas *Institutionen des Deutschen Privatrechts,* 2 vols. Leipzig, 1885–86.

Hewitt, Margaret *Wives and Mothers in Victorian Industry.* London, 1958.

Holdsworth, W. S. *A History of English Law,* 16 vols. London 1903–.

Kelso, Ruth, *Doctrine for the Lady of the Renaissance.* Urbana, 1956.

Kuczynski, Jurgen *Studien zur Geschichte der Lage der Arbeiterinnen in Deutschland von 1700 bis zur Gegenwart.* Berlin, 1963.

———. *The Rise of the Working Class,* English translation by C. T. A. Ray. London, 1967.

Lallier, R. *De la condition de la femme dans la famille athénienne au Ve et au IVe siècle.* Paris, 1875.

Lipinska, Melania *Les femmes et le progrès des sciences médicales.* Paris, 1930.

Macqueen, John, F. *A Practical Treatise on the Law of Marriage, Divorce and Legitimacy.* London, 1860.

Mead, K. C. H. *A History of Women in Medicine.* Haddam, 1938.

McArthur, E. A. 'Women Petitioners and the Long Parliament,' *English Historical Review,* 24, 1909.

O'Malley, Ida Beatrice *Women in Subjection. A Study of the Lives of Englishwomen before 1832.* London, 1933.

Paoli, U. E. *La donna greca nell' antichità* Florence, 1955.

Parent-Duchâtelet, Dr. A. J.-B. *De la prostitution dans la ville de Paris,* 2 vols. Paris, 1857.

Picard, Roger *Les salons littéraires et la société française.* New York, 1943.

Pinchbeck, Ivy *Women Workers and the Industrial Revolution, 1750–1850.* London, 1930.

Portemer, Jean 'La femme dans la législation royale aux XVIIe et XVIIIe siècles,' in *Mélanges Petot.* Paris, 1958.

Reicke, Ilse   *Die Frauenbewegung. Ein Geschichtlicher Uberblick*, Leipzig, 1929.

Reynier, Gustave   *La femme au XVIIe siècle: ses ennemis, ses défenseurs.* Paris, 1929.

Richardson, L. M.   *The Forerunners of Feminism in French Literature.* Baltimore, 1924.

Rodocanachi, E.   *La femme italienne à l'epoque de la Renaissance.* Paris, 1907.

Rousselot, Paul   *Histoire de l'éducation des femmes*, 2 vols. Paris, 1883.

Rover, Constance   *Women's Suffrage and Party Politics in Britain, 1866–1914.* London, 1967.

Stenton, D. M.   *The English Woman in History.* London, 1957.

Stobbe, Otto   *Handbuch des Deutschen Privatrechts*, 5 vols. Berlin, 1882–85. See especially vols. 4–5.

Sullerot, Evelyn   *Histoire et sociologie du travail féminin.* Paris, 1968.

Tamassia, Nino   *La famiglia italiana nei secoli decimoquinto e decimosesto.* Milan, 1910.

Thibert, Marguerite   *Le féminisme dans la société française, 1830–1850.* Paris, 1926.

Thomas, Edith   *The Women Incendiaries.* London, 1967.

——*Les femmes en 1848.* Paris, 1948.

Thomas, Keith   'Women and the Civil War Sects,' in T. Aston, ed., *Crisis in Europe, 1560–1660.* New York, 1967.

Thomson, George   *Studies in Ancient Greek Society.* London, 1949.

Villiers, Marc de   *Histoire des clubs de femmes et des Legions d'Amaziones, 1793–1848–1871.* Paris, 1910.

Weinhold, Karl   *Die Deutschen Frauen in dem Mittelalter*, 2 vols. Vienna, 1882.

Zetkin, Clara   *Zur Geschichte der proletarischen Frauenbewegung Deutschlands.* Berlin, 1958.

Acknowledgments

Extracts from the Authorized Version of the Bible which is Crown Copyright are reproduced with permission.

Grateful acknowledgment is made for permission to quote the following copyright material:

Doubleday & Co Inc. for extracts from *The Book of the Courtier* by Baldassare Castiglione, translated by Charles S. Singleton and Edgar de N. Mayhew;

Fortress Press for extracts from *Luther's Works*, 'Sermons', vol. 51, edited by John W. Doberstein;

The Hogarth Press and the Translator's Literary Estate for extracts from *Malleus Maleficarum* by Kramer and Sprenger, translated by H. Montague Summers;

The Johns Hopkins Press for extracts from *Gynecology* by Soranus of Ephesus, translated by Owsi Temkin;

The University Presses of Oxford and Cambridge for extracts from the *New English Bible,* second edition;

Princeton University Press for extracts from *The Theodosian Code and Novels and the Sirmondian Constitutions,* translated by Clyde Pharr;

The University of Pennsylvania Press for extracts from *The Burgundian Code,* translated by Katherine Fischer Drew.

Source index

Subject index